Nicholas Rowe
and
Christian Tragedy

The Penance of Jane Shore in St. Paul's Church, by William Blake. Courtesy of The Tate Gallery, London

Nicholas Rowe
and
Christian Tragedy

J. Douglas Canfield

A University of Florida Book

The University Presses of Florida
Gainesville ❧ 1977

The University Presses of Florida is the scholarly publishing agency for the State University System of Florida. The publication of this book was assisted by the American Council of Learned Societies under a grant from the Andrew W. Mellon Foundation.

Library of Congress Cataloging in Publication Data

Canfield, John Douglas, 1941–
    Nicholas Rowe and Christian tragedy.

    Includes bibliographies and index.
    1.   Rowe, Nicholas, 1674–1718—Criticism and
interpretation.   I.   Title.
PR3671.R5C3   822'.5   76–39917
ISBN 0–8130–0545–0

For Pam and Robbie
  —they endured.

Preface

HIS IS A STUDY of the meaning and the merit of Nicholas Rowe's tragedies, examined in their historical context. By "Christian tragedy" I mean tragedies that mirror a Christian Weltanschauung. Tragedy is whatever any age makes it. The size of the category swells or shrinks accordingly. In the English Renaissance through the Restoration into the eighteenth century, plays were generally divided between "comedies" and "tragedies," the latter usually treating in an elevated style high-born characters involved in suffering and evil and loss—whether or not the plays end happily, whether or not they meet Aristotle's criteria, much less Nietzsche's. Christianity does not preclude any of these things, certainly, and its basic, "comic" pattern of fall and redemption, which some take to be inimical to tragedy, is a general pattern of history, to which the pattern of an individual's life may or may not conform. After all, Macbeth falls never to rise again, yet Scotland is redeemed, as if to prove life signifies much more than nothing.

A far more important pattern for the individual in Christian art is that of *trial*. As this study argues, Rowe's tragedies, in the tradition of earlier English tragedy, borrow the metaphor from Scripture and Christian apologetics and employ it over and over as a shaping pattern, the ultimate trial being the temptation to despair, the most serious—and most sinister—temptation of man in the Christian scheme. This and other similar patterns, infused as they are with Christian language, imagery, and thought, are what make the tragedies of Nicholas Rowe Christian.

Not that they are therefore true, or reflect ontological reality. Rowe obviously thought they did. But in our post-Kantian—indeed, post-

Heideggerian—age, perhaps the best we can say is that Rowe's fictions take their meaning from the larger, dominant fiction of his age, the Christian myth. His words refer to another set of words. His poetical justice, for example, pretends to reflect providential justice, which is itself—as are all human notions of justice—poetical. Once we conclude that "reality" is a fiction, however, we must then realize that fiction is our reality: the projections of human consciousness are all we've got. Fiction, then, is no longer a pejorative term. We must take it seriously, and, as literary critics especially, we must construct our own fictions carefully, aware of our limitations, as out of necessity we scribble notes toward yet other fictions.

Accordingly, in this study I have adopted the critical fictions that seem to me to account most fully for my conscious experience of the intentionality (in the phenomenological sense) of Rowe's consciousness as projected toward me in the stimuli of the text. The critical principles (by changing a word, I thus legitimate them) are those of formalism and the history of ideas. In other words, I have accepted a formal imperative as a necessary fiction: whatever their ontological status, we must treat verbal artifacts *as if* they were integral objects, for that allows us, I think, to get the most out of them. And I also assume that, since they use words (not to mention body language on the stage), they are therefore meaningful; that they are *about* states of mind and states of affairs, rooted in their own historical time; and that those meanings are more or less ascertainable, within vague but nevertheless present parameters (*Jane Shore* is *not* a play about Watergate, however much the two Richards have in common). Why else read them? And why write about them? So ontology and epistemology finally yield to the fictions of common sense, and I set out not to save Rowe's plays for Christianity but to interpret their play of words as objectively as I can.

With regard to the merit of Rowe's plays, I have done an evaluative analysis only of the plays which warrant it. Why kick a man when he's down? When Rowe is up, however, I have tried to show how and why. Perhaps such an analysis will convince others that he is worth reading, not because of his place in literary history or in the history of ideas but because of his occasional felicitous marriage of theme and form and language. For convenience's sake, I originally used as my text the 1792 edition of *The Works of Nicholas Rowe, Esq.*, apparently the most readily available edition of the plays—until the 1971 reprinting of the 1720 edition of *The Dramatick Works of Nicholas Rowe, Esq.*, which was not picked up by the standard bibliographies and came to my attention only after this study was accepted for publication with the quotations thoroughly woven into its fabric. I apologize for not using the more authoritative text. Also, Landon Burns' recent monograph, *Pity and Tears: The Tragedies of Nicholas Rowe* (Salzburg, 1974), which reprints his dissertation almost verbatim, came to my attention too late for me to alter my references from dissertation to book. Moreover, in the four-and-a-half-year lag between submission and publication of this study in its present form, I have attempted to incorporate references to recent work bearing directly on my reading of Rowe and Restoration tragedy; but, for expedience's sake, I have not included ancillary material, such as several recent and important books on Dryden and especially two excellent related studies, Martin Battestin's *The Providence of Wit: Aspects of Form in Augustan Literature and the Arts* (Oxford, 1974), with whose formalistic approach I am in fundamental agreement, and Robert Hume's *The Development of English Drama in the Late Seventeenth Century* (Oxford, 1976), with whose affective approach I am in fundamental disagreement. Battestin corroborates the findings of Aubrey Williams and Hume those of Eric Rothstein, to both of whom I do refer.

I have used the following forms of reference: parenthetical citations in the text (where I have tried to place most references to avoid the annoyance of brief notes); footnotes at the ends of chapters, containing only author, short title, and an occasional date where necessary; and a bibliography of works cited, which may be consulted for full titles and publishing information. To streamline further, I have adopted the abbreviations *f* and *ff*, except where exact termination must be identified (and I have eschewed redundant plurals, as in "pp. 218 ff," which I render "p. 218 ff"). Because my edition does not number lines, I cite act, scene (where applicable), and page numbers (e.g., II.iii, p. 39) and note every change of page as soon as it occurs. Finally, I have silently corrected accidentals and transposed italics in prefaces, prologues, epilogues, and the like in the body of the study, but for scholarship's sake I have reproduced the text of the appendix as exactly as possible. A fully annotated edition of this sale catalogue of Rowe's library awaits a critical edition of the entire canon of his works.

This volume was begun as a dissertation at the University of Florida. For help in the revision I am grateful to the following: the staffs of the William Andrews Clark Memorial Library and the Henry E. Huntington Library, for bibliographical assistance; the Regents of the University of California, for financial assistance; Ethel Wallis, Stan Scott, and Renata Landres, for research assistance; and Henry Ansgar Kelly, Henry

Knight Miller, and Ben Ross Schneider, for careful critical readings of
the manuscript.

For help all along the road to this book, I am especially grateful to
the following: John Logan, Richard Sewall, and Cleanth Brooks, who
guided my initial steps toward an appreciative understanding of literature in general and tragedy in particular; the late W. K. Wimsatt, who
introduced me to the theory behind Restoration tragedy; the late D. C.
Allen, who introduced me to the thought behind it; and Aubrey Williams, who taught me how to read it. From start to finish of the study
proper, Professor Williams has been my rod and my staff, a fact I acknowledge with appreciation and affection.

J. Douglas Canfield

Contents

Introduction

ICHOLAS ROWE is an important literary figure simply because he was the first biographer and editor of Shakespeare, as most of us know. He is also important as the translator of Lucan's *Pharsalia* into what Samuel Johnson called "one of the greatest productions of English poetry,"[1]* as most of us do not know. But his greatest importance in his own time—as it should be in ours—is that he was the major tragedian of the early eighteenth century and became poet laureate in 1715 on that basis. Nearly all of his tragedies were initially successful, and after Shakespeare's, three of them—*Tamerlane, The Fair Penitent,* and *The Tragedy of Jane Shore*—were among the most popular of the century.[2] Historically, Rowe's she-tragedies—*The Fair Penitent, Jane Shore,* and *Lady Jane Gray*—influenced not only the development of English and continental domestic tragedy but also Richardson and the development of the novel (*Clarissa* is obviously indebted to *The Fair Penitent*).[3] Because of their popularity and their historical importance, the four plays mentioned are still being edited and anthologized anew (see Bibliography A), and one or another is still being taught in dramatic surveys of the period.

Popularity and literary history aside, however, Rowe's tragedies deserve to be studied for their intrinsic meaning and merit. His *Ulysses* is one of the better classical tragedies of the many attempted in this neoclassical age, and his she-tragedies are the best tragedies of the entire century. In them Rowe achieves the naturalness of diction and the smoothness of verse for which he has been traditionally praised,[4] plus a fine weave of metaphoric and allusive patterns and a keenness of characterization, as in his famous "gay Lothario." The she-tragedies are, fur-

*Notes to the introduction begin on page 8.

1

thermore, engaging examinations of the central human problems of
suffering and sin.

Yet Rowe's tragedies have received meager attention from
twentieth-century scholarship. The only full-length studies are dissertations, and these are primarily concerned with Rowe's life, his sources,
and his position in the history of English drama as a transitional figure
between "heroic" and "sentimental" tragedy, or as an exemplar of the
"pathetic" mode. In analyzing the plays themselves, when not merely
sketching characters or summarizing plots, critics have concentrated
almost entirely on Rowe's techniques of arousing pity in his audience.
Thus the criticism is most often affective instead of cognitive, and
Rowe's tragedies simply do not seem to have been read for their full
meaning.[5] Some critics have discussed, in most instances briefly and
tangentially, Rowe's "moralizing," but even then they have divorced
the ethical from any metaphysical foundation.[6] In his volume of *The
Oxford History of English Literature,* Bonamy Dobrée goes so far as to
say of Rowe's tragedies that "one essential part of tragedy, the metaphysical sense, was missing"; for that matter, "in none of the plays of the
period is there any metaphysical idea, no great theme which makes the
observer say, 'This is what happens to man!' "[7] In his *Restoration
Tragedy,* Eric Rothstein argues that "theology does not set its mark in
any real way" on later Restoration tragedy (implicitly including Rowe,
whom he mentions throughout) as it becomes more affective and its
"serial" form becomes detached from plot and thus from a mimetic reflection of metaphysical reality (pp. 117, 158 f, and passim). "All conduct in these plays," writes Rothstein, "proceeds from an ethical rather
than a religious . . . basis" (p. 131). Although in his recent and generally
excellent *Restoration Serious Drama* Geoffrey Marshall admits that *Jane
Shore* is a "fundamentally religious play" concerning "salvation" and
"penance" (p. 220), because of his emphasis on character throughout his
study he consistently portrays the "seriousness" of Restoration tragedy
—and the Christianity upon which it often depends in the plays—in
strictly ethical terms: "Restoration plays are concerned with the path
through *this* life. . . . [The playwrights] assume that every man must
make himself right before the world will be right. They believe that
character, that ethos, is everything that counts. They are therefore distinguished from writers who find the answer to the morally good life in
terms of any of the following: revelation, institutions, [etc.]. . . . The
Christian figures [in these plays] . . . do not attempt to convert the audience to a faith, but to show the advantages of a Christian way of life. . . .

The Restoration image of man, in outline, is not very different from the image of man in the Renaissance, with perhaps one significant difference —the Restoration man is a secular creature. He may have intimate ties with the divine or the macrocosmic or the metaphysical, but the plays make little of that. They focus instead on his worldly anguish and the possibilities, such as they are, for his worldly redemption, salvation, and peace" (pp. 30, 34 f, 65).

On the other hand, Rowe's physician and first biographer, James Welwood, assures us that Rowe was an intensely religious man, one who studied philosophy and theology diligently: "He had a good Taste in Philosophy, and having a firm Impression of Religion upon his Mind, he took great delight in Divinity and Ecclesiastical History, in both which he made great Advances in the times he retir'd into the Country, which were frequent. He expresst on all Occasions his full Perswasion of the Truth of Reveal'd Religion."[8] Welwood also assures us that religion is a primary concern in Rowe's plays: "It may be justly said of them all, that never Poet painted *Virtue* or *Religion* in a more charming Dress on the Stage, nor were ever *Vice* and *Impiety* better expos'd to Contempt and Hatred. There runs through every one of them an Air of Religion and Virtue" (p. xx). This religious dimension has either been denied or almost totally neglected in criticism of Rowe's tragedies, and yet, I submit, it is this dimension—in its metaphysical even more than its ethical aspects —which is the most apposite to their full understanding. For the trage- dies of Nicholas Rowe are *Christian* tragedies; that is, the solution which they dramatically proffer to the problems of suffering and sin and con- comitant metaphysical doubt is the traditional Christian solution, that man must above all avoid the nihilistic sin of despair and must trust im- plicitly in the Providence of God—in His justice and in His mercy. That Providence, as it manifests itself in the formal design of Rowe's tragedies, is the supreme metaphysical reality—eminently and imma- nently involved in "what happens to man," and upon which Christian ethics, at least as Christians view the world, is necessarily dependent.

PART 1

Five of Rowe's seven tragedies—*The Ambitious Stepmother, Tamerlane, Ulysses, The Royal Convert,* and *Lady Jane Gray*—concentrate on the figure of the suffering innocent. Tragedy with such a protagonist has generally put off most modern readers because of its polarization of good and evil and its lack of hamartia; but this particular type of tragedy, like the tragicomedy which was so popular in the seventeenth century and with which it has so much in common, is really the other side of the coin to revenge tragedy in its theme of God's distributive—rather than primarily retributive (or vindictive)—justice. In Rowe's plays, as in so many of the type, the solution to the problem of suffering innocence is to trust in the providential care and justice of God, Who eventually rewards and punishes according to deserts—if only in the hereafter—and Who ultimately brings good out of evil—if only in the eschaton.

As Herschel Baker points out in *The Wars of Truth*, "The doctrine of providence has always served to justify the apparent evils of a world that, though sunk in sin and temporality, must somehow be adjusted to the hypothesis of a theocratic universe" (p. 13), and he relates how the doctrine was strenuously maintained throughout the Renaissance (p. 12 ff). In his study of Renaissance atheism, *Doubt's Boundless Sea*, Don Cameron Allen notes that in answer to the growing threat of free thinking, and particularly deism, "the sections on theodicy in antiatheist books grew more and more extended" as the seventeenth century progressed and that, accordingly, the English "were being very vigorous in their defense of special Providence," or God's particular intervention into the lives of men (p. 146 f). This intense activity—culminating in eighteenth-century optimism—was quite naturally reflected in the imaginative literature of the period, most notably, of course, in Milton's *Paradise Lost*, whose theodicy Rowe constantly echoes. And in the major tragedians of the seventeenth century, Rowe found ample precedent for the Christian tragedy of suffering innocence.

The major tragedian for Rowe and his contemporaries was, of course, William Shakespeare. Shakespeare's histories and tragedies constantly raise questions of suffering innocence and cosmic justice, and as numerous critics have argued (and as I am firmly convinced), those plays commonly portray a providentially ordered universe where suffering is not meaningless and evil does not go unpunished. From Richmond's defeat of Richard III at the chronological end of the tetralogies; to the "special providence" in *Hamlet* which alone can right the state of Denmark and the world; to Cordelia's and Edgar's redemptive actions and Malcolm and Macduff's final triumph; to the providential accidents of *Cymbeline* (considered a tragedy throughout the seventeenth century and in Rowe's own edition, *The Works of Mr. William Shakespear*, q.v.), most of Shakespeare's serious plays, not to mention his comedies, are theodicean. In the Restoration period Shakespeare's subtle and complex treatment of theodicy was oversimplified by those infamous adapters with their strict and constricting interpretation of poetic justice. When examined thematically, as has seldom been done, several of the alterations in three of the most popular adaptations reveal attempts to further justify Providence. In Davenant's operatic version of *Macbeth*, a new emphasis is placed on trust in God, and Macduff becomes even more explicitly the agent of divine justice. In Tate's *The History of King Lear*, Providence is continually invoked; Edgar explicitly becomes God's Champion, and Cordelia interprets the happy ending thus: "Then there are Gods, and Vertue is their Care."[9] In Cibber's *The Tragical History of King Richard III*, against Richard's threat to world order the need for trust in Providence is stressed, from Henry VI's submission to "Heav'ns Will" (I.i.89), to the frequent appeals to Heaven, to the appearance of the ghosts "By Heavens high Ordinance" (V.v.35), to Richmond's role as God's Champion (V, passim).

Critics have only begun to see that one of the dominant themes in the tragedies and heroic plays (if not the entire canon) of the major dramatist of the Restoration, John Dryden, is also trust in providential justice.[10] Nearly all these plays focus on the problem of suffering innocence, and they are filled with challenges to, complaints against, and justifications of Providence, with the fiercest challenges coming perhaps from Dryden's villainesses, Zempoalla, Lyndaraxa, and Nourmahal; the most poignant complaints from Aureng-Zebe, Almeyda, and Cleomenes; and the most signal justifications from Tiresias and Saint Catharine. In the opening of Act V of *All for Love*, Charmion epitomizes the problem of suffering innocence (or at least misfortunate virtue) in Dryden's tragedies when she says of Cleopatra's suffering,

> Be juster, Heav'n: such virtue punish'd thus,
> Will make us think that Chance rules all above,
> And shuffles, with a random hand, the Lots
> Which Man is forc'd to draw.[11]

Yet whether already present, or acquired gradually as in *The Conquest of Granada*, faith in Divine Providence is tested and ultimately vindicated against those who scorn it—even if, as in the instances of Saint Catharine, Towerson, and Cleomenes, the test is death. That Dryden would attempt to adapt Milton's great theodicy to drama in *The State of Innocence* should not be at all surprising.

There are other major precedents in seventeenth-century tragedy for Rowe's theodicean solution to the problem of suffering innocence.

Webster's *The Duchess of Malfi* and Tourneur's *The Atheist's Tragedy*
are the best examples in the Jacobean period. In the Restoration some
of Otway's tragedies are theodicean, certainly *Alcibiades* and *Don
Carlos*.[12] The same is true of Lee's *Mithridates* and *Lucius Junius Brutus*
and of Settle's *The Empress of Morocco*. Finally, just a few years before
Rowe's advent on the stage, Congreve wrote his popular tragedy, *The
Mourning Bride*, which concludes,

> Seest thou, how just the Hand of Heav'n has been?
> Let us that thro' our Innocence survive,
> Still in the Paths of Honour persevere;
> And not from past or present ills Despair:
> For Blessings ever wait on vertuous Deeds;
> And tho' a late, a sure Reward succeeds.[13]

The same conclusion is echoed over and over in Rowe's five dramatic
theodicies.

PART 2

In Rowe's two most famous plays—*The Fair Penitent* and *Jane Shore*—
the focus is not primarily on the problem of suffering innocence but on
the problem of sin and repentance. The major theme remains, nevertheless, trust in Providence—in God's mercy as the key to expiation and
atonement. Rowe's sinful heroines, either early or late, follow the path
of repentance to a human forgiveness which is itself emblematic of divine. The central importance to Christianity of the doctrine of repentance is epitomized in the authorized Anglican sermon "An Homily of
Repentance, And of True Reconciliation unto God": "There is nothing
that the Holy Ghost doth so much labour in all the Scriptures to beat
into mens heads, as Repentance, amendment of Life, and speedy return-
ing unto the Lord God of Hosts. And no marvel why: For we do daily
and hourly by our wickedness and stubborn disobedience, horribly fall
away from God, thereby purchasing unto our selves (if he should deal
with us according to his justice) eternal damnation."[14] Accordingly, the
themes of repentance and forgiveness permeate medieval and Renaissance literature, including seventeenth-century English tragedy. With
regard to that kind of tragedy which focuses on the problem of repentance, however, there is a particular tradition out of which Rowe's plays
emerge.

Nearly all of Rowe's modern critics place *The Fair Penitent* and *Jane Shore* in the Renaissance-Restoration tradition of "domestic" tragedy.[15] Indeed, both are adaptations of domestic tragedies by Massinger and Heywood, respectively,[16] and Rowe announces in the prologue to *The Fair Penitent* that he is abandoning "the fate of Kings and Empires" for "an humbler theme," a "melancholy tale of private woes" (*Works*, I, 156). But the important resemblance between Rowe's two tragedies and the domestic tradition is that they have the same religious dimension which both Henry Hitch Adams and Charles Howard Peake have shown to be predominant in seventeenth- and early eighteenth-century domestic—or "homiletic"—tragedies.[17] Both critics argue very cogently that the meaning of these plays is heavily influenced by the contemporary theological concepts which are reflected throughout, so that the plays become something like "adjuncts to the pulpit" (Peake, passim). Adams offers a formula for the genre, which, if it is too sweeping, at least applies in the majority of instances: "The typical domestic tragedy followed a pattern, the sequence being: sin, discovery, repentance, punishment, and expectation of divine mercy" (p. 7). This pattern is roughly that to which Rowe adheres in his two domestic tragedies. His most important predecessor in this kind of tragedy is Thomas Heywood. The repentance of Heywood's sinful heroines in *A Woman Killed with Kindness*, *The English Traveller*, and *Edward IV*, and their final appeals to their husbands—and to Heaven—for forgiveness, anticipate Rowe, who in fact adapted Heywood's treatment of Jane Shore in his own most polished play. But Rowe is more subtle in his treatment of the pattern than most of his predecessors, including Heywood, and his plays are much more than mere "adjuncts to the pulpit." Through his excellence of characterization and through his powerful expression of mental and spiritual anguish, his two best plays transcend didactic formulae and become good art.

Looming behind Rowe is another and far greater predecessor in the tragedy of repentance—John Milton. In *Samson Agonistes*, Samson finally overcomes despair and places his "trust" in "the living God" and "his final pardon / Whose ear is ever open; and his eye / Gracious to re-admit the suppliant."[18] Samson's crucial turning point is his encounter with Dalila, where he resists the very temptation to which he had succumbed—a pattern repeated in both *The Fair Penitent* and *Jane Shore*. For that matter, Milton's tragedy sheds light upon all of Rowe's, for besides being a penitence play, it is a dramatic theodicy as well. Milton's conclusion may well serve as an epigraph for Rowe's tragedies:

All is best, though we oft doubt,
What th'unsearchable dispose
Of highest wisdom brings about,
And ever best found in the close. (vs. 1745 ff)

It is in the light of these traditions and themes, I submit, that the tragedies of Nicholas Rowe must be read. As will become apparent in the
course of this study, Rowe was intimately acquainted with the works of
several of the authors I have mentioned, but the important point is that
from these major predecessors he inherited not so much sources as forms
of tragedy that embody the Christian vision of a providential universe,
a vision which was under attack, as Herschel Baker's, Don Cameron
Allen's, and others' studies have shown,[19] by nearly all the new *isms* un-
leashed by the Renaissance and the Reformation: not only atheism, but
determinism and predeterminism, Machiavellianism and Hobbism, Epi-
cureanism and deism—anything that denied the immanence of Providence and the efficacy of prayer. Perhaps this attack inspired Rowe, like
Milton before him and his friend Pope after him, to justify the ways of
God to men and to exhort them to trust in divine justice and mercy.
Howbeit, this study attempts to show at least that Rowe's tragedies indeed *assert eternal Providence* in answer to the metaphysical dilemmas
of suffering innocents and sinners alike.

NOTES TO THE INTRODUCTION

1. "The Life of Nicholas Rowe," conveniently prefixed to Rowe, *Works*, I, 10°.
(The pagination being separate but not Roman, I distinguish it with an asterisk.)
2. See Emmett L. Avery, "The Popularity of *The Mourning Bride* in the London
Theatres in the Eighteenth Century," p. 115 f. For Rowe's general success, see Donald
B. Clark, "Nicholas Rowe," who discusses the success of each tragedy in each chapter
and who tabulates performances in Appendix C.
3. Rowe's influence on later English drama and on Richardson is well known. His
influence on continental drama is not, but witness the number of foreign translations
and adaptations (listed in James R. Sutherland, ed., *Three Plays*, by Nicholas Rowe, p.
42; Ferdinand H. Schwarz, *Nicholas Rowe's* Fair Penitent, p. 14 f; and Willy Budig, *Untersuchungen über* Jane Shore, p. 76) and see the inadequate but suggestive general
sketch in Alfred Behrend, *Nicholas Rowe als Dramatiker*, p. 62 ff. Continuing German
interest in Rowe is evidenced by the spate of early-twentieth-century dissertations listed
below (Bibliography A, criticism) and by the recent German reprint of Bell's and Inchbald's editions of Rowe's she-tragedies, also listed below (Bibliography A, collected editions).
4. See, e.g., the most famous praise, that of Samuel Johnson, "The Life of Nicholas
Rowe."

5. See Bibliography A, criticism, and subsequent citations in my text. A more specific review of this criticism would be both tedious and irrelevant, since my approach is radically different from the bulk of it.

6. See especially Frank J. Kearful, "The Nature of Tragedy in Rowe's *The Fair Penitent*," and his dissertation, "The Rhetoric of Augustan Tragedy," ch. ii. His criticism is still mainly affective, however; he concentrates on Rowe's pathetic and didactic appeals to his "middle-class" audience. But see Richard H. Dammers, "Female Characters and Feminine Morality in the Tragedies of Nicholas Rowe," a 1971 dissertation that is subsequent to my own "Nicholas Rowe's Christian Tragedies" (1969). Dammers mentions some of Rowe's religious themes while concentrating, obviously, on other matters. His own review of this criticism, "Recent Scholarship on Nicholas Rowe," overlooks not only mine (which is not included in *Dissertation Abstracts* but is cited in a few places, including a dissertation Dammers does review) but several other dissertations and theses (also, with one exception, not included in *DA* but cited in the standard bibliography in this field, Carl J. Stratman et al., eds., *Restoration and Eighteenth-Century Theatre Research: A Bibliographical Guide, 1900–1968*).

7. *English Literature in the Early Eighteenth Century, 1700–1740*, pp. 241, 243. In "Pathos and Personality in the Tragedies of Nicholas Rowe," Malcolm Goldstein concurs in denying Rowe's plays any "high seriousness of purpose" whatsoever (p. 185).

8. In Rowe, trans., *Lucan's* Pharsalia, p. xxiv. For probable evidence of Rowe's reading, see the numerous volumes of philosophy, theology, and ecclesiastical history and polity in *A Catalogue of the Library of Nicholas Rowe, Esq.*, appended to this study.

9. V.vi.97, in *Five Restoration Adaptations of Shakespeare*, ed. Christopher Spencer. All the references to the adaptations are to this edition.

10. See Anne T. Barbeau, *The Intellectual Design of John Dryden's Heroic Plays*, and Gail H. Compton, "The Metaphor of Conquest in Dryden's *The Conquest of Granada*."

11. V.i.1 ff, in *John Dryden: Four Tragedies*, ed. L. A. Beaurline and Fredson Bowers.

12. See John David Walker, "Moral Vision in the Drama of Thomas Otway."

13. V.ii.317 ff, in *The Complete Plays of William Congreve*, ed. Herbert Davis. See Aubrey Williams, "The 'Just Decrees of Heav'n' and Congreve's *Mourning Bride*."

14. In *Certain Sermons or Homilies*, p. 334 f. These were the official Anglican sermons originally appointed to be read every Sunday, and as Donald Greene has pointed out, they were published forty to fifty times at least in the seventeenth century ("Augustinianism and Empiricism," p. 45n).

15. The quotation marks indicate the arbitrariness of the generic limitations, which can be stretched to include tragedies of the nobility such as *Othello, The Duchess of Malfi*, and *Venice Preserved*, or restricted to tragedies of the native common folk.

16. Viz. Massinger and Field, *The Fatal Dowry*, and Heywood, *Edward IV*. Rowe had one volume each of Massinger and Heywood in his library, probably (since most of his sources have been found there) containing these plays (*Catalogue*, quarto 70).

17. Adams, *English Domestic or, Homiletic Tragedy 1575 to 1642*, and Peake, "Domestic Tragedy in Relation to Theology in the First Half of the Eighteenth Century."

18. Vss. 1140 and 1171 ff, in *Complete Poems and Major Prose*, ed. Merritt Y. Hughes. All quotations from Milton's poetry are from this text.

19. See, e.g., Peake, ch. i; Adams, ch. ii; Roy W. Battenhouse, *Marlowe's* Tamburlaine, p. 86 ff; and J. Paul Hunter, *The Reluctant Pilgrim*, ch. iii. Cf. the following statement concerning the great contemporary French bishop, Jacques-Bénigne Bossuet, and the doctrine of Providence: "De tous les dogmes chrétiens, c'est celui que Bossuet a défendu avec le plus de rigueur, parce qu'il était le plus vivement combattu par les athées" (F. Gendrot and F.-M. Eustache, eds., *Auteurs français*, p. 266). The same doctrine, the editors note, inspires the whole of Bossuet's *Les Oraisons funèbres* and *Le Discours sur l'histoire universelle*.

One

The Trial of the Innocent

I   Prolegomena
The Ambitious Stepmother,
"Poetical Justice," and
"The Trial of Man"

HOUGH AN OBVIOUS apprentice work, Rowe's first tragedy, *The Ambitious Stepmother,* produced in 1700, reveals at once both his literary promise and one of his major themes, the problem of suffering innocence. The play ends with a dilemma: although the principal virtuous characters are dead,[1]* the new king Artaban insists, "The Gods are great and just" (*Works,* I, 78 [V.ii]). That this ending presented a problem for at least some of Rowe's contemporaries is evident from the Dedication: "Some people, whose judgment I ought to have a deference for, have told me, that they wished I had given the latter part of the story quite another turn; that *Artaxerxes* and *Amestris* ought to have been preserved, and made happy in the conclusion of the play; that besides the satisfaction which the spectators would have had to have seen two virtuous (at least innocent) characters rewarded and successful, there might have been also a more noble and instructive moral drawn that way" (p. 4). Perhaps one of these dissatisfied persons was Charles Gildon, whose *A New Rehearsal, or Bays the Younger* (1714), voices such a criticism—a criticism which could well have been offered at the time of the play's production.[2] Through the mouths of his fictional critics, Gildon says that the death of Cleone "is contrary to Poetic Justice, and the Rules of Providence," and that there is "as little Reason that *Amestris* or *Artaxerxes,* shou'd die, both Sovereignly Virtuous, and yet Miserable"; his position is summed up thus: "The Deaths of *Cleone, Amestris,* and *Artaxerxes,* provoke our Indignation, as having done nothing at all to deserve those Incredible Misfortunes; so that instead of *Fear* and *Pity,* the true aim of all Tragical Action, it [the play] moves only Horror [at the misfortune

*Notes to this chapter begin on page 40.

13

of the virtuous] and Satisfaction [at that of the wicked]; and indeed
every where endeavors to abolish the Notion of a particular Providence,
and so is Impious."[3] The comment of one recent critic shows that the
difficulty with the ending persists: "Artaban, in his final speech, claims
that 'The Gods are great and just,' . . . but this is just what the last act
has proved not true. If it were, then the pathos Rowe wanted to create,
and in fact succeeds rather well in portraying, would be almost impossible. This kind of pathos is created rather by undeserved suffering and
unjust action by 'the Gods,' or what Artemisa calls 'the Hand of
Chance.' "[4] If these critics are right; if the play does "abolish the Notion of a particular Providence, and so is Impious"; if the outcome for
the virtuous and the vicious alike depends only on the caprice of
"Chance"; if, in short, the play proves that the gods are not just, then
not only is the judgment of Artaban contradicted, but the faith of the
other virtuous characters in the play is belied, and the scorn of the
usurpers is justified. For throughout the play the usurpers insist that the
gods do not care, while the virtuous insist that they do.

i

From the beginning it is clear that for the usurpers, religion is nothing
more than a tool to placate and manipulate the populace. When the
statesman Mirza proposes seizing Artaxerxes and Memnon in the temple
of the Sun-god on that feast day which is the "most venerable" of all
"sacred times," the high priest Magas balks at the "profanation" and
raises the fear of "the vengeance of the Gods" (II.ii, p. 31 f). Mirza rebukes him thus:

> The Gods shall certainly befriend our cause,
> At least not be our foes, nor will they leave
> Their happy seats (where free from care and pain,
> Bless'd of themselves alone, of man regardless,
> They loll serene in everlasting ease)
> To mind the trivial business of our world. (p. 32)

Thus Mirza's gods are those infamous deities of the Epicureans and their
seventeenth-century atheistical disciples, who denied Divine Providence and consequently were vigorously attacked by clergy, scholars,
and poets alike.[5] After the sacrilege, Magas exclaims in terror, "Every
God / Seems from his shrine to threaten us with vengeance" (III.iii,
p. 45). Yet Mirza simply accuses him of being "superstitious" and of

fabricating "monsters"—the "coward's vice." When Magas later describes to Mirza the righteous indignation of the mob, who vow "revenge" upon their "slighted" gods (V.i, p. 64), Mirza merely sends him out to placate them by indulging their "fancy for religion" with the "gaudy shew" of a sacred procession, an "apt amusement for a crowd" (p. 65).

On the other hand, the virtuous characters continually assert that the gods do care. To the flattering Magas, Memnon says, "The Gods, 'tis true, are just, and have, I hope, / At length decreed an end to my misfortunes" (II.i, p. 21). At the end of their encounter, Memnon warns Magas of divine retribution (p. 24), and in disgust with the corruption of the priesthood, calls upon the "awful powers" to assert their "justice" (p. 25). In the first encounter between Artaxerxes and his usurping stepmother, she ironically echoes Memnon's earlier words and hypocritically invokes the "thunders" of the "righteous pow'rs, whose justice awes the world" (II.ii, p. 27). But Artaxerxes roundly rebukes her:

> Thy priest instructs thee,
> Else sure thou hadst not dar'd to tempt the Gods,
> And trifle with their justice.

Later, to quiet Amestris' fears that their bridal bliss will be destroyed, Artaxerxes says assuredly, "Doubt not the Gods, my fair, whose righteous power / Shall favour and protect our virtuous loves" (III.ii, p. 39).

When they are captured a moment later, Artaxerxes challenges the Sun-god, from whom by virtue of his royalty he claims descent: "Canst thou behold, and not avenge thy race?" (III.iii, p. 45). The indignant Memnon correctly concludes that Mirza "laughs / At the fictitious justice of the Gods, / And thinks their thunder has not wings to reach him" (p. 46). In response Mirza prophesies that Memnon soon will renounce the gods and be renounced by them. With supreme confidence in "the Gods" and in himself Memnon hurls Mirza's challenge back in his teeth. And when Amestris concludes that "There are no remedies for ills like ours" except to "indulge our grief" and wait for the gods "to end our woes in immortality" (p. 47), Artaxerxes exclaims,

> Ha! say'st thou? Gods! Yes certain there are Gods,
> To whom my youth with reverence still has bow'd,
> Whose care and providence are virtue's guard;

Think then, my fair, they have not made us great,
And like themselves, for miserable ends. (p. 47 f)

Yet after the three captives have been led off to their temple-prison,
Mirza muses,

This night let 'em despair, and ban, and rage,
And to the wooden deities within
Tell frantic tales. (p. 48)

Frantically complain they do, along with Artaban and Cleone, throughout the fourth act (q.v.); whether to "wooden deities" is the question.
Finally, in Act V Amestris complains,

Will ye not hear, ye ever-gracious Gods?
(Since sure you do not joy in our misfortunes,
But only try the strength of our frail virtue.)
Are not my sorrows full? (sc. ii, p. 66)

In contrast, as he prepares to ravish Amestris, Mirza speaks of a Jove
who would "lay aside his providence" for similar pursuits, and when
Amestris cries to the "awful Gods" for "lightning" to "blast him" (p. 69),
Mirza replies,

Oh no! Your Gods have pleasures of their own;
Some mortal beauty charms the wanton *Jove*,
Within whose arms he revels, nor has leisure
To mind thy foolish screaming.

She continues to call on the gods, complaining, "Is there no hope of aid
from Gods or men?" When in desperation she kneels to beg Mirza that
he do anything but dishonor her, Mirza gloats,

Thou art, thou must be mine, nor heaven, nor earth,
Nor the conspiring power of hell shall save thee. (p. 70)

Thus the play is permeated with the question of whether the gods
care, a fact which establishes the question as a major—if not the major—
theme. At the end, although Amestris is not raped, she is murdered, and
Memnon asks pointedly, "What has thy innocence done to merit this?"

(p. 74). Their momentary hope shattered, Artaxerxes and Memnon kill themselves. These events temporarily shake even Artaban's confidence in divine justice, and he complains, "Then virtue is in vain, since base deceit / And treachery have triumph'd o'er the mighty" (p. 77).

ii

Artaban finally concludes, however, that the gods *are* just, and the report of Magas' death is the decisive factor. Artaban immediately tells Cleanthes, his general and the bearer of the report, to ponder the "recent story of this night" and he too will "wonder" at and "confess" the justice of the gods, whom Artaban addresses thus:

> Well have you mark'd,
> Celestial powers, your righteous detestation
> Of sacrilege, of base and bloody treachery. (V.ii, p. 78)

In other words, he interprets the overthrow of the usurpers as a well-marked providential judgment. In the Dedication, Rowe maintains that their overthrow observes "that which they call the poetical justice" (p. 5). The point is that for this and all of Rowe's plays, as indeed for the tradition whence he writes, poetic and providential justice are the same.

In recent years, two seminal articles by Richard H. Tyre and Aubrey Williams[6] have rescued the concept of poetic justice from its interpretation as a mere dramaturgical contrivance to effect a happy ending, to illustrate a moral, or even to escape from the realities of suffering and evil.[7] They have shown that in the time of Rowe, especially in the writings of Thomas Rymer, John Dennis, and Charles Gildon, and throughout the Renaissance as well (if not the entire Western tradition), the concept had a metaphysical foundation. As Williams puts it, the best critics and playwrights of the entire seventeenth century considered poetic justice to be "fully referential to an ontological reality that was truly immanent in all earthly events. If poesy were to reflect the essential realities of man and his world, it had to image forth, they thought, the order of cosmic justice which they and the majority of persons in their age believed in. The imaging of that Divine Reality of Justice is 'poetical justice' " (p. 553). Dennis states the matter very strongly: "Poetick Justice would be a Jest if it were not an Image of the Divine, and if it did not consequently suppose the Being of a God and Providence."[8]

In his recent and important book, *Restoration Tragedy: Form and the Process of Change*, Eric Rothstein admits that "poetic(al) justice is

the dramatic analogue to Divine Providence" in the "fabulist," or plot-
oriented, theory of Rymer and his tradition (p. 5), and that his demand
for that justice "reflected a commitment to 'nature,' a metaphysically
informed 'nature' which tragedy should map out" (p. 182). Yet after
Rymer, Rothstein sees a new affectivism arising in both theory and practice which is inimical to "dramatic forms that mirror Providence"
(p. 118). No doubt critics wrote more about affective matters then as
they wrestled with the theory of catharsis, and no doubt playwrights
like Lee, Otway, and Banks became more sensational. But Rothstein
simply does not prove that Restoration tragedies thus surrendered integral form to "serial" form—that is, a form which mirrors physical and
metaphysical reality to a form which dispenses with plot and presents
merely a series of interchangeable scenes designed to titillate the audience (ch. i). As he admits, the theoretical shift was one of "emphasis"
and still "a copious number of early eighteenth-century critics reiterated the fabulist theories" (p. 23), a number which included not only
minor critics like James Drake, who throughout his *Antient and Modern
Stages Survey'd* (1699) bases his answer to Jeremy Collier on the primary importance of formal design, but also such major critics as Dennis
and Gildon, whose names Rothstein carefully does not mention, for they
weaken his case considerably.[9]

What dilutes Rothstein's case most is his illogical shifting of ground
between formal and affective concerns, as in this passage: "The rhetorical basis of tragedy had changed. To be persuasive, pleasure had to be
deeply satisfying; to be satisfying, it demanded sensationalism; and sensationalism, in turn, bludgeoned the sense of a providential whole out of
recognition. For although logically the fabulist theory was tenable even
after the older assumptions about tragic pleasure had shrunk in promi-
nence, playgoers accustomed to looking for a succession of sensations
rather than for overall order must have found it difficult to perceive a
continuing and exact Providence animating the whole" (p. 8 f). Must
sensationalism necessarily destroy overall design? Rothstein himself here
admits that no *logical* connection exists between affective and formal
matters, yet he speculates on a totally unempirical assertion about the
habits and desires of playgoers and what they might have had difficulty
observing.

In his rage for generalization, I think, Rothstein has simply not
carefully read later Restoration tragedy, particularly that of Dryden,
Congreve,[10] and Rowe. For the proof of whether a Restoration playwright departed from the very long "fabulist" tradition lies in the de-

sign of the individual plays themselves. Leaving affective concerns aside, then, let us examine the design of *The Ambitious Stepmother* on formal grounds to see whether Rowe was right to insist that it follows poetic justice, in the traditional mimetic sense, the theoretical foundation for which he most probably knew, since the sale catalogue of his library (q.v.) contains the relevant works of Jonson, d'Aubignac, Rapin, Rymer, Dennis, Gildon, and Blackmore.

At the end of Rowe's play Artaban sees in the defeat of the usurpers that the gods have marked well their "righteous detestation / Of sacrilege, of base and bloody treachery." For the punishments inflicted on the usurpers are remarkably appropriate to their crimes. The corrupt priest Magas is destroyed in the midst of his hypocritical and sacrilegious procession by the "superstitious" mob he is attempting to appease. Moreover, the function of the mob as the gods' avenger is explicit. In the beginning of Act IV, immediately following the sacrilege in the temple, Cleanthes has said that while the "fearful crowd" dreads "the anger of the Gods," the "wise, who know th'effects of popular fury," expect "vengeance" from the crowd itself (sc. i, p. 49). Ironically, the "wise" are both right and wrong, as is obvious in Cleanthes' later report of the "fate" Magas "merited" (V.i, p. 78):

> on a sudden, like a hurricane,
> That starts at once, and ruffles all the ocean,
> Some fury more than mortal seiz'd the crowd;
> At once they rush'd, at once they cry'd revenge;
> Then snatch'd and tore the trembling priest to pieces.
> What was most strange, no injury was offer'd
> To any of the brotherhood beside,
> But all their rage was ended in his death:
> Like formal justice that severely strikes,
> And in an instant is serene and calm.

Details such as the "hurricane," the "fury more than mortal," the crying "revenge," the strangeness and uniqueness, and the reference to "formal justice" seem calculated to leave no doubt in the audience's minds (as they do not in Artaban's) about the import of the entire account: this is not only a fitting fate, but a manifestation of the Hand of Heaven. It appears that Memnon's earlier appeal for divine retribution upon this evil

priest has finally been answered—by the "formal justice" of the gods,
working, as usual, through secondary causes that serve as the instruments of their Providence.

The imagery of serenity and calmness that ends Cleanthes' report—
and the play—can also be seen to have supernatural and providential
significance when viewed in relation to the imagery of darkness and imminent chaos that has persisted from the opening description of the
dying Arsaces. Magas says that "an universal horror" seized him as he
watched the King:

> The chearful day was every where shut out
> With care, and left a more than midnight darkness,
> Such as might ev'n be felt. (I.i, p. 9)

The "few dim lamps" only added to the dismalness, which is contrasted
to the "majestic fire" the King's eyes once had. There seems to be a
metaphoric analogy between the demise of the King and the chaotic
absence of the Sun-god, whom he represents on earth[11] and who is the
very principle of order and harmony in the universe (III.iii, p. 43). On
this holiest of holy days, when, as Magas says, "Pernicious discord
seems / Out-rooted from our more than iron age" (II.ii, p. 31), discord
is far from "Out-rooted." It is imminent. And not merely because the
King is dying, but because he is dying without securing the succession
of the rightful heir. The usurpers are tampering with the very order of
the universe, the very law of nature, as Memnon makes clear. In a scene
marked with several references to the impending "universal ruin"
(II.i, p. 21 f), Memnon rebukes the usurpers and their plot thus:

> Can I, can they, can any honest hand,
> Join in an act like this? Is not the elder
> By nature pointed out for preference?
> Is not his right inroll'd among those laws
> Which keeps the world's vast frame in beauteous order[?] (p. 23)

It is extremely significant that the King dies at the moment of the sacrilegious capture in the very Temple of the Sun, for the crime is at once
against the gods themselves, against their "race" (the King and his law-
ful successor), and consequently against the principle of order, both in
heaven and on earth. The King's death presages the demise of order and
the advent of chaos. Accordingly, after the sacrilege Magas reports to

Mirza that the temple "reels" and "Nods at the profanation" (III.iii, p. 45), and he later describes in apocalyptic terms the "Infernal discord" that threatens the city (V.i, p. 64), while in "confus'd disorderly array" the crowd marches on the palace, crying,

> religion is no more,
> Our Gods are slighted, whom if we revenge not,
> War, pestilence, and famine will ensue,
> And universal ruin swallow all.

Magas' death at the hands of this mob, then, must be seen in terms of the "revenge" of this slight to the gods in order to save the world from chaos. The mode of his death and the ordered calm that follows it both imply a providential judgment.

The manifestation of Providence in the death of Magas enables Artaban, and should urge the audience, to reflect on the entire story of the night and *a fortiori* to see also the fates of Mirza and Artemisa as providential. Like Magas', their punishments are remarkably appropriate to their crimes. Mirza is killed in the act of his own lust; moreover, the instrument of his death is the maiden he is attempting to ravish and at whose cries for heavenly assistance he contemptuously scoffs. In the Dedication Rowe himself points out the appropriateness of the Queen's punishment: "The Queen is deposed from her authority by her own son; which, I suppose, will be allowed as the severest mortification that could happen to a woman of her imperious temper" (p. 5). Thus, lust is punished by virgin innocence and usurpation by deposition. Both the punishments and their modes, then, are signs of poetical—and providential —justice.

The fate of the usurpers is appropriate not only to their particular crimes. It is appropriate to their entire philosophy. Mirza's attitude toward religion and the gods is shown to be woefully mistaken. But this attitude is also the basis for the usurpers' moral and political philosophy. Where there are no gods who care, self-interest becomes the guiding principle. Artemisa explicitly calls "self-interest" the "first and noblest law of nature" (IV.i, p. 54). According to this view, mankind is divided into the "wise" and the "foolish." In the passage just cited, Artemisa is inveighing against Artaban's "foolish honour," which she calls a "ridiculous notion." From the opening scene of the play Mirza has delineated

this philosophy: "The wise and active conquer difficulties / By daring
to attempt 'em" (p. 12). Thus they overcome "Valiant fools" like Memnon, who are but the "tools" of statesmen (p. 13):

> Dull heavy things! Whom nature has left honest
> In mere frugality, to save the charge
> She's at in setting out a thinking soul.

The prime example in the play of such a "thinking soul," of course, is
Mirza himself, who conceives evil plots in his mind "at once compleatly
form'd" in the fashion of the typical Satan-Machiavel (II.ii, p. 31; cf.
p. 33 and I.i, p. 10). By such a "fine project of the statesman's brain,"
"wit" overcomes "courage" and "boasted prowess" (II.ii, p. 33). Furthermore, Mirza predicts the conversion of the Pretender (Artaban) to
the philosophy "that only fools would lose / A crown for notionary principles" (III.ii, p. 42). When Artaban refuses to gain the throne dishonor-
ably, Artemisa asks the "honourable fool" if he has forgotten the "wise
arts of empire" and the "worth of power" in favor of a "notion," an
"empty sound of virtue," a "dry maxim, / Which pedants have devised
for boys to canvas" (IV.i, p. 50 f). So the "wise" are opportunistic, self-
interested nominalists—or Hobbists—and the enemies not only of religion but of all traditional morality. Theirs is a morality of expediency,
and their politics is based upon it.

As Artemisa implies, the politics of the "wise" is the politics of
"power." Earlier Magas argues,

> Unbounded pow'r, and height of greatness give
> To Kings that lustre, which we think divine. (II.i, p. 23)

He thus denies the relationship between the King and the Sun-god
which is stressed throughout the play. The boldest and most naked assertion of the doctrine of power is Artemisa's justification of her husband's
murder: "Pow'r gives a sanction, and makes all things just" (I.i, p. 15).
Mirza echoes this doctrine when he begs Amestris to "think on power,
on power and place supreme," and then she will consent to violate her
bridal bed (V.ii, p. 67). Unchecked power is the goal of the usurpers, and
the end justifies any means to obtain it. The political philosophy of the
"wise," then, is a poetic exaggeration of the theories of Machiavelli and
Hobbes, which, as Louis Teeter has shown, had become amalgamated
in the Restoration, and which were seen as a threat to the Christian

vision of world order.[12] In the tradition of Shakespeare and Dryden, Rowe is attacking those who, as a consequence of their denial of the spiritual and the providential—Mirza believes that "mankind is govern'd" only by the "finer arts" of the "wise" (III.ii, p. 42)—subscribe to a politics of *de facto* power, in which the most cunning can seize power and hold it with impunity.

In her opening speech—"Be fix'd, my soul, fix'd on thy own firm basis" (I.i, p. 14 f)—Artemisa carries the self-interested philosophy of the "wise" to its logical conclusion: total reliance on self instead of the gods. Her self-assertion is the height of pride and tantamount to the assumption of divinity. Rowe drives the point home by having Mirza approach her as a goddess, an attribution she implicitly accepts (p. 15).[13] Again in Act IV Artemisa assumes the language and the prerogatives of divinity: she asks Artaban,

> Is not thy power the creation of my favour,
> Which in precarious wise on me depending,
> Exists by my concurrence to its being? (sc. i, p. 52)

Finally she concludes in the ultimate of blasphemous self-assertion, "I am fate in *Persia*, / And life and death depend upon my pleasure" (p. 53). Artaban's retort ("The world would be well govern'd, should the Gods / Depute their providence to women's care") makes it clear that Artemisa is assuming powers which belong to Providence alone.

Appropriately, the irony of the usurpers' defeat is precisely their inability to control events and their utter dependence on a fortune or a fate that ultimately proves to have a providential pattern. At the beginning Mirza wishes he could delay fate in the approaching death of Arsaces (I.i, p. 9), for,

> My royal mistress *Artemisa*'s fate,
> And all her son, young *Artaban*'s, high hopes,
> Hang on this lucky crisis. (p. 10)

Speaking of the temporary truce between the princes, Mirza exclaims,

> Most fortunate event! which gives us more
> Than ev'n our wishes could have ask'd. This truce
> Gives lucky opportunity for thinking. (II.ii, p. 31)

After Arsaces' death and the capture of Artaxerxes in the temple, Artemisa exhorts Artaban to "seize" fortune "While she is thine, or she is lost forever" (IV.i, p. 51). When Artaban rejects his mother's advice, Mirza warns,

> meddling fortune,
> (Whose malice labours to perplex the wise)
> If not prevented, will unravel all
> Those finer arts, which we with care have wove. (p. 54)

As he has said earlier, "The wise should not allow / A possibility to fortune's malice" (III.iii, p. 48).

Yet Mirza allows fortune the possibility of undoing him and his faction. Consumed by lust, he becomes careless and, ironically, unprovidential. Magas, fearful of the wrath of the people, taxes Mirza with underestimating the crowd's reaction to the capture of Artaxerxes and pleads with him to accompany the procession which is to placate the crowd, since they hold his "wisdom in most high regard": "Th'occasion is well worth your care and presence" (V.i, p. 65). But Mirza refuses, and we have already noted the subsequent fate of that procession. Mirza is about his own undoing, too. He is enraptured with the "fatal beauty" of Amestris (III.iii, p. 44). Struggling with himself, he says,

> Remember, statesman,
> Thy fate and future fortunes now are forming,
> And summon all thy counsels to their aid,
> Ev'n thy whole soul.

Nevertheless, he soon turns to rationalizing his lust: the "wise" are free to "indulge" in a little lustful "riot," he argues, as long as they desist before it dulls "the faculty of thinking" (p. 49). Thus begins the fall of the "thinking soul." Finally, his "fine arts" are "Unravel'd all" (V.ii, p. 70). He cries out in agony,

> Malicious fortune!
> She took the moment when my wisdom nodded,
> And ruin'd me at once. O doating fool! (p. 72)

Artemisa sums up the irony of his fall in terms of fate and chance:

> Could not all thy arts,
> That dol'd about destruction to our enemies,
> Guard thy own life from fate? Vain boast of wisdom,
> That with fantastic pride, like busy children,
> Builds paper towns and houses, which at once
> The hand of chance o'erturns, and loosely scatters! (p. 76)

It is not, however, either "fate" or "fortune" or the "hand of chance" that overturns Mirza. His death and its mode are remarkably appropriate not only to his particular crime but to everything he represents as the "thinking soul." This appropriateness alone argues for the presence of the Hand of Heaven. But what is more, the presence of that hand is explicit. Over Mirza's dead body Artaxerxes exclaims, "O all ye juster powers!" (p. 73). Memnon depicts Mirza's soul in hell, and Amestris says,

> and now he stands
> Arraign'd before the dread impartial judges,
> To answer to a long account of crimes.

After she has recounted the latest of those crimes, Artaxerxes complains, "O ye eternal rulers of the world, / Could you look on unmov'd?" (p. 74). In his next breath he answers his own question: "But say, instruct me, / That I may bow before the God that sav'd thee." Amestris' reply makes fully explicit the intervention of Providence:

> Sure 'twas some chaster pow'r that made me bold,
> And taught my trembling hand to find the way
> With his own poniard to the villain's heart.

Artemisa's fall is similarly ironic, and similarly appropriate to her philosophy. Immediately after laying claim to the regency of fate, she warns her son thus:

> The patience ev'n of Gods themselves has limits,
> Tho' they with long forbearance view man's folly,
> Yet if thou still persists to dare my power,
> Like them I may be urg'd to loose my vengeance,
> And tho' thou wert my creature, strike thee dead. (IV.i, p. 53)

As before, Artemisa is trifling with the truth, and her blasphemous analogy portends the vengeance that waits for her, for in good Pauline tradition, it is her wisdom that is the "folly," and that which the usurpers have called "folly" is the real wisdom. Artemisa senses a power controlling events at cross-purposes to her will:

> Some envious pow'r above, some hostile *Demon*,
> Works underhand against my stronger genius,
> And countermines me with domestic jars.
> Malicious chance! When all abroad was safe,
> To start an unseen danger from myself! (p. 53 f)

Mirza may call this *"Demon"* "meddling fortune," and Artemisa may call it "Malicious chance," but all the indications in the play are that they are wrong. Just like Mirza's dagger, the instrument of Artemisa's undoing comes, appropriately, from herself: her own son. Such "remarkable concurrences," to borrow a standard phrase from seventeenth-century homilies on Providence, can only be the signs of the Hand of Heaven.

So in their "fantastic pride" Mirza and Artemisa have overreached themselves, as do most of the villains of Christian literature, in accordance with that vision of the nature of the universe which sees evil as willy-nilly contributing to a good that is providentially ordained. Ironically, they spin out of themselves, out of their self-centered and blasphemous philosophy, their own destruction. Artemisa's final threat to Artaban shows her clinging to delusions of grandeur:

> When I assert the pow'r thou dar'st invade,
> Like Heaven I will resolve to be obey'd,
> And rule or ruin that which once I made. (V.ii, p. 78)

The curse falls back upon Artemisa herself. Since she will not be ruled, that "Heaven," which has destroyed her faction and thereby passed judgment upon its perversity, will inevitably "ruin" her. In the punishment of the usurpers, then, the justice of the gods has been unqualifiedly, and most appropriately, asserted. Neither the necessity of fate nor the fortuity of chance, to which the usurpers continually allude, but rather Divine Providence governs their "fates."[14]

While the fate of the usurpers implies providential justice, the fate of the virtuous seems to contradict it. According to Gildon, their deaths violate "Poetic Justice and the Rules of Providence." And yet Rowe claims to have "strictly observed" poetic justice (Dedication, p. 5), which, as we have seen, implies Providence. The key to the enigma is that in Rowe's day there were different opinions about how *much* justice poets had to distribute in imitation of Providence, perfect distribution being the innovation. As Corneille puts it in his "Discours du poème dramatique" (1660), such perfect distribution "n'est pas un précepte de l'art, mais un usage que nous avons embrassé, dont chacun peut se départir à ses périls" (*Œuvres complètes*, ed. André Stegman, p. 823). In fact, from the dawn of criticism very few theorists have ever prescribed, without qualification, perfect distributive justice as a rule for tragedy. Plato and Aristotle may have obliquely implied it, but only after the Renaissance does such a rule find its few uncompromising supporters: besides Rymer, Dennis, Gildon, Blackmore, and Collier, cited earlier, they are Georges de Scudéry, Edward Filmer, and the author of *The Stage Acquitted*.[15] Almost all the other critics who speak of a poetic justice mean merely the punishment of the wicked.[16] Even those critics usually cited for the development of the strict interpretation—Jean de Mairet, Jean Chapelain, La Mesnardière, d'Aubignac, Corneille, and Dryden—all qualify it in some way.

In his preface to *La Silvanire* (1631), Mairet merely distinguishes his tragicomic ending (where everyone is happy) from that which Aristotle describes (sig. õõ ij^r). In his prefatory letter to Marino's *Adone* (1623), Chapelain says merely that in the dénouement of a poem (as distinguished from an historical account) "the good man is recognized as such and the wicked man is punished, since their actions result from virtue or vice whose nature it is to reward or to destroy those who follow them" (Elledge and Schier, p. 12 f). If he means the kind of choric recognition Horace describes (*De Arte Poetica*, vs. 196 ff, Loeb), he is not really prescribing "reward" in the strict sense, just as he does not later in *Les Sentiments de l'Académie française sur la tragi-comédie du* Cid (1638), where he argues merely for "la punition" of vice (in *La Querelle du* Cid, p. 360 f).

La Mesnardière does lay down this maxim: "*Que les plus iustes Tragedies sont celles où les forfaits ont leurs punitions légitimes, & les vertus leurs recompenses*" (*La Poëtiqve*, p. 223). Yet he qualifies his maxim thus: "Si toutefois la Fable est telle que le Poëte n'ait pas lieu d'y recompenser la Vertu, il doibt pour le moins faire en sorte que les

Personnes vertueuses soient loüées publiquemēt par quelqu'vn des personnages qui obserue & qui admire leurs glorieuses actions. . . . Si la Fable ne permet pas qu'ils ["des Vices"] reçoiuent à l'heure mesme les punitions qui leur sont deuës, il faut qu'ils soient menacez de la Iustice divine par quelqu'un des personnages qui exagere & qui deteste leur honteuse difformité" (p. 223 f). D'Aubignac and Corneille merely echo La Mesnardière, but the actual phrasing is important, because these are the critics Rowe probably would have known on this subject (see *Catalogue*, quarto 50 and octavos 135, 169) rather than La Mesnardière or even Dryden (see below). In *The Whole Art of the Stage*, d'Aubignac writes, "One of the chiefest, and indeed the most indispensible Rule of Dramatick Poems, is, that in them Virtues always ought to be rewarded, or at least commended, in spight of all the Injuries of Fortune; and that likewise Vices be always punished, or at least detested with Horrour, though they triumph upon the Stage for that time" (p. 5; cf. p. 35 f). In the "Discours du poème dramatique," Corneille writes, "Celle-ci [la vertu] se fait toujours aimer, quoique malheureuse, et celui-là [le vice] se fait toujours haïr, bien que triomphant" (*Œuvres complètes*, p. 823).[17]

Dryden's seeming demand in *Of Dramatic Poesy* (1668) for perfect distribution of poetic justice[18] is belied both in some of his tragedies (*Tyrannick Love, Amboyna,* and *Cleomenes,* if not *Oedipus* and *Don Sebastian*) and in his later theory. He is talking only about punishment of the wicked when he discusses "poetical justice" in the Preface to *An Evening's Love* (1671) and in "The Grounds of Criticism in Tragedy" (1679).[19] In "Heads of an Answer to Rymer" (1677), Dryden's notes toward the "Grounds of Criticism in Tragedy," he walks a tightrope between strict poetic justice and unrewarded virtue. Obviously influenced by the French theorists just mentioned, Dryden writes that if the true end of tragedy is the reformation of manners, then "not only pity and terror are to be moved as the only means to bring us to virtue, but generally love to virtue and hatred to vice; by shewing the rewards of one, and punishments of the other; at least by rendering virtue always amiable, though it be shown unfortunate; and vice detestable, tho' it be shown triumphant."[20] The reason for Dryden's qualification is immediately clear: "The punishment of vice and reward of virtue are the most adequate ends of tragedy, because most conducing to good example of life. Now pity is not so easily raised for a criminal . . . as it is for an innocent man, and the suffering of innocence and punishment of the offender is of the nature of English tragedy" (p. 218). Yet Dryden acknowledges that if the protagonist is "altogether innocent, his punish-

ment will be unjust" (p. 219), and that Aristotle "places tragedies of this
kind in the second form" (p. 218). In obvious consternation, Dryden
wants his poetic justice and his pity too.[21] And that brings us to Rowe's
own important theoretical pronouncements in the Dedication to *The
Ambitious Stepmother.*

Like Addison after him,[22] Rowe admits that "tragedies have been
allowed . . . to be written both ways very beautifully" (p. 4), but he is
opposed to the *demand* for perfect distributive justice (even to the point
in his later tragedies of not punishing the wicked on stage). And like
Dryden before him,[23] Rowe sees "the suffering of innocence and punishment of the offender" as in the "nature" if not of English tragedy at least
of many successful tragedies: "As for that part of the objection, which
says, that innocent persons ought not to be shewn unfortunate; the success and general approbation, which many of the best tragedies that
have been wrote, and which were built on that foundation, have met
with, will be a sufficient answer for me" (p. 5). Examples of such tragedies are among the most prominent on Rowe's London stage—many by
Shakespeare, Dryden, Lee, Otway, Banks, and Southerne, as Addison
was later to point out in *Spectator* 40. Indeed, the usual practice in
English Renaissance tragedy—and Western tragedy up to that time generally—provides a punishment for the wicked but not a temporal reward
for the innocent. In other words, tragedy up to Rowe had almost always
shown that *sin will out* by the workings of divine justice, whether or
not the innocent survive.

It is in the light of that tradition, then, that Rowe considers "poetical justice" to be "strictly observed." Furthermore, like Dryden, Rowe
wanted his poetic justice and his pity too: "But since terror and pity
are laid down for the ends of tragedy by the great master and father of
criticism, I was always inclined to fancy that the last and remaining
impressions, which ought to be left on the minds of an audience, should
proceed from one of these two. They should be struck with terror in
several parts of the play, but always conclude and go away with pity;
a sort of regret proceeding from good-nature, which, though an uneasi-
ness, is not altogether disagreeable to the person who feels it. It was this
passion that the famous Mr. *Otway* succeeded so well in touching, and
must and will at all times affect people, who have any tenderness or
humanity. If therefore I had saved *Artaxerxes* and *Amestris,* I believe
(with submission to my judges) I had destroyed the greatest occasion for
compassion in the whole play" (p. 4 f). Other critics have shown the
foundations and subsequent developments of this affective (and very un-

Aristotelian) theory,[24] but the question before us is whether, as Rothstein argues, such affective concerns militate against the reflection of providential order. Does Rowe's "pity," obtained by withholding justice from virtuous characters, undercut what we have seen to be the thematic function of his "poetical justice" in the punishment of the usurpers? I contend that, far from being inimical to providential justice, such a tragedy as Rowe's *The Ambitious Stepmother* can and does image forth a providential universe in its design, precisely by means of the suffering of the innocent.

iii

In "The Grounds of Criticism in Tragedy," Dryden argues that the misfortunes of the "most virtuous, as well as the greatest," show that not even the innocent are safe from the "turns of fortune" (*Essays*, I, 245). He probably took the idea from his chief source, Rapin, who says undeserved misfortune teaches that the "favors of fortune and the grandeurs of the world are not always true goods" (Elledge and Schier, p. 279). D'Aubignac mentions similar lessons, which, by implication, can be taught by showing virtue either rewarded or unrewarded: that the "favours of Fortune are not real Enjoyments"; "that Happiness consists less in the possession of worldly things, than in the despising of them; that Virtue ought to seek its recompence in its self" (p. 5). There are many similar passages from other critics, but the point is that it is a commonplace of Judeo-Christian thought, from the Book of Job to Anglican theology, that no man is guaranteed a temporal recompense for his virtue, though Providence may grant him one. Throughout this tradition, life has been viewed as a *trial* in which man merits an eternal reward or punishment. In that trial, the things of this world are not reliable, because they are subject to the caprice of fortune. Man must, therefore, patiently rely solely on Divine Providence, which provides the necessary grace to meet the trial. The metaphor of trial is thus central to Judeo-Christian theodicy and runs throughout Scripture and tradition, from "the trial of the innocent" in Job[25] to "the trial of man" in Milton (*PL* I.366). Perhaps the most famous biblical *topos* is this one:

> Blessed *be* the God and Father of our Lord Jesus Christ, which according to his abundant mercy hath begotten us again unto a lively hope by the resurrection of Jesus Christ from the dead,

To an inheritance incorruptible, and undefiled, and that fadeth not away, reserved in heaven for you,

Who are kept by the power of God through faith unto salvation ready to be revealed in the last time.

Wherein ye greatly rejoice, though now for a season, if need be, ye are in heaviness through manifold temptations:

That the trial of your faith, being much more precious than of gold that perisheth, though it be tried with fire, might be found unto praise and honour and glory at the appearing of Jesus Christ.[26]

In Rowe's time, answering the theodicean complaint that the good are often not rewarded in this life, Bishop William Sherlock could write "what is commonly said upon this occasion": "That this world is not the place of Judgment, but a state of Trial, Probation, and Discipline; where good men many times suffer, not so much in Punishment of their sins, as to exercise their Faith and Patience, and to brighten their Vertues, and to prepare them for greater Rewards" (*A Discourse Concerning the Divine Providence*, p. 147 f). Archbishop James Ussher argues that the trial of the innocent in this life *assures* us of such rewards: "The most godly having the remnant of sin that dwelleth in their mortall bodies, deserve everlasting condemnation, and therefore in this life are subject to any of the plagues of God; as for that they are sharplier handled oftentimes then the wicked, it is to make triall of their patience, and to make shew of the graces he hath bestowed upon them, which he will have known, and that it may be assured that there is a Judgment of the world to come, 2 Thess. I. wherein every one shall receive according to his doing in this life, either good or evill."[27] Furthermore, argues John Donne early in the century, such a trial produces God's champions on the stage of the world: "*Militia, vita*; our whole life is a warfare; God would not chuse *Cowards*; hee had rather we were valiant in the fighting of his battels; for battels, and exercise of valour, we are sure to have. . . . And therefore *think it not strange, concerning the fiery triall, as though some strange thing happened unto you* [1 Pet. 4:12]; Make account that this world is your Scene, your Theater, and that God himself sits to see the combat, the wrestling."[28]

In his recent book, *Microcosmos: The Shape of the Elizabethan Play*, Thomas B. Stroup has traced, through Western thought and drama up to the late seventeenth century, the metaphor of the world as a stage, in which the metaphor of trial is inherent. Stroup writes, "It seems a far cry from Plotinus to Ficino to John Bunyan, but it is a clear one: the same figure has for all of them the same meanings and value. God the artist, stage-builder, and producer, puts on his cosmic drama and tests his creature, man. In this way they explain the presence of evil in the world and the suffering of the innocent" (p. 22). Thus the metaphor, especially as adopted into the Christian tradition, has a theodicean function that leads man to an acceptance of "the transitory nature of this life" (p. 13). Stroup argues that the metaphor was responsible for the structure of medieval and Renaissance drama, and from it emerges what he calls the "testing pattern"—"the trial or proving of a man," which is administered by Providence and "follows the pretty well-recognized pattern of Christian tests" (p. 179 f; see ch. vi entire). According to how the test is endured, the pattern carries with it the promise of reward or punishment, if not in this life, at least in the next (p. 181). Purporting to treat only the Elizabethan play (to 1642), Stroup traces this pattern right up to the time of Rowe: "Provided for in the ancient concept of the world as stage, this testing motif developed into a pattern in both the mystery and the morality plays and descended as a shaping force in the Elizabethan drama. Although it is apparent in all sorts of plays, it was perhaps most effectively used in tragedy. In those tragedies in which the protagonist succeeds in his quest, though he loses his life, one may discern the special pattern of the career of the Christian hero, a Dante, a Red Cross or a Guyon, Adam and Eve, a Jesus in *Paradise Regained*, or a Samson" (p. 206).

The "testing pattern" does not cease with Milton, however. Rather, I submit, it remains, with its still very Christian metaphysical orientation, the basic pattern of tragedy throughout the Restoration and early eighteenth century, from Dryden to Rowe at least to Lillo. Certainly it is the basic pattern of Rowe's tragedies. In *The Ambitious Stepmother*, the metaphor of trial is central. Memnon boasts to Mirza that he can face "with ease" even death, if "the Gods" so will "in trial" of his "virtue" (III.iii, p. 46). Amestris later plaintively asserts of the "evergracious Gods" that surely they "do not joy in our misfortunes, / But only try the strength of our frail virtue" (V.ii, p. 66). The metaphor reveals the very pattern of the play, the trial not only of virtue—as it was to become in subsequent melodrama—but of faith. In answer to Memnon's boast, Mirza cynically says, "Rest well assur'd, thou shalt have cause to try / Thy philosophic force of passive virtue" (III.iii, p. 46). And throughout, the virtuous are severely tested by malice and misfortune, but mostly by what was considered in the Christian tradition the most crucial trial of man: the temptation to despair, to lose trust in Divine Providence. For such distrust can lead to an eternal loss of grace and thus the loss of a human soul. That loss is the subject of the great Christian tragedies of Faustus and Macbeth, while victory over despair is the triumph of the Duchess of Malfi, of Hamlet and Samson, despite their deaths.[29]

Throughout this tradition, darkness, especially that of a prison or dungeon atmosphere, has been associated with despair. Some of the more famous literary treatments are those of Job, of Boethius, of Chaucer's Palamon and Troilus, of Spenser's Redcrosse Knight, of Shakespeare's King Lear, of Milton's Samson, and of Bunyan's Christian. The association is especially prevalent in the tragedy of suffering innocence, where a prison is often the scene of a crucial theodicean complaint, as in Shakespeare's *Cymbeline* (V.iv), Webster's *The Duchess of Malfi* (IV.i), Tourneur's *The Atheist's Tragedy* (III.iii), Settle's *The Empress of Morocco* (III.ii), Congreve's *The Mourning Bride* (III ff), and many of Dryden's tragedies.[30] In Rowe's *The Ambitious Stepmother*, the "*Night Scene of the* Temple *of the* Sun" (IV.iii, p. 56) exploits this traditional motif of the prison of despair. Though he feels it is "in vain," Artaxerxes gives vent to his "rage" and "swelling passion," and utters a poignant complaint, vacillating between trust and distrust of the gods, while Memnon indicts the "malice" of "fate" and the "damn'd reverse of fortune" (p. 56 f). Both go so far as to contemplate suicide (p. 57). Faced with the horrible thought of Amestris' rape, Artaxerxes even threatens to "blaspheme" those gods on whom he earlier so vociferously protested to rely (p. 59). He aptly describes his condition and the correspondence between the external scene and the internal state of his soul:

> This horrid night suits well my soul,
> Love, sorrow, conscious worth, and indignation
> Stir mad confusion in my lab'ring breast
> And I am all o'er chaos.

The threat of the "universal ruin" of nature (II.i, p. 21) is paralleled in the play by the threat of the eternal ruin of a human soul.

Into this "huge holy Dungeon" with "Not one poor lamp to cheer the dismal shade" enters Cleone with her "*dark lanthorn and key*" to help them escape (IV.iii, p. 59). When Memnon asks, "Ha! whence this gleam of light?" Artaxerxes says more than he knows: "Fate is at hand, lets haste to bid it welcome, / It brings an end of wretchedness." It is

not the fate either imagines, for Cleone is "the minister of a happier
fate" (p. 60). But Artaxerxes and Memnon misinterpret Cleone's mission,
and she is forced to kill herself to convince them of her innocence and
sincerity. Yet, through her sacrifice, the light Cleone brings performs its
symbolic function: as Memnon holds the lantern above her dead body,
Artaxerxes says,

> A beam of hope
> Strikes thro' my soul, like the first infant light
> That glanc'd upon the chaos. (p. 63)

Cleone has provided these desperate men with more than the literal
"key" which "amidst the tumult of this night" opens them a "way" out
of their prison (p. 62): she has brought the light of "hope" into the darkness of despair. Thus it appears that their complaint to the gods has been
heard.

In the meantime, Amestris' faith and virtue are being severely tried.
Thinking her husband and father dead, she complains, "Are not my sorrows full? can ought be added?" (V.ii, p. 66). She too is maddened with
"raging sorrow" and longs for "vengeance" on Mirza (p. 68). When
Mirza threatens her, she desperately begs to die since life has no more
meaning for her and she has suffered the worst. Yet something *can* "be
added" to her afflictions that is worse even than death. It is Mirza's ra-
pacious lust. As he pursues her, she challenges the "awful Gods" to
"blast him" with "lightning" (p. 69), and when none is forthcoming, she
pathetically whimpers, "Is there no hope of aid from Gods or men?"[31]
Finally, calling on Diana and Juno, she gains the strength and, the implication is, the grace from those "ever-gracious Gods," to stab Mirza
and to save herself from rape. As we have noted before, she openly
attributes that strength to "some chaster power." It appears, then, that
her virtue has met the test and that Providence has "sav'd" her from
Mirza's "most brutal outrage" to her "honour" (p. 74). The gods, it
seems, *have* answered her prayer—and Artaxerxes'—that she be not dis-
honored. And yet she dies.

Amestris' death is not an indictment of Providence, any more than
that of Cordelia or Webster's Duchess. Dennis himself wrote the following: " 'Tis true indeed upon the Stage of the World the Wicked
sometimes prosper, and the Guiltless suffer. But that is permitted by the
Governour of the World to show from the Attribute of his infinite Justice that there is a Compensation in Futurity, to prove the Immortality

of the Human Soul, and the Certainty of Future Rewards and Punishments" (*Critical Works*, II, 49). In opposition to Dennis' demand for perfect distributive justice on the stage itself, and in accordance with the bulk of tradition, Rowe chose here to picture the world closer to the literal truth of history than to the ideal truth of philosophy (poetry containing both, according to Aristotle and his Renaissance interpreters). But if the play imitates life more closely than Dennis or Gildon would like, still it points to an afterlife, however shadowy may be its apprehension in the pre-Christian world of the play (as in *King Lear*). The immortality of the soul is stressed throughout Rowe's play (as indeed it was throughout the Renaissance and especially in answer to the neo-Epicureans and the Hobbists of the Restoration[32]). We have already noted Amestris' faith in the "immortality" promised by the gods, who "behold" the "sufferings" of these innocents (III.iii, p. 47). The most explicit statement about the immortality of the soul occurs in the "Hymn to the Sun" (written by Rowe's school chum, William Shippen):

> What is the soul of man, but light,
> Drawn down from thy transcendent height?
> What but an intellectual beam?
> A spark of thy immortal flame?
> . . . .
> Since then from thee at first it came,
> To thee, tho' clogged, it points its flame;
> And conscious of superior birth,
> Despises this unkindred earth. (p. 43)

This is the traditional imagery—not only Persian, but also Platonic and especially, for a Christian audience, Johannine—for man's participation in the eternal source of light: "The true Light, which lighteth every man that cometh into the world."[33]

Finally (with regard to immortality), upon hearing the news of Arsaces' death (the description of the dying King which opens the play is, after all, something like a *memento mori*), Artaban says,

> 'Twas time the soul should seek for immortality,
> And leave the weary body to enjoy
> An honourable rest from care and sickness. (IV.i, p. 50)

Thus, not only is the human soul immortal, but death is actually not an evil but a good, because it releases man from his trial. This metaphor of death as rest for the just is a traditional theodicean answer to the problem of death, and it runs throughout Christian literature (e.g., *The Divine Comedy, The Pardoner's Tale, King Lear, Gulliver's Travels*), but nowhere is it more explicit than in *Paradise Lost* (God is speaking of man after the Fall):

> I at first with two fair gifts
> Created him endow'd, with Happiness
> And Immortality: that fondly lost,
> This other serv'd but to eternize woe;
> Till I provided Death; so Death becomes
> His final remedy, and after Life
> Tri'd in sharp tribulation, and refin'd
> By Faith and faithful works, to second Life,
> Wak't in the renovation of the just,
> Resigns him up with Heav'n and Earth renew'd. (XI.57 ff)

So, in the Christian vision, death becomes—not an indictment of Providence—but rather a *proof* of Providence, and in Rowe's play, with its stress on the immortality of the soul, the inevitable suggestion is that Amestris' constancy of virtue during her trial has merited her such an awakening.

Yet despite the manifestation of Providence in the defense of Amestris' honor, Artaxerxes and Memnon lose their renewed hope when she dies. Their "philosophic force of passive virtue," as Mirza has called it, is found wanting when tested to the extreme, and Artaxerxes and Memnon despair. Though he forbears to curse the gods as he has threatened (after all, Amestris' "honour" has not been "ruin'd"), Artaxerxes sinks to earth in self-loathing and stabs himself (V.ii, p. 74 ff). Ironically, he has forgotten to "bow before the God that sav'd" Amestris, and the imagery of gloom, annihilation, and hell underscores his despair. Memnon, on the other hand, does explicitly renounce the gods, as Mirza has prophesied (p. 76). He then dashes out his brains, and Artemisa concludes, "Fierce despair / Has forc'd a way for the impetuous soul" (p. 77). Again ironically, Artaxerxes and Memnon kill themselves just as the usurpers are defeated in what we have already seen to be a manifestation of Providence. Despite their personal loss in the death of Amestris, all is not lost, and while their plight is pitiful, their solution is damnable —yet it is certainly understandable, and that tension is at the heart of

Christian tragedy and distinguishes it from formal theology or theodicy. Such tension makes us, along with Shakespeare's Edgar, want to *speak what we feel and not what we ought to say.*

iv

The last virtuous character mentioned in Gildon's indictment of *The Ambitious Stepmother* is Cleone. It could perhaps be answered that she too commits suicide. But her death appears, upon closer scrutiny, to be quite different in motivation from Artaxerxes' and Memnon's and to be far from a violation of "Poetic Justice and the Rules of Providence." It is instead an act of self-sacrifice which is in sharp contrast to the self-interest of her father Mirza and of the rest of the usurpers. In the first act Mirza describes Cleone as

> By nature pitiful, and apt to grieve
> For the mishaps of others, and so make
> The sorrows of the wretched world her own. (sc. i, p. 15 f)

Of course, Cleone's melancholy has another source besides her compassionate nature's response to human misery. Her tears are for her "unregarded love" of Artaxerxes as well. Yet despite this more immediate motivation for her tears, Cleone's compassion seems really a part of her nature, as her father suggests, and she appears to mean it when she tells Artaban that she grieves at the "miserable state of human kind" (III.i, p. 36). It is her compassion for the "poor Amestris," as well as her love for Artaxerxes, that leads her to pray for them to the "gentle powers, who view our cares with pity" (IV.ii, p. 55). Furthermore, despite her fears and doubts and the apparent inevitability of death, Cleone goes forth to "save" Artaxerxes in a genuine spirit of self-sacrifice (p. 56).

To the suspicious Memnon and Artaxerxes, Cleone utters a sacred oath, calling on the present "awful God" to damn her if she have "any thought but" Artaxerxes' "safety" (IV.iii, p. 62). Stabbing herself as a last resort, she says to Artaxerxes that she has given him

> the last,
> And only proof remain'd that could convince you
> I held your life much dearer than my own.

Through this total self-sacrifice, Cleone (like Arsaces) finally obtains peace and "everlasting rest" from her war with her passions (p. 63).

Moreover, her sacrifice could atone for her father's sins and even more, as Artaxerxes says:

> Why hast thou stain'd me with thy virgin blood?
> I swear, sweet saint, for thee I could forgive
> The malice of thy father, tho' he seeks
> My life and crown; thy goodness might atone
> Ev'n for a nation's sins.

Memnon agrees:

> Sure the Gods,
> Angry ere while, will be at length appeas'd
> With this egregious victim.

As we have seen, the light that she has brought symbolically becomes "the first infant light / That glanc'd upon the chaos," giving hope to the despairing and providing them with the "key" out of their prison.

The suggestion of this accumulated imagery is that Cleone's sacrifice is that kind of which Christ speaks: "Greater love hath no man than this, that a man lay down his life for his friends" (John 15:13). The very diction—the *forgiveness* for her father, the *atonement* "Ev'n for a nation's sins," the *appeasement* of the gods, all obtained by this "egregious victim"—seems designed to invoke the Atonement itself, the fulfillment of the ultimate promise of the care of the gods: "For God so loved the world, that he gave his only begotten Son, that whosoever believeth in him should not perish, but have everlasting life" (John 3:16). Thus, by imagistically suggesting the Atonement, Cleone's sacrifice reinforces the primary lesson of the play: the need for absolute trust in Divine Providence. Moreover, the light that her death brings—"the first infant light / That glanc'd upon the chaos"—symbolizes more than just the light of hope that momentarily redeems Artaxerxes from the internal "chaos" of his despair. As we have noted before, the Persian imagery of light is also Johannine, and because of the accumulation of allusions, it seems to me inescapably to suggest the light of the Creative Word of God, in Whom "was life; and the life was the light of men. And the light shineth in darkness; and the darkness comprehended it not" (John 1:4 f). In effect, Cleone's sacrifice suggests the promise of redemption from the chaos (both external and internal) that threatens throughout the play. It presages the restoration of order and harmony, and, as Cleone came forth out of the loins of Mirza, it presages the intervention of Providence to bring forth good out of evil.

Artaban's conclusion, then, is justified by more evidence than he sees. Not only the punishment of the wicked, but also the care for Amestris' honor and the significance of Cleone's sacrifice indicate that "The Gods are great and just." Furthermore, the accession of Artaban to the throne represents the restoration of order. Throughout the play Artaban has reverenced the gods. He acknowledges no superiors but them and relies on their justice to reward his merit (IV.i, p. 50). Accordingly, he refuses to obtain the crown by underhanded means but would follow the "paths of honour" and "do as a King ought," armed against his mother's threats by his "own innate virtue" (p. 53). At the end the deposed Queen inveighs against Artaban's self-assertion:

> Thou talk'st as if thy infant hand could grasp,
> Guide, and command the fortune of the world;
> But thou art young in pow'r. (V.ii, p. 78)

Unlike his mother, however, Artaban has learned that another hand commands the fortune of the world, and he resolves to build his reign in imitation of divine justice:

> May this example guide my future sway:
> Let honour, truth and justice crown my reign,
> Ne'er let my Kingly word be given in vain,
> But ever sacred with my foes remain.
> On these foundations shall my empire stand,
> The Gods shall vindicate my just command,
> And guard that power they trusted to my hand. (p. 78 f)

All the other providential judgments in the play imply that the gods have indeed entrusted Artaban with the power of the throne, and the fact that he gains it not through his own defeat of Artaxerxes in combat as he had prophesied (IV.i, p. 53), but through wondrous events, reinforces that implication. He becomes the divinely established symbol of the repudiation of the usurpers and their philosophy; a symbol of the inevitable triumph of "honour, truth and justice"; a symbol of the ultimate (if sometimes posthumous) vindication of suffering innocence. Artaban's final declaration is nothing but complete trust in Providence, and that, after all, is the message of the play, for the world it images—

however much a vale of tears and trials—is indeed a world governed by a just and "gracious" God.

Thus *The Ambitious Stepmother* is Rowe's first, but neither his last nor his best dramatic theodicy. The play is obviously trite and sensational and at times positively lugubrious in plot and language. It provides, nevertheless, an excellent introduction to the patterns and themes with which Rowe was working. There is no doubt, in my mind at least, that the play is, in its formal design, a Christian tragedy in the fullest metaphysical sense. Its most important aesthetic quality is that once we see this design of the whole, then all the parts fit: imagery; plaintive rhetoric; allusions; setting (particularly the temple-prison); all the ethical, political, and metaphysical motifs; and especially the ending. In short, despite Rowe's immaturity, his first play is a unified whole, already a successful marriage of form and theme. Contrary to prevailing opinion, then, Rowe's techniques are not gratuitous but integral and therefore meaningful. Seeing their function in this early apprentice work prepares the way to understanding his later plays.

Notes to Chapter I

1. These include *Prince Artaxerxes*, the rightful heir to the throne of Persia; *Amestris*, his bride and the daughter of his faithful general and friend, Memnon; *Memnon* himself, who has been exiled, allegedly for murdering the Machiavellian Mirza's brother Cleander, but really to get him and the young prince out of the way of the usurping stepmother, Artemisa, and her son, Artaban; and *Cleone*, the daughter of Mirza, who is in love with Artaxerxes but beloved by Artaban.

2. Cf. Alfred Schwarz, "The Literary Career of Nicholas Rowe," p. 60.

3. Because it includes comments on all of Rowe's plays, I have used the 1715 edition, *Remarks on Mr. Rowe's* Tragedy of the Lady Jane Gray, *and all his other Plays*, edited by George L. Anderson as "Charles Gildon's *A New Rehearsal, or Bays the Younger*," p. 52 ff. Gildon is willing to excuse the death of Memnon because he did kill Cleander (though Memnon defends himself on that charge while admitting partial guilt in the murder of Tiribasus, Artemisa's husband [II.ii, p. 27 f]), but he cannot forgive Rowe for allowing Orchanes to go free and Artemisa to remain alive (p. 53). The fact that Orchanes is reported killed (V.ii, p. 77) shows that Gildon did not study the play carefully and suggests that his analysis and evaluation of Rowe may be untrustworthy on all levels.

4. Landon C. Burns, Jr., "The Tragedies of Nicholas Rowe," p. 46.

5. For the anti-Epicurean movement in seventeenth-century England, see especially Charles T. Harrison, "The Ancient Atomists and English Literature of the Seventeenth Century," sec. 2, and George D. Hadzits, *Lucretius and His Influence*, p. 284 ff. For further evidence of the neo-Epicurean movement itself, see Thomas F. Mayo, *Epicurus in England (1650–1725)*, and Wolfgang B. Fleischmann, *Lucretius and English Literature, 1680–1740*.

6. Tyre, "Versions of Poetic Justice in the Early Eighteenth Century," and Wil-

liams, "Poetical Justice, the Contrivances of Providence, and the Works of William Congreve." Both critics were anticipated by three important, unpublished (even by University Microfilms), and therefore sadly neglected dissertations: Charles H. Peake, "Domestic Tragedy in Relation to Theology"; J. Leland Rudé, "Poetic Justice: A Study of the Problem of Human Conduct in Tragedy from Aeschylus to Shakespeare"; and Thomas A. Hart, "The Development and Decline of the Doctrine of Poetic Justice from Plato to Johnson."

7. See Sarup Singh, *The Theory of Drama in the Restoration Period*, p. 64 ff, and Eugene Hnatko, "The Failure of Eighteenth-Century Tragedy," passim, for some of the latest (and most wrong-headed) of these interpretations.

8. *The Critical Works of John Dennis*, ed. Edward N. Hooker, I, 183. Williams and Tyre maintain, along with Singh and Michael A. Quinlan, *Poetic Justice in the Drama*, that the concept is traditional in England, and Rudé shows that, indeed, poetic justice is traditional in tragedy itself, for tragedy is ever concerned with the problem of justice and retribution and it has ever (at least through to the Renaissance) rationalized its retribution in terms of divine justice. Cf. Hart, who recognizes the metaphysical foundation of poetic justice in much Renaissance practice and theory (through to the first half of the eighteenth century), but who finally sees disproportionate punishment as an indictment of divine justice. Cf. also John D. Ebbs, *The Principle of Poetic Justice Illustrated in Restoration Tragedy*, who, along with Singh and Quinlan, completely fails to explain this metaphysical dimension. Even Rudé backs off from it in his fear of imputing a didactic function to tragedy, particularly Shakespeare's.

Those who still doubt the metaphysical foundation of poetic justice or, especially, the depths of its roots in English and continental theory should consult the following critics, who equate poetic with divine justice: Martin Bucer, *De Regno Christi* (1551), in E. K. Chambers, *The Elizabethan Stage*, IV, 189; William Bavande, *A Woork of Ioannes Ferrarius Montanus* (1559), in Chambers, IV, 190; Antonio Minturno, *L'Arte Poetica* (1564), in Allan H. Gilbert, ed., *Literary Criticism: Plato to Dryden*, p. 292; Lodovico Castelvetro, *The Poetics of Aristotle* (1571), in Gilbert, p. 349; George Puttenham, *The Arte of English Poesie* (1589), in G. Gregory Smith, ed., *Elizabethan Critical Essays*, II, 35; Thomas Nashe, *Pierce Penilesse* (1592), in Chambers, IV, 239; Ben Jonson, Prefatory Epistle to *Volpone* (1607), in *Ben Jonson*: Volpone, ed. Alvin B. Kernan, p. 32, where the "justice" the poet is enjoined to "imitate" is surely divine; Jules de La Mesnardière, *La Poëtiqve* (1640), pp. 23 ff, 107 f; François Hédelin, abbé d'Aubignac, *La Pratique du théatre* (1657), trans. as the very popular *Whole Art of the Stage* (1684), p. 5 f; René Rapin, *Réflexions sur la poétique* (1674), trans. by Rymer himself the same year as *Reflections on Aristotle's Treatise of Poesy in General*, in Scott Elledge and Donald Schier, eds., *The Continental Model*, p. 278. The relevant passages in Rymer, Dennis, and Gildon are cited in Peake, p. 115 f, Tyre and Williams, passim. As corroborative passages from a couple of Rowe's contemporaries, see also Sir Richard Blackmore, *Prince Arthur* (1695), first page of the Preface (no sig.), recto and verso; and Jeremy Collier, *Second Defence of the Short View* (1700), p. 83.

Tyre and Ebbs point to several modern critics who have seen the connection between poetic and providential justice in Elizabethan drama, including William L. Courtney, *The Idea of Tragedy in Ancient and Modern Drama*, p. 67 ff; Richard G. Moulton, *Shakespeare as a Dramatic Artist*, p. 245; and Lily B. Campbell, *Shakespeare's Tragic Heroes*, ch. i, passim. Ebbs himself sees that poetic justice is equated with Providence in *Samson Agonistes* in his article "Milton's Treatment of Poetic Justice in *Samson Agonistes*." See also Roy W. Battenhouse, *Marlowe's* Tamburlaine, who says that poetic justice is providential throughout Elizabethan tragedy and even makes the following extravagant claim in the light of the metaphor of the world as a stage: "Drama was the chief form of Elizabethan art largely because Providence was the central dogma of Elizabethan religion" (p. 126). Henry H. Adams, *English Domestic or, Homiletic Tragedy*, sees that poetic justice in Elizabethan domestic tragedy is providential but denies that it is so for

Rymer and the Restoration (p. 18 f). Peake, Tyre, and especially Williams have convincingly proved that it is.

9. Rothstein does mention Dennis earlier but implies that as he adopted more affective theories in his "later" criticism (Rothstein only takes us up to 1698), he neglected "fabulist" theories (p. 18). This is simply not the case. Dennis continued to demand forms which mirror Providence, from *The Advancement and Reformation of Modern Poetry* (1701) to his letter to the *Spectator* (1711) to *An Essay on the Genius and Writings of Shakespear* (1712), passim. In 1713, which takes us pretty nearly through the career of Rowe, Dennis wrote one of his strongest statements on the mimetic function of poetic justice: " 'Tis certainly the Duty of every Tragick Poet, by an exact Distribution of a Poetical Justice, to imitate the Divine Dispensation" (*Remarks upon Cato*, in *Critical Works*, II, 49).

10. See Aubrey Williams' answer to Rothstein on Congreve, "Poetical Justice," p. 546 f, as well as his formal analysis of *The Mourning Bride* in "The 'Just Decrees of Heav'n,' " especially p. 13 ff, where Williams appeals to the formal theories of James Drake. See also Peake's entire dissertation, which argues exactly the contrary to Rothstein on late seventeenth- and early eighteenth-century tragedy; he sees theology as setting its hand in a very heavy way upon this tragedy.

11. See the "Hymn to the Sun" (III.iii, p. 43 f), and the numerous references to the semidivinity of the royal family, e.g., I.i, p. 16 ff; II.i, p. 23 f; III.ii, p. 40.

12. "The Dramatic Use of Hobbes's Political Ideas," *ELH*, 3 (1936), rpt. in H. T. Swedenberg, Jr., ed., *Essential Articles for the Study of John Dryden*, p. 341 ff. For the anti-Hobbesian movement, see especially Samuel I. Mintz, *The Hunting of Leviathan*. Cf. John A. Winterbottom, "The Place of Hobbesian Ideas in Dryden's Tragedies," *JEGP*, 57 (1958), rpt. in Swedenberg, p. 374 ff; and Anne T. Barbeau, *The Intellectual Design of John Dryden's Heroic Plays*.

13. The sexual overtones seem to heighten the perversity of their blasphemous relationship; cf. Artaxerxes' intimation that Mirza was at one time Artemisa's paramour (II.ii, p. 30).

14. The doctrine of Providence was, in Anglican apologetics as well as the entire Christian tradition since Augustine's *The City of God*, the mean between fate and fortune, which were seen, at best, as agencies of Providence. See Peake, ch. i, passim.

15. For Plato, as for Collier, the prescription is somewhat irrelevant, for both really want to ban the stage; they seem to feel the harm has already been done to an audience, whatever the ending of a play (see especially *Republic* III, and Collier's various *Defences*). For Aristotle (*Poetics* xiii), and for Rymer, Dennis, and Gildon, the prescription is also somewhat qualified, for none thinks that tragic protagonists should ever be completely innocent; but for these critics, it seems obvious that if one were to portray an innocent person on the stage, he would have to reward him in the dénouement. See de Scudéry, *Observations sur* Le Cid (1637), in Arnaud Gasté, ed., *La Querelle du* Cid, p. 79 f; Filmer, *A Defence of Plays* (1707), p. 43; *The Stage Acquitted* (1699), p. 93 f. Cf. Philip Massinger, *The Roman Actor* (1626), who implies strict poetic justice (I.i.20 ff, in Gilbert, p. 570).

16. See the references above (n. 8) to Bucer, Bavande, Minturno, Castelvetro, Puttenham, Nashe, and Rapin, in none of whom is there the demand for the reward of the innocent. Ben Jonson's *Sejanus* speaks for itself. See also Jacopo Mazzoni, *On the Defense of the* Comedy (1587), in Gilbert, p. 399 f; Henry Chettle, *Kind Harts Dreame* (1592), in Chambers, IV, 244; Thomas Heywood, *An Apology for Actors* (1612), in Gilbert, p. 558; Gérard-Jean Vossius, *Poeticarum Institutiorum* (1647), as quoted in Edith G. Kern, *The Influence of Heinsius and Vossius upon French Dramatic Theory*, p. 126 (Heinsius himself in *De Tragoediae Constitutione* [1611] does not insist on any kind of poetic justice); John Oldmixon, *Reflections on the Stage* (1699), p. 117; *A Vindication of the Stage* (1698), p. 20, which implies that vice should always be punished but says nothing of virtue; James

Drake, *Antient and Modern Stages*, who seems to recommend strict poetic justice (p. 122), but then finds *The Orphan* and *Hamlet* acceptable despite unrewarded virtue (p. 204 ff) and suggests that the way to satisfy poetic justice in *Cleomenes* is merely to have the vicious die too (p. 213 f; cf. Peake, p. 113). Passages usually cited as prescribing strict poetic justice I have found to be generally either (a) statements recommending the *praising* of virtue and *blaming* of vice—e.g., Plato, *Laws* II; Giraldi Cinthio, *On the Composition of Romances* (1549), in Gilbert, p. 271; and most comic theorists—or (b) purely descriptive statements—e.g., Julius C. Scaliger, *Poetices Libri Septem* (1561), p. 146; Benedetto Varchi, *Lezzioni* (1590), p. 576; Sir Philip Sidney, *The Defense of Poesie* (1583), in Gilbert, p. 425; Sir William Temple, "Of Poetry" (1690), in *Five Miscellaneous Essays*, ed. Samuel H. Monk, p. 187; and William Congreve, *Amendments of Mr. Collier's False and Imperfect Citations* (1698), in The Mourning Bride, *Poems, and Miscellanies*, ed. Bonamy Dobrée, p. 453—or (c) statements only about comedy—e.g., George Farquhar, *A Discourse upon Comedy* (1702), in *The Complete Works*, ed. Charles Stonehill, p. 343; and the anonymous author of *A Comparison between the Two Stages* (1702), ed. Staring B. Wells—or (d) statements with important qualifications (see below).

17. These important qualifications in La Mesnardière, d'Aubignac, and Corneille have been noted by René Bray, *La Formation de la doctrine classique en France*, p. 81, and Edward N. Hooker in Dennis, *Critical Works*, II, 436.

18. Of Dramatic Poesy *and Other Critical Essays*, ed. George Watson, I, 38, 47—hereafter cited as *Essays*.

19. *Essays*, I, 151 f, 245; see Hooker in Dennis, II, 437.

20. *Essays*, I, 213; Sarup Singh has noticed the similarity to Corneille (p. 75).

21. See Baxter Hathaway, "John Dryden and the Function of Tragedy," p. 671; and Singh, p. 74 ff. Cf. Lewis M. Magill, "Poetic Justice: The Dilemma of the Early Creators of Sentimental Tragedy." See also Rothstein, p. 13 ff, with whom I disagree emphatically when he concludes from the "Heads" that "virtue now receives its rewards not because God loves it and cherishes it, but because the pit and boxes do" (p. 15). This is again a confusion of affective and formal concerns; despite his admission that Dryden's shift from "traditional fabulist attitudes" is only one "in stress, in degree, in intensity, in tone; not in kind" (p. 18), Rothstein concludes from the absence of explicit reference to Providence that poetic justice must now be rationalized in terms of public desire. Rothstein's assertions are belied not only by his faulty logic but by Dryden's own practice in *All for Love, Don Sebastian,* and *Cleomenes,* where the outcomes are specifically rationalized in terms of Providence (or "Heaven").

22. *Spectators* 40 and 548 (putative authorship), in *The Spectator*, ed. G. Gregory Smith, I, 147, and IV, 279. Burns notices the similarity between Rowe's and Addison's positions on poetic justice, at least on this point (p. 15); cf. Amrik Singh, "The Argument on Poetic Justice (Addison *versus* Dennis)."

23. Of course, Rowe could not have known the passage in Dryden since it was not published till 1711 (*Essays*, I, 211).

24. See Hathaway, "John Dryden and the Function of Tragedy," and "The Lucretian 'Return Upon Ourselves' in Eighteenth-Century Theories of Tragedy"; Earl R. Wasserman, "The Pleasures of Tragedy"; A. Owen Aldridge, "The Pleasures of Pity"; and Rothstein, ch. i entire. The appeal to pity, to Christian charity, perhaps gained its impetus from the current Latitudinarian attack on the Calvinist and Hobbesian views of the nature of man. See Peake, p. 56, and Ernest L. Tuveson, "The Importance of Shaftesbury," both of whom show, in answer to Ronald S. Crane's classic article, "Suggestions toward a Genealogy of the 'Man of Feeling,' " that the Latitudinarians' insistence on innate benevolence did not deny, as did Shaftesburianism, the inclination toward evil which resulted from Original Sin. From their constant allusion to the Fall throughout their drama, it appears that Dryden's theory of "concernment" and Rowe's appeal to "good-nature" are in the Latitudinarian tradition. Cf. Rothstein, p. 20, who sees a "be-

nevolist philosophy" underlying Rowe's statement, and Eugene Waith, "Tears of Magnanimity in Otway and Racine," p. 19, who sees it as a "prime example" of "sentimen-
talism." But Rowe's plays simply do not espouse philosophical benevolism or senti-
mentalism, however literally "sentimental" they may be in their appeal to "tenderness
or humanity." In the criticism of Restoration and eighteenth-century drama, as Geoffrey
Marshall has recently and ably argued (*Restoration Serious Drama*, p. 211 ff), we must
begin to use such terms as "benevolist" and "sentimental" with more precision—or else
abandon them altogether.

25. 9:23 (Authorized Version, whence all Biblical quotations are taken). See Blackmore's Preface to *A Paraphrase on the Book of Job* (in Rowe's library, *Catalogue*, fol. 116),
where he gives the traditional exigetical interpretation that the story of Job is one of a
providential trial in order to justify the ways of God to men (passim).

26. 1 Pet. 1:3 ff. See Samuel Clarke, *Seventeen Sermons*, p. 370, who in a sermon
entitled "The *Present* Life, a State of *Probation* in order to a Future Life" points out that
the metaphor of "the purifying and *Trying* of *Metals* by *Fire*" is common in Scripture,
and who gives many citations.

27. *A Body of Divinitie*, 4th ed. rev. (1653), p. 108, the edition Rowe possessed
(see *Catalogue*, fol. 41).

28. *The Sermons of John Donne*, ed. Evelyn M. Simpson and George R. Potter, VI,
108. For further proof that the metaphor was commonly used in contemporary apologetics, see, e.g., Clarke, p. 364 ff; Symon Patrick, *The Works*, ed. Alexander Taylor, IX,
197 f; Isaac Barrow, *The Theological Works*, ed. Alexander Napier, III, 63, 86, 138 f;
Richard Kingston, *A Discourse on Divine Providence*, p. 91, a copy of which Rowe
possessed (*Catalogue*, oct. 336); and John Tillotson, *The Works*, I, 687.

29. See Kilbee C. Brittain, "The Sin of Despair in English Renaissance Literature,"
for a thorough and excellent treatment of despair in Western thought and literature
through Shakespeare.

30. Though this type of scene occurs often in Dryden's tragedies, nowhere is it
dealt with more fully and more intensely than in Acts IV and V of *Cleomenes*.

31. We must not allow the triteness either of this scene or of its language to obscure
its meaning. Amestris' cries of "Unhand me, villain!" and "Save me" must be seen in the
context of the play's dominant theme of theodicy. She is not calling merely for her "hero"
to save her; she is challenging the very justice of the gods. Whatever became of the rape
scene in subsequent melodrama does not negate its function here.

32. See Don Cameron Allen, *Doubt's Boundless Sea*, ch. v, passim; Harrison on
neo-Epicureanism; and Mintz on Hobbism.

33. John 1:9. The similarity between Persian and Judeo-Christian imagery has
always been obvious, although in Rowe's day, the latter was thought to have influenced
the former, and not vice-versa, as is the case. See Rustom Masani, *Zoroastrianism*, pt. 1,
ch. i. Rowe is obviously capitalizing on the similarity.

II   Protagonist as Champion

Tamerlane and *Ulysses*

 N TWO OF HIS subsequent tragedies of suffering innocence, *Tamerlane* (1701) and *Ulysses* (1705), Rowe presents us with a protagonist who is unmistakably a Champion of Divine Justice. The title-character in each play acts, as much as a man can, as the agent of Providence in the vindication of the innocent. But each is ultimately effective only through an act of self-sacrifice similar to that of Cleone in *The Ambitious Stepmother*. Thus, like Milton, Rowe continues to portray such vindication as the result of a higher heroism than simply that of the pagan epic hero. *Tamerlane* and *Ulysses* are very similar, then, in thematic development, though quite unequal, I think, in aesthetic value, *Ulysses* being far the better play and one of the better classical tragedies of the period. Whatever their merit, however, the meaning of these two plays as dramatic theodicies is manifest in their formal design.

i

Tamerlane (*Works*, I, 81 ff) was one of the most popular plays of the early eighteenth century,[1]° a fact critics have long attributed to the play's political significance. In *The Politics of Drama in Augustan England*, for instance, John C. Loftis points out that *Tamerlane* is "an allegorical eulogy" of King William III (p. 31). Indeed, in the Dedication Rowe tacitly admits that the characterization of Tamerlane is an implicit panegyric on William (just as the Dedication itself is an explicit panegyric), and for almost a century the play was performed annually on William's birthday and on the anniversary of his landing in England

°Notes to this chapter begin on page 73.

45

(November 4 and 5, respectively). Rowe himself notes similarities between William's and Tamerlane's characters and even their "stories"
(p. 85), and critics have since conjectured whether there are not similarities to other historical personalities as well.[2] It is at least certain that
there is an analogy between Bajazet and Louis XIV, that infamous vio-
lator of "all the most solemn engagements of public faith" whom Rowe
describes in the Dedication (p. 84 f).

Loftis sees even more political significance in the play. In its
immediate historical context, he argues, *Tamerlane* is a "call to arms"
at the beginning of the Wars of the Spanish Succession: "The dramatic
action projects an English Whig's wish: that William would promptly
defeat the forces of Louis and take him personally a captive." As such,
the play dramatizes "war-inspired Francophobia" (p. 32). Moreover,
according to Loftis, the play is propagandistic in a more general sense:
"The frequency with which the play was performed in the first half of
the eighteenth century would suggest that it was a chief vehicle by
which Whig—and Lockeian—ideas on constitutional theory and religious toleration were disseminated" (p. 34). Thus he attributes Rowe's
obvious exaggerations of contemporary history to this function: "Rowe
was writing propaganda, not political theory, and consequently a convincing confrontation of political philosophies does not emerge. The
French conception of monarchy is distorted; for whatever the liabilities
of the French theory of absolutism, it represented no such diabolical
capriciousness as Rowe would suggest" (p. 32 f).

While Loftis is fairly correct in his assessment of the play, he does
not, perhaps because his thesis is limited, suggest the fuller ramifications
of Rowe's exaggerations, especially Bajazet's "diabolical capriciousness." Though *Tamerlane* is admittedly a political allegory,[3] it transcends propaganda. Through the same process of analogy that charac-
terizes Augustan poetry of praise and blame, Rowe's Tamerlane and
Bajazet come to represent much more than either historical or contemporary personalities. Bajazet becomes a satanic figure and Tamerlane God's Champion, and their conflict becomes emblematic of the
eternal struggle between good and evil.[4]

In "The Source and Characterization of Nicholas Rowe's *Tamerlane*,"
Donald B. Clark has shown that Rowe's primary source for the story
and the characterization of Tamerlane and Bajazet was not, as might be

expected, either Marlowe's play or his sources—both of which had been virtually forgotten—but Richard Knolles' *The General Historie of the Turkes* (1603), a history whose popularity is demonstrated in the number of editions and revisions it received in the seventeenth century.[5] Unlike Marlowe's historians, Knolles depicts Tamerlane as a model prince with even a special reverence for Christianity;[6] Bajazet is, on the other hand, still the cruel tyrant par excellence (p. 203 ff). But what Clark has failed to emphasize is that, in the tradition of Tudor Historiography, where history is viewed as the working out of God's plan,[7] Knolles portrays Tamerlane's victory over Bajazet as a manifestation of providential justice. For Tamerlane was a champion "by God himselfe appointed" (p. 213): "Hee was sent from heaven to punish his [Bajazet's] rashnesse, and to teach him, that the proud are hated of God, whose promise is to plucke downe the mightie, and raise up the lowly" (p. 217). Thus Tamerlane's title, "Scourge of God."

Several times Knolles reiterates the lesson of "the just judgement of God against the arrogant follie of the proud" (p. 221), and his last reiteration is the most important, because it carries the process of analogy the furthest. He reports that Tamerlane told the Greeks he came not to conquer but to aid them, and that "his upright meaning therein, was the greatest cause, That God from above had beheld his power, and thereby brused the head of the greatest and fiercest enemie of mankind that was under heaven." As it did vaguely in the phrase, "to plucke downe the mightie, and raise up the lowly," Knolles' language here unmistakably echoes Scripture: "And I will put enmity between thee [the snake] and the woman, and between thy seed and her seed; it shall bruise thy head, and thou shalt bruise his heel" (Gen. 3:15); again, "And the God of peace shall bruise Satan under your feet shortly" (Rom. 16:20). Through the allusion, Knolles has implicitly made Tamerlane a figure of the Messiah and Bajazet a figure of Satan. Such a use of implied analogy may be called the process of typification, whereby Knolles has related his characters and their conflict to archetypes in the Christian myth.

Rowe adopts Knolles' typification into his play. Not only does he make Tamerlane and Bajazet model king and typal tyrant, but at the very outset he establishes the archetypal nature of their conflict. In the prologue he reviews the history reported in Knolles, characterizing Tamerlane and Bajazet accordingly. Then he says that Bajazet was given sway,

Till Heav'n, the growing evil to redress,
Sent *Tamerlane* to give the world a peace. (p. 87)

Thus Tamerlane "sav'd mankind." In the opening scene of the play the
world looks to Tamerlane as a redeemer, and Mirva says,

Well has our holy *Alha* mark'd him out
The scourge of lawless pride, and dire ambition,
The great avenger of the groaning world.
Well has he worn the sacred cause of justice
Upon his prosp'rous sword: approving Heav'n
Still crown'd the right'ous warrior with success;
As if he said, go forth, and be my champion,
Thou most like me of all my works below. (p. 89)

As Tamerlane enters, the Prince of Tanais exclaims that he "Comes like
the proxy of inquiring Heav'n, / To judge and to redress" (p. 91). As he
prepares for battle, Tamerlane prays to the "great spirit" that "fires"
his "soul" to assist his "sword" in "the cause of Heav'n and injur'd
Earth"(p. 96 f). After his triumph, Tamerlane disdains the homage paid
to him and attributes his success to Heaven, content to be known only
as "Heav'n's happy instrument, / The means of good to all my fellow
creatures" (II.ii, p. 104).

Thus, like Knolles, Rowe has made his hero God's Champion in
what amounts to a holy war. Furthermore, as George W. Whiting has
shown in "Rowe's Debt to *Paradise Lost*," Rowe has patterned Bajazet
after Milton's Satan and perhaps even Tamerlane after Milton's Messiah
(p. 272 ff). Whiting maintains that "it is not absurd to suggest a parallel
between Tamerlane and the Son of God," especially in Mirva's speech,
concluding, "go forth, and be my champion, / Thou most like me of
all my works below" (Whiting, p. 272). Tamerlane is certainly, like
Milton's Messiah, God's Champion, and he is certainly Christ-like in
his mercy and humility (as we shall further see), but Whiting seems on
firmer ground when he says, "If Tamerlane reminds one of Christ, Satan
is even more unmistakably the prototype of Bajazet" (p. 273). He proceeds to point to several of the numerous passages where Bajazet is compared to the "fallen archangel" both explicitly and implicitly (p. 273 ff).
In an apposite passage he does not mention, the satanic analogy is clear.
Tamerlane says to Bajazet in amazement, "Thou would'st scale Heav'n"
(II.ii, p. 106):

> Thou vain, rash thing,
> That with gigantic insolence, hast dar'd
> To lift thy wretched self above the stars,
> And mate with pow'r almighty: Thou art fall'n!

Although Whiting does not discuss their function, the allusions he has marked enable us to see the ultimate dimension of Rowe's exaggeration by analogy. On this typological level, *Tamerlane* conforms to an eternal pattern. It is a reiteration of God's triumph over Satan, another manifestation of His Providence. Like Satan, Bajazet threatens the very fabric of universal order, as Arpasia makes clear in the opening of Act V:

> Some ruling fiend hangs in the dusky air,
> And scatters ruin, death, and wild distraction,
> O'er all the wretched race of man below. (p. 140)

But, as Tamerlane insists, "Heav'n is watchful o'er its worshippers" (III.ii, p. 123), and he insists again at the end of the play that Providence has acted, through him, to deliver the "wretched race of man" from this satanic evil:

> Behold the vain effects of earth-born pride,
> That scorn'd Heav'n's laws, and all its pow'r defied:
> That could the hand, which form'd it first, forget,
> And fondly say, I made myself be great:
> But justly those above assert their sway,
> And teach ev'n Kings what homage they should pay,
> Who then rule best, when mindful to obey. (p. 149)

Like the great epic it echoes, then, and the central Christian myth it images, Rowe's *Tamerlane* is a theodicy which dramatically asserts the intervention of Providence to stem the spread of prosperous vice. As in *Paradise Lost*, however, the dramatic conflict in *Tamerlane* is not only between contending armies that emblematically represent the cosmic forces of good and evil. Against that background the play also dramatizes a struggle between the philosophies of Tamerlane and Bajazet: between mercy and revenge; between tolerance and prejudice; between compassion and hatred; in short, between Christian altruism and satanic (or Hobbesian) self-interest.

Like Knolles', Rowe's Tamerlane has a special reverence for Christianity. Indeed, some of his followers are increasingly jealous of the influence of his "Christian minion," Axalla (IV.i, p. 128), whom his soul attends "like a prophet, / That waits the inspiration of his God" (I, p. 92). The extent of this influence can be seen in Tamerlane's forgiveness of the Moslem Dervise who tries to assassinate him for his tolerance of the Christians: Tamerlane says to him,

> Now learn the difference 'twixt thy faith and mine;
> Thine bids thee lift thy dagger to my throat;
> Mine can forgive the wrong, and bid thee live.
> Keep thy own wicked secret, and be safe;
> If thou continu'st still to be the same,
> 'Tis punishment enough to be a villain.
> If thou repent'st, I have gain'd one to virtue,
> And am, in that, rewarded for my mercy. (III.ii, p. 123)

Later the Dervise complains to Bajazet's confederates that Tamerlane's forgiveness argues an abandonment of Islam for a "new faith":

> 'Tis what his Christian favourites have inspir'd
> Who fondly make a merit of forgiveness,
> And give their foes a second opportunity,
> If the first blow should miss. (IV.i, p. 127)

In this "new faith" Tamerlane rejects the revenge code of Islam and the hypocrisy of its priesthood (III.ii, p. 122 ff). Appealing to Providence's own toleration of the "fair variety" of "different faiths," he rejects the attempt by any religious group to convert by force (p. 121 f). What is more, Tamerlane the Conqueror is opposed to war, considering it a "fell monster" (I, p. 91); he goes into battle "unwillingly" and only because Bajazet forces his hand (p. 93). Astounded by Bajazet's "Causeless" hatred and his unnatural, blasphemous pride and ambition (II.ii, p. 105), Tamerlane brands him a "monster" and expounds his own contrasting ambition to "fix" his "name,"

> by peace,
> By justice, and by mercy; and to raise
> My trophies on the blessings of mankind. (p. 106)

Thus Tamerlane represents a New Law (like that of the Christians) which is antithetical to Bajazet's inordinate hatred and pride.

This conflict between values becomes crystallized into one contrast (with *Paradise Lost* still very much in the background): mercy versus revenge. When Bajazet describes the cruel and merciless treatment Tamerlane would have received at his hand (p. 106 f), though strict "justice" and "vengeance" demand the same punishment for him, Tamerlane instead would give him the chance to reform, "that thou may'st learn / What man should be to man" (p. 107). Here again, then, as in his forgiveness of the Dervise, Tamerlane is merciful in order to reform the sinner, if possible. For, as he says, he is devoted to the "True greatness" of reforming the world (III.ii, p. 126). Like the Dervise, Bajazet rejects Tamerlane's mercy, calling him a "vain fool" and crying, "Thy folly on thy head!" (II.ii, p. 108). Tamerlane justifies his folly thus:

> Great minds (like Heav'n) are pleas'd in doing good,
> Tho' the ungrateful subjects of their favours
> Are barren in return.

Tamerlane insists that virtue is its own reward, and his mercy is seen to be "folly" only in the eyes of the worldly, who disparage those who "fondly make a merit of forgiveness." In other words, as in *The Ambitious Stepmother*, Rowe is alluding to that tradition of Christian folly which has its roots in the epistles of Saint Paul.

Bajazet answers Tamerlane's mercy with revenge and hatred. On the way to his dungeon of living hell and despair (see the descriptions on pp. 108 and 111), Bajazet encounters Arpasia and Moneses, the Greek lovers whom he had captured and who had masqueraded as brother and sister until Bajazet forced Arpasia to marry him in Moneses' absence. Spurned by both, Bajazet takes delight in the "revenge" of leaving Moneses to hear in "horror" of the rape of his betrothed (p. 110 f). Later Bajazet rejects Axalla's offer to "atone / The fatal breach" between him and Tamerlane and thus "To buy mankind a peace" (III.i, p. 117); answering Axalla's promise to obtain the return of Bajazet's crown in exchange for his daughter's hand, Bajazet demands "the *Tartar*'s head" to "sate" his "revenge" (p. 119). And he commands Selima to emulate his hatred:

> Henceforth, unless thou mean'st to cancel all
> My share in thee, and write thyself a bastard,

Die, starve, know any evil, any pain,
Rather than taste a mercy from these [Christian] dogs. (p. 117)

In Act V, against his captive Queen and his own daughter, Bajazet
displays his merciless cruelty at its fullest. With his "wrath" and "vengeance" he attempts to pierce Arpasia's "swelling heart" (p. 142), and
asserting in hypocritical self-righteousness, "Here, mercy, I disclaim
thee," he subjects her to a torture so cruel that it does indeed break
her heart (p. 143 ff). Then, disdaining the escaped Axalla's reported
pledge of "mercy" (p. 147), he turns on Selima, who arranged the escape, to "tear" her "to pieces" in "answer" to his "great revenge."
Appropriately, Bajazet is foiled in the midst of his last attempt at vengeance, and his abuse of mercy is now finally and fittingly repaid by its
withdrawal from him in favor of "righteous vengeance": as Tamerlane
says,

Mercy at length gives up her peaceful scepter,
And justice sternly takes her turn to govern. (p. 148)

Bajazet's recalcitrance finally calls forth the world's "keenest sword,
/ To cut up villainy of monstrous growth." In poetic justice, Tamerlane
administers a punishment "equal to Bajazet's crimes"—the very caging
Bajazet had planned for Tamerlane—so that Bajazet can be

borne about, in public view,
A great example of the righteous vengeance
That waits on cruelty, and pride like thine. (p. 149)

As Bajazet is led off desperately vowing to kill himself and to curse
Tamerlane with his "parting breath," Tamerlane confirms the poetic
justice done on him to be explicitly providential: "But justly those
above assert their sway."

In view of the deaths of the innocent Moneses and Arpasia, however, Tamerlane's merciful attitude and his final victory in justice may
appear to be vitiated. Ironically, Tamerlane—"whose word next
Heav'n's, / Makes fate at second hand" (I, p. 98); who is "The Sovereign
judge of equity on earth" (II.ii, p. 112); and "before whose awful throne
/ Th'afflicted never kneel in vain for justice" (III.ii, p. 123)—is unable
from the beginning to redress the evil done this pair, which stands
"bleeding fresh" and calls aloud to Heaven "for justice" (II.ii, p. 109).

Tamerlane bids Moneses forget "these lesser cares" and join him in reforming the world (III.ii, p. 126). Confronted with Arpasia's beauty and
virtue, however, Tamerlane himself complains:

> When sorrow dwells in such an angel form,
> Well may we guess that those above are mourners;
> Virtue is wrong'd, and bleeding innocence
> Suffers some wond'rous violation here,
> To make the saints look sad. Oh! teach my power
> To cure those ills which you unjustly suffer,
> Lest Heav'n should wrest it from my idle hand,
> If I look on, and see you weep in vain. (IV.ii, p. 129)

Though he is God's own Champion on earth, Tamerlane is powerless
to help Arpasia and Moneses, and their story, as well as their complaints
and his, raises the problem of suffering innocence with a special poignancy in this otherwise transparent dramatic theodicy.

The solution that the play offers is once again couched in the
metaphor of life as a trial. From the moment of their capture on the way
to be married, Moneses and Arpasia, who are both Christians, have been
tempted to despair. Arpasia describes their situation as hopeless:

> Our woes are like the genuine shade beneath,
> Where fate cuts off the very hopes of day,
> And everlasting night and horror reign. (II.ii, p. 111)

Arpasia wills to resist despair, however. Since the evil cannot be re-
dressed on earth and since, on the other hand, she has sworn to maintain
her marital faith, she clings to the hope that "Heav'n" will be "gracious"
and take her to "that blest place / Where the good rest from care and
anxious life" (p. 113). To sustain Moneses' "failing faith," she describes
to him a "tract of endless joys" and provides them both with a "hope"
to build on as they endure their ordeal, the trial of the innocent. Unlike
the Stoic heroines Lucrece and Portia, Arpasia espouses the higher
Christian heroism to "Live . . . And dare to be unhappy" (IV.ii, p. 129).
Yet they both gradually languish into a spiritual sloth where, porten-
tously, "all the glorious lights of Heav'n look dim" as they await "the
long night" in "sad society" (p. 135 f).[8]

They are not permitted to languish thus, however; they must still
face the supreme trial of martyrdom. And for Arpasia this is no ordinary

trial by fire. She must watch her beloved be cruelly "butcher'd" in her sight (V, p. 142). She prays to "holy martyrs" for heavenly assistance and appears to be armed with a "sacred spirit," but like Mirza in *The Ambitious Stepmother*, Bajazet challenges her fortitude, asserting that she talks her virtue well but dares not meet the danger. Significantly he concludes, "This moment is the trial." As she begins to fail, though, Moneses, who rises from lassitude to meet the test, becomes her example and instructs her in the Christian *ars moriendi*:

> Since thou art arm'd for all things, after death,
> Why should the pomp and preparation of it
> Be frightful to thy eyes? (p. 144)

The readiness is all, he insists with Hamlet and Edgar, and he goes to prove it.

The anguished Arpasia breaks down into impatience and "distraction": "Ye moralists, / Ye talkers, what are all your precepts now?" She screams for "Avenging lightnings," till human "Nature" can endure "no more" and she expires (p. 144 f). Critics of the ilk of Gildon would say that her death impugns Providence or that Rowe's sensationalism here undercuts his attempt to mirror Providence in the overall design. But despite her momentary impatience, Arpasia dies peacefully. In traditional Christian imagery, after wandering "bewilder'd with misfortunes" (p. 145), she finally reaches her "home," which must be that "blest place" she has prayed for, "Where the good rest from care," for she lies down in "peaceful slumber." We are led to infer that she has been granted that "peace" promised by the "gentle spirit" who whispers to her earlier (p. 140). It is a peace that is not languished into, however, but is earned through an excruciating trial, from which she is finally released. Moreover, Arpasia has said that she would live to triumph over Bajazet a moment, and she does so when she says, "I am now beyond thy cruel pow'r." Bajazet's reaction expresses the ironic limitations of that power:

> What is royalty?
> If those that are my slaves, and should live for me,
> Can die, and bid defiance to my pow'r.

The point is, as it was from Job and Plato to Milton, that no tyrant, not even Satan himself, has power over the mind.[9] God allows the satanic

Bajazets of the world to severely try, but not to coerce, the souls of men. For the soul is inviolable and thus can endure the gravest test.

Tamerlane's inability to redress the injuries of Moneses and Arpasia, or to save their lives, argues the necessity of retribution in the afterlife that the couple so ardently expects. To recall the words of Dennis—and the homiletic tradition they echo—suffering innocence "is permitted by the Governour of the World to show from the Attribute of his infinite Justice that there is a Compensation in Futurity, to prove the Immortality of the Human Soul, and the Certainty of future Rewards and Punishments" (*Critical Works*, II, 49). Tamerlane's final victory seems the external ratification of the hope for ultimate providential justice, and Arpasia's prayer for "Avenging lightnings" seems answered, for at last "justly those above assert their sway." Furthermore, the death of Moneses and Arpasia is the play's ultimate confirmation of Tamerlane's boast that the virtuous "(like Heav'n) are pleas'd in doing good," even if they receive no reward in this life. What appears folly in the eyes of the world is actually the highest kind of heroism, even if, paradoxically, its victory is attained only through death. But the play's firmest guarantee of the peace in which Moneses and Arpasia trust seems to be the self-sacrifice of Selima. Tamerlane is enabled to foil Bajazet's plot only because Selima sets her beloved Axalla free at the risk of her own destruction. Through Selima, then, the world obtains a peace—a peace of justice and order which points to that for Moneses and Arpasia beyond.

Throughout the play Selima is associated with imagery of peace, and even her name means *peace* in Arabic.[10] Early in the play, impressed by Tamerlane's beneficence, Selima utters a speech that emphasizes the supremacy of Christian over martial virtues and that constitutes a prayer for peace:

> Where shall my wonder and my praise begin!
> From the successful labours of thy arms?
> Or from a theme more soft, and full of peace,
> Thy mercy, and thy gentleness? oh, *Tamerlane*!
> What can I pay thee for this noble usage
> But grateful praise? So Heav'n itself is paid.
> Give peace, ye pow'rs above, peace to mankind;
> Nor let my father wage unequal war,
> Against the force of such united virtues. (p. 93)

Her prayer is not immediately answered, however, and she is forced
into a conflict between her love for Axalla and her duty to her father.
Together Selima and Axalla approach Bajazet and through their love
attempt to "buy mankind a peace," if he will only let their marriage
"atone / The fatal breach" between him and Tamerlane (III.i, p. 117).
Bajazet answers, however, by making it a duty for Selima to hate Axalla
and all Christians as her father's "foes": "Hate shall be pious in thee"
(p. 119). At her father's sentence Selima complains, "Undone for ever! /
Now tyrant duty, art thou yet obey'd?" Axalla knows, nevertheless, that
she is incapable of fulfilling such a duty: he has said earlier,

> Hate is not in thy nature: thy whole frame
> Is harmony, without one jarring atom. (I, p. 98)

Accordingly, when Axalla is later condemned to death by Bajazet,
Selima begs for his life and wins a momentary reprieve. She prays,
"Some angel whisper to my anxious soul / What I shall do to save him"
(IV.ii, p. 138). It appears that Providence answers her prayer, for she
conceives the ruse whereby Axalla escapes. And her action must also
be interpreted as a love to mankind ("to buy mankind a peace"), for
she must know that Axalla will return with Tamerlane to defeat her
father.

Yet she still attempts to save her father, too. Just as before she
would have maintained the balance between love and duty by remaining constant to Axalla though separated from him—"ev'n duty shall not
force me to be false" (III.i, p. 115)—so now she insists that even though
she has disobeyed her father, she has not "betray'd" him:

> I made the gentle, kind, *Axalla* swear,
> Your life, your crown, and honour would be safe. (V, p. 147)

She is willing to seal this gesture of peace even with her life. Though she
will not sacrifice Axalla to duty, she will sacrifice herself:

> Plunge the ponyard deep!
> The life my father gave shall hear his summons,
> And issue at the wound.

Her last words as he is about to kill her are, significantly, a prayer—"That
Heav'n may guard my royal father" (p. 148)—and a request for his final

blessing. It seems no exaggeration to say that Bajazet's final rejection of his own daughter is a rejection of the spiritual peace she represents.

Since Tamerlane insists that through his force "justly those above assert their sway," Axalla's arrival in the nick of time implies a providential intervention and a final divine judgment between Christian charity and inhuman cruelty. Selima's loving self-sacrifice has freed Axalla to arouse Tamerlane's sword as the instrument of Heaven's justice. From Bajazet himself, then, comes the ultimate agent of peace. Emblematically, as in *The Ambitious Stepmother*, Rowe has dramatized the basic Christian theodicean principle that out of evil comes forth good, and like Cleone's (and Christ's), Selima's sacrifice represents the promise of that principle and the pledge of eternal reward and peace for virtue and suffering innocence.

We have come a long way from William III, but then what greater compliment than to compare him to one of God's greatest Champions; to show him to be ultimately Christ-like and his enemy satanic; in short, to place him in the perspective of an eternal pattern. Rowe's *Tamerlane* goes far beyond the topical to the typological. It is not just an "allegorical eulogy" but an image of the eternal victory of good over evil, not just by the old heroism of a "Scourge of God" but by the new heroism of Christ. The play is a justification of the ways of God—and especially the Son of God—to men.

ii

In the introduction to the recent Twickenham edition of Pope's Homer, Robert Fagles maintains that the two great early English translations of the *Odyssey*—Chapman's and Pope's—are both theodicies.[11] For Chapman, Fagles refers us (p. ccxviii) to George DeForest Lord's excellent study, *Homeric Renaissance: The* Odyssey *of George Chapman*, which argues that the "dynamic allegory" in Chapman's translation is Ulysses' spiritual regeneration and that Ulysses' reunion with divine grace (symbolized by Pallas Athena) enables him to triumph at his return to Ithaca (ch. iii). Thus the dominant theme in Chapman is "man's relation with the gods" (p. 79), and Ulysses' suffering is justified as the process of establishing the proper relationship.

That Pope's translation is a theodicy is obvious from the very opening of the poem, when Jove, as Pope's note expresses it, "vindicates his divinity" (*Odyssey* I.45n):

Perverse Mankind! whose Wills, created free,
Charge all their woes on absolute Decree;
All to the dooming Gods their guilt translate,
And Follies are miscall'd the crimes of Fate. (I.41 ff)

Pope's note on Jove's entire speech is explicit: "This passage is . . .
worthy of a Christian; it shews us that the Supreme Being is sovereignly
good; that he rewards the just, and punishes the unjust; and that the
folly of man, and not the decree of Heaven, is the cause of human calamity" (I.41n). As Fagles points out, through his sufferings and trials[12]
"Augustan Odysseus" has come to rely on that Supreme Being: "Finally,
full circle from the man who courted disaster with Polyphemus,
Odysseus is willingly 'resign'd to Providence,' " and he now at his return "allies with Pallas to purify his land" (p. ccxiii).

In *The Ulysses Theme*, W. B. Stanford describes the traditional
treatments of Ulysses' return thus: "The third phase of Ulysses's career,
his return to Ithaca, as described in the *Odyssey*, provided little scope
for controversy in the post-Homeric tradition. . . . He returns as a King
to claim his rightful kingdom and as a husband to rescue his wife from
insolent suitors. Poetic justice prevails. The good are rewarded: the bad
are punished. Ulysses is clearly the leader of the good party" (p. 193).
Poetic justice certainly prevails in the Augustan *Odyssey*. A note
adapted from Bishop Eustathius, the twelfth-century commentator on
Homer, explains that since Antinous is "the first in guilt, he is the first
in punishment": "This is an act of Poetical justice" (II.95n). And it is
poetic justice in the Renaissance-Restoration-Augustan sense—that is,
providential justice. From Penelope (XXIII.61 ff), to the shades of the
suitors (XXIV.209), to Medon (XXIV.515, 517n), all attribute Ulysses'
victory to the intervention of Heaven. Laertes concludes, "almighty
Jove! / Heav'n rules us yet, and Gods there are above" (XXIV.409 f).
The poem ends, as it began, with the manifestation of Providence, for
Jove intervenes in Ulysses' final battle (XXIV.580 ff).

Pope's *Odyssey* reflects the culmination of a whole tradition of
Christian influences, not the least of which was Chapman's Christian-
Platonic theodicy. Itself a collaboration, Pope's translation can be taken
as representative of the Augustan view of Homer's great epic: thus
Fagles' phrase "the Augustan *Odyssey*." It is not surprising, then, that
only a few years earlier, Pope's friend Nicholas Rowe,[13] a man of the
same era and an heir to the same Christian and Homeric traditions,
would render the return of Ulysses as theodicy.

Rowe's *Ulysses (Works,* II, 1 ff) begins with the question of Providence. Telemachus' opening lines complain of his condition in the absence of Ulysses and of justice:

> O *MENTOR!* urge no more my royal birth,
> Urge not the honours of my race divine,
> Call not to my remembrance what I am,
> Born of *Ulysses*, and deriv'd from *Jove*;
> For 'tis the curse of mighty minds opprest,
> To think what their state is, and what it should be;
> Impatient of their lot they reason fiercely,
> And call the laws of Providence unequal. (I, p. 7)

Mentor counters this complaint by instructing Telemachus to restrain his passions and "To wait the leisure of the righteous Gods" till one day he will "bow, and bless thy fate, and own the Gods are just." Mentor says of the suitors,

> Doubt not but all their crimes, and all thy wrongs
> Are judg'd by *Nemesis* and equal *Jove*;
> Suffer the fools to laugh and loll secure,
> This is their day,—but there is one behind
> For vengeance and *Ulysses*. (p. 9)

The much-injured Ulysses himself, disguised as the beggar Aethon, advises Telemachus to bear his injuries and indignation (as he himself has done) in expectation of "That day of recompence and righteous justice."

Upon her entrance Penelope renews the central question of the play: How can the gods allow the virtuous to suffer for so long the adversity of fate and the perversity of men? She reminds the suitors of what she has suffered—"From *Troy*, the winds and seas, the Gods and you"—all for her Ulysses (p. 14). She complains,

> Are not my wrongs gone up to Heav'n against you?
> Do they not stand before the throne of *Jove*;
> And call incessant on his tardy vengeance? (p. 15)

In response to his threats against Telemachus, Penelope promises to marry Eurymachus, but she regains her fortitude and attempts to kill

herself as the only way both to save her honor and to escape witnessing
Telemachus' death. When she is disarmed by Aethon and constrained
by Mentor and Eumaeus, she sinks down in despair and complains bitterly against both gods and men:

> Cast not thy eyes up to yon azure firmament,
> Nor hope relief from thence, the Gods are pitiless,
> Or busy in their heav'n, and thou not worth their care;
> And oh! oh! cast 'em not on earth, to seek
> For succour from the faithless race of man. (III, p. 37)

Penelope's complaint is the archetypal crisis of faith which is at
the heart of the problem of suffering innocence. Rowe balances her
doubt against the hope of others and finally against the testimony of
the gods themselves. As he has done with Telemachus, Mentor now instructs her to rely on Providence:

> Far be that thought, to think you are forsaken;
> Gods and good men shall make you still their care.

Eumaeus seconds him with a prediction of an imminent Doomsday,
"That good we daily pray'd for, but pray'd hopeless" (p. 38). Such a day
is the theodicean promise, and Mentor marks its advent:

> And hark! vindictive *Jove* prepares his thunder,
> Let the wrong-doer and the tyrant tremble!
> The Gods are present with us.

At that moment the beleaguered faithful are granted a theophany.
Pallas descends to mark the return of justice, and the three pray for vindication. As she reascends, Pallas' smile appears an "omen," and "to
the left auspicious rolls the thunder" to mark Ulysses' triumphal entry,
"*magnificently armed and habited*" (p. 39). The import is clear. Ulysses
is the agent of "vindictive *Jove*," his Champion, and justice is impending. The day has come.

As Penelope's (and later Telemachus') continual praising of the
gods attests (p. 39 f), Ulysses' return is indeed providential. He is under
the guidance of Jove, who provides him the "opportunity" to seize his
"right" and "empire" (p. 40). Moreover, as the continual references to
Ulysses as "God-like" insist, he is explicitly the representative of Jove.

He tells Telemachus,

> Justice instructs her sword to this right hand,
> And I will see it faithfully employ'd. (p. 43)

The last description of the suitors, who have been portrayed throughout as blasphemous, is the final justification of their fate: Ulysses prepares to

> invade yon' drunkards,
> Immerst in riot, careless, and defying
> The Gods as fables, start upon 'em sudden,
> And send their guilty souls to howl below,
> Upon the banks of Styx. (p. 44)

The return of Ulysses proves that the gods are anything but "fables." By Telemachus' "fatal error," however (V, p. 56), Ulysses' cause is nearly lost and Providence nearly thwarted (so it would seem). Antinous seizes Penelope and bids Ulysses "In vain to *Pallas* and to *Jove* complain" (IV, p. 56). Indeed, Eumaeus does complain, and even Mentor expects only death, "That last relief, that refuge of despair" (V, p. 56 f). In contrast, Ulysses eschews despair and utters the supreme theodicean statement of the play:

> To doubt if there be justice with the Gods,
> Or if they care for ought below, were impious.
> Oft have I tried, and ever found 'em faithful,
> In all the various perils of my life,
> In battles, in the midst of flaming *Troy*,
> In stormy seas, in those dread regions where
> Swarthy *Cimmerians* have their dark abode,
> Divided from this world, and borderers on hell;
> Ev'n there the providence of *Jove* was with me,
> Defended, chear'd, and bore me thro' the danger;
> Nor is his pow'r, nor is my virtue less,
> That I should fear this rude tumultuous herd. (p. 63)

Pallas' assistance throughout the *Odyssey*, then, stands as the proof of the care and the justice of Providence, Which must be trusted again at this crisis.

Confronting the rebellious Antinous, Ulysses actually goes so far as to disdain the help of the gods (p. 64). But Antinous spitefully grants him divine assistance: "Invoke those friendly Gods whose care thou art, / And let them save thee" (p. 65). Ulysses rightly brands him a "defier of the Gods" and attacks. Ulysses' boast is not justified, however, for he is *not* "alone sufficient" to defeat Antinous, and the gods must help. It is not Ulysses but Telemachus who wins the day. Ulysses interprets the significance of Telemachus' arrival:

> Celestial Pow'rs! ye guardians of the just!
> This wond'rous work is yours, and yours be all the praise.

The truth of this interpretation is witnessed even by Antinous: "Thou and thy Gods at last have got the better" (p. 66). The point is that the gods *do* care and that man must rely on them for justice. The overall design of the play unmistakably images a providential universe.

Penelope's and Ulysses' final comments are even more instructive of the theodicean argument of the play. She runs to Ulysses and exults,

> At length the Gods have prov'd us to the utmost,
> Are satisfied with what we have endur'd,
> And never will afflict nor part us more.

Similarly, Ulysses says to Telemachus,

> 'Tis true the gracious Gods are kind at last,
> And well reward me here for all my sorrows past. (p. 67)

Thus Providence does grant Ulysses and Penelope an earthly reward for their virtue—but not before they have endured their trial of suffering. The pattern is basically the same as in *The Ambitious Stepmother* and *Tamerlane*—trial and providential judgment. Yet Rowe's *Ulysses* does not focus on the trial of the central hero. Ulysses has already been tried in the half of the *Odyssey* not represented but briefly alluded to in his remarks at his reunion with Penelope and in his references to his sufferings throughout. Instead the play focuses on his vengeance and vindication, in the process of which he himself, as the representative of justice, tries others, especially Penelope and Telemachus. In the

Odyssey, Minerva praises Ulysses for his prudence in not, as soon as he reaches Ithaca, rushing home to wife and son as other men would have done:

> Not thus *Ulysses*; he decrees to prove
> His subjects faith, and Queen's suspected love. (XIII.383 f)

Unlike Homer, Rowe does not stress the actual testing of the suitors for any redeeming virtues, although he does portray Aethon as a railer who attempts in vain to goad the suitors to reform. Rowe does, however, stress the trial of Ulysses' Queen and then of his son, and the play can be roughly divided accordingly.

The Greek for Pope's "to prove / His . . . Queen's suspected love" is σῆς ἀλόχου πειρήσεαι (*Od.* XIII.336, Loeb). With the personal genitive, the verb (the Ionic future infinitive form of πειράω) means *to make trial of* a person, in this case Ulysses' *spouse*. Perhaps taking his cue from this line,[14] Rowe has expanded the metaphor into a full-fledged and severe trial for Penelope. Having witnessed Penelope's rebuff to the suitors, Aethon extolls her exemplary virtue, which has already undergone twenty years of trial: "O matchless proof of faith and love unchang'd" (I, p. 16). At this point he is convinced of her truth. There is no "suspected love" here. Yet Eurymachus raises a doubt, and Ulysses resolves that Penelope "must be try'd" (p. 19).

Penelope's trial is that of Racine's Andromaque: a wife's honor versus a mother's love.[15] In Racine's play, Andromaque must agree to marry Achilles' son Pyrrhus or else Hector's and her son Astyanax will be sent with Oreste back to the Greeks to be killed. To save her son she finally yields, but plans to kill herself once his safety is assured "par des nœuds immortels," the marriage bonds (vs. 1092). She is reprieved by Pyrrhus' death. In Rowe's play, Penelope is forced to the same extremity. She passes the test of solicitation and indignantly rebukes Aethon's pandering, but Eurymachus abandons persuasion and threatens to kill Telemachus. Aethon comments aside, "That stroke was home —now, virtue, hold thy own" (II, p. 29), and Penelope demands such strictness from herself (p. 31). But like Andromaque's, her trial is even more demanding than her own death, and "A mother's mourning for her only son" causes her to yield. She is immediately aware of the cost, and pathetically, she exits murmuring that she gave her son a second birth "at a price too great" (p. 33).

Despite Mentor's insistence on the "unequal terms" under which

Penelope has struggled, Aethon concludes that her virtue is already
"abandon'd, lost and gone" and that she is now a "Cursed object" (III, p.
34 f). Yet Eumaeus proves to be right: her compliance was only "one
unheeded word, / Forc'd from her in the bitterest pangs of sorrow" (p.
35). The distraught Penelope is no longer hesitant. Unlike Andromaque,
she has no perfect solution to save both her honor and her son. For the
model of fidelity, the marriage itself would be a pollution. There is no
way out. As Ulysses has demanded (p. 34), since she cannot conquer,
she chooses to die—to preserve her virtue and to "shield" herself from
the piteous spectacle of Telemachus' murder (p. 36 f). Her trial is over,
and calling himself a "trifler," Ulysses stays her hand. The ensuing theophany is a sign that the disconsolate Penelope has been more than
sufficiently proved; indeed, as her pitiful, desperate complaint indicates,
she has reached the limits of human endurance. At last "vindictive *Jove*"
is ready to reward and punish. Only the trial of Telemachus remains.[16]

Telemachus, "whose temper / Is open as the day, and unsuspect-
ing" (I, p. 10), is led by the false Antinous to forsake "The fierceness,
rage, and pride of youth" that suit his condition and to become "the
love-sick youth [that] dotes ev'n to death / Upon the *Samian* Princess"
(II, p. 22). So Telemachus in his naivety has allowed himself to be distracted from the primary business at hand—the assumption of his role as
Ulysses' son in the chaotic state of Ithaca. We recall his opening complaint to Mentor:

> Call not to my remembrance what I am,
> Born of *Ulysses*, and deriv'd from *Jove*;
> For 'tis the curse of mighty minds opprest,
> To think what their state is, and what it should be.

Moreover, Telemachus' love leads him rash and overhasty into an illicit
marriage, for Semanthe is a virgin dedicated to Diana—thus her fits and
starts during and after the ceremony (II, p. 23 ff). Her portentous dream,
wherein Diana condemns her marriage and her father's corpse takes
Telemachus' place, is expressive of Semanthe's guilt and prophetic of
the fate of the marriage. Semanthe and Telemachus do not heed the
dream, however. He tells her not to "dread the anger of the awful Gods,"
since she is "Safe" in her "native unoffending innocence" (p. 25). Yet
a bit like Adam and Eve, they steal away from the "watchful eye" of
Aethon, who recognizes their flirtation with "folly" (p. 26) and drives
home the import of their actions:

> This *Samian* King is happy in his arts:
> His daughter, vow'd a virgin to *Diana*,
> Is brought to play the wanton here at *Ithaca*:
> No matter for religion; let the Gods
> Look to their rites themselves.

When he later reveals himself to Telemachus, Ulysses makes "harsh mention" of his love to remind him of what he owes to "honour" (III, p. 42). Telemachus is boldly assertive and would be tried in battle, but Ulysses has a greater trial for him: to defend his mother against Semanthe's father. When he warns Telemachus, "With powerful opposition shalt thou strive" (p. 44), the audience is aware, as Ulysses himself must be, that the struggle will be not only against the power of Eurymachus but also against the power of Telemachus' love for Semanthe.

As he kneels to kiss his father's sword, like Corneille's Rodrigue, Telemachus responds to his charge by wagering what the French would call his *gloire*:

> I swear—And may my lot in future fame
> Be good or evil but as I perform it.

Yet again like Rodrigue, Telemachus hesitates momentarily. His wedding night, which he has promised to Semanthe and to love (II, p. 26), he gives over only grudgingly to honor (IV, p. 46). From the first sight of Eurymachus he attempts to avoid the fatal confrontation to which he has pledged himself. Finally, in the climax of the problem of his identity and his "nature," Telemachus becomes what his heritage has destined him to be:

> Nay then 'tis time to speak like what I am,
> And tell you, Sir, you must not, nor you shall not [pass]. (p. 48)

He dispels the last hesitation and becomes the champion not only of his mother's honor but also of "the Gods" themselves (p. 49). As he kills Eurymachus, he reignites the "heav'nly fire" that had nearly grown "extinct within" him.

Telemachus' trial is by no means over, however. Like Chimène, Semanthe adopts the code of honor that has destroyed her father and rejects love, along with its concomitant mercy and forgiveness, in favor of "blood, destruction and revenge" (p. 53). As she leaves cursing those who would still believe in love, Telemachus moans,

> Now arm thee for the conflict, oh my soul,
> And see how thou canst bear *Semanthe's* loss. (p. 54)

The burden is too great to bear. He is immediately overwhelmed by the thought that his father's "cruel policy" has been responsible for his loss, and he rushes, desperately "Careless of all," into battle to be killed (p. 55). At the same moment, he breaks his vow to his father and thereby fails his test after all—a failure with consequences far more serious than the loss of Semanthe. For he leaves Penelope unattended, allowing her to be seized and carried off to a citadel where she appears to be destined the object of another Trojan War: "*Troy* and *Hector* are reviv'd again" (p. 56).

Telemachus has failed not only because of his despondency but because he has yielded his secrets to a false friend, Antinous. At the beginning of the play, Aethon instructs the distraught Telemachus (whom he significantly calls his "son") how to patiently await the "day of recompence and righteous justice":

> Learn thou, my son, the cruel arts of courts;
> Learn to dissemble wrongs, to smile at injuries,
> And suffer crimes, thou want'st the power to punish;
> Be easy, affable, familiar, friendly,
> Search, and know all mankind's mysterious ways,
> But trust the secret of thy soul to none. (I, p. 9)

Aethon is, of course, the perfect embodiment of the lesson he gives, for he is the disguised Ulysses, famous for his worldly wisdom, stealth, and craftiness. Throughout the play, moreover, and throughout the entire Odyssean tradition, secrecy is established as a primary virtue, and both of Telemachus' parents are its exemplars. As mentioned earlier, Minerva in the epic praises Ulysses for his secrecy at his return, without which he would have been destroyed by the suitors. He uses his secrecy to test his followers, the suitors, and his wife, and to await his divinely occasioned opportunity for vindication. In the meantime, as he tries Penelope in the play, he suffers the "racking, racking, pain of secret thought"

(II, p. 31). Secrecy has been equally important to Penelope. Through "The riddle of her mystic web" (I, p. 11)—through what Polydamas the suitor calls "the secret malice of the night" which "Undid the labours of the former day"—she fooled the suitors for four years. For twenty years she has "preserv'd" the "heav'nly train" of marital virtues in her "secret soul" (II, p. 31). Now, even at the moment of ecstatic joy at Ulysses' return, she must yield to Mentor's call for secrecy and abandon her lord again for a while: Mentor says,

> Think where you are, what eyes malicious chance
> May bring to pry into the happy secret,
> Untimely to disclose the fatal birth,
> And rashly bring it immature to light. (III, p. 40)

Howbeit unwittingly, Telemachus does exactly what Mentor has feared, precisely because he does not heed Aethon's advice. Beseeching him to "heal" the "cares" that the son of Ulysses cannot escape (I, p. 10), Telemachus trusts Antinous with the "dear secret" of his soul—his love for Semanthe (p. 9)—and allows himself to be seduced into a secret and illicit marriage with her. Ironically, he hides his marriage from Aethon, who is in secret both his father and, as Ulysses makes clear at their reunion (III, p. 41), his truest friend. While the newlyweds steal away from his watchful eye, Aethon comments,

> Ha! what so close? how cautious to avoid me!
> As who should say, old man you are too wise,
> What has my youth to do with your instructions. (II, p. 26)

Unaware of the marriage which makes the trial even more severe, Ulysses prepares to teach Telemachus a lesson. With grave irony, he promises Eurymachus for *his* secret marriage with Penelope a priest "try'd in these pious secrets" and "sworn to secrecy," one who is his "friend of ancient date" and "now in *Ithaca*" (II, p. 34)—meaning, of course, himself! But he sends instead Telemachus, who, if he is not actually sworn to secrecy by Ulysses, at least has been instructed in it by Aethon.

Not only does Telemachus reveal the secret of *his* soul to his false friend, but he reveals his father's "fatal secret" too (IV, p. 45): Antinous exclaims,

The King return'd? so long conceal'd in *Ithaca*?
Aethon the King? What words can speak my wonder?

This is the "fatal secret" upon which depends not only Telemachus'
own life but that of all his "royal race." For Telemachus reveals that
which the secret workings of his parents are parallel to, guided by, and,
in effect, representative of—the secret workings of Providence Itself:

Yes, my *Antinous*, 'tis most amazing,
'Tis all the mighty working of the Gods,
Unsearchable and dark to human eyes.

Like Milton's Samson, Telemachus has "profan'd / The mystery of
God" by his "Shameful garrulity."[17] Telemachus' phrase "the fatal
secret" links Mentor's image of the providential "fatal birth" with his
later naming of Telemachus' "fatal error." By rashly bringing the design
of Providence "immature to light," Telemachus loses much more than
Semanthe: he loses the "prize" for which Ulysses has yearned in his
wanderings and has fought now at home (V, p. 56). Since the beginning
of the Trojan War, Penelope has remained the very model of virtue in
a world replete with strife. Just as order is about to be restored, Telemachus allows the original act of rape to be repeated, and the world
slips again into chaos and despair.
    Telemachus' despair is the greatest. In traditional Jobish fashion,
he curses the day he was born (V, p. 59). Although he accepts the divine "justice" of his punishment (p. 60), he seeks to be annihilated, and
he begs Semanthe to "Complete th'imperfect vengeance of the Gods."
Semanthe refuses, however, and reverses her earlier repudiation of
mercy for revenge. Despite the "cruel" (read *retributive*) decree of the
gods that they must part forever (p. 62), Semanthe, in implied contrast
to Corneille's Chimène, sacrifices her pride and sense of honor for "One
last, one guilty proof" of love. Like Ulysses, keeping the secret of her
soul and practicing "just deceit" (p. 66), she accuses Antinous of killing
her father and turns her countrymen upon him, with Telemachus at
their head. Thus her action not only redeems Telemachus from his desperate sloth but also redeems the world from his "fatal error," from a
new Trojan War, and it allows the "fatal birth" of Providence to be

brought *mature* to light. As Mentor says, "Heav'n has approved the fraud of fond affection"—

> A turn so happy, and so unexpected,
> None but those over-ruling pow'rs who caus'd it,
> Could have foreseen.

And finally, since the ultimate "safety" results from Semanthe's love and not from Ulysses' righteous vengeance, it can be seen that once again Rowe, like Milton, asserts the New Testament heroism of love and sacrifice as superior to the ancient heroism of revenge and force of arms. Ulysses' justice is implemented and superseded by Semanthe's mercy. And once again in Rowe, the daughter of a pernicious villain saves the world: out of evil comes forth good.

Amidst the "wonder" and the "joy" at the victory made possible by Semanthe's love and at the end of suffering for Ulysses and Penelope enters the penitent Telemachus. He throws himself at his father's feet:

> Here let me kneel, and with my tears atone
> The rash offences of my heedless youth.
> Here offer the first trophies of my sword,
> And once more hail my father King of *Ithaca*. (p. 66 f)

These first trophies being Eurymachus and Antinous, his action marks both his initiation into manhood and the atonement of his "fatal error." He has now resumed his proper relationship to his "race divine"—to both Ulysses and Jove—and is reintegrated into the order which they represent. Yet Telemachus still complains to his father (and who would not say justifiably so?):

> Joy like the chearful morning dawns on all,
> And none but your unhappy son shall mourn.

Ulysses' only answer is to explain what it means to be a man:

Like thee the pangs of parting love I've known,
My heart like thine has bled—But oh! my son,
Sigh not nor of the common lot complain,
Thou that art born a man, art born to pain;
For proof, behold my tedious twenty years
All spent in toil, and exercis'd in cares.

Telemachus himself has spoken earlier of "all those miseries mankind is born to" (IV, p. 52), and now he is fully aware that, along with the legacy of semidivinity (his "race divine"), he—like everyman—inherits a legacy of suffering. It is the curse of all men "To think what their state is, and what it should be." Nevertheless, the design of the play insists that the "laws of Providence" are not "unequal." Using his own life as an example, Ulysses can declare to Telemachus, " 'Tis true the gracious Gods are kind at last." Just as the trial of suffering is passed on from generation to generation, so also is its theodicean solution: absolute trust in Divine Providence, Which vindicates at last. Armed with this faith, Telemachus must go forth on his own odyssey of toil and care, of suffering and trial, keeping the secret of his soul till his own "day of recompence" arrive. For he, like each of us, is the new Ulysses.

iii

Ulysses is a far better play than not only *The Ambitious Stepmother* and *Tamerlane* but also most of the English classical plays of this neoclassical age. Many were attempted but few are choice: Dryden's *All for Love* and *Cleomenes*, and Lee's *The Rival Queens* and *Lucius Junius Brutus*. In my opinion, Rowe's play is inferior to Dryden's but at least equal to Lee's. *Ulysses* is a good play because Rowe captures something of the aura of his sources in Homer, Corneille, and Racine and because his characters are not the usual one-dimensional heroes and villains. His Ulysses is not the all-perfect champion (Christian or Stoic); he is great in virtue and in soul but a bit too suspicious, too vindictive, a "trifler" with virtue, even a boaster of too much self-reliance at the end. Penelope is magnificent in both her indignant disdain and her impatient complaint. Semanthe is a second-rate Chimène but nevertheless approaches Cornelian quality in her rejection of Telemachus and love in Act IV and in her resignation and redemptive love in Act V. Telemachus is also a complex hero, and Rowe portrays with force and credibility both his triumph over Eurymachus and his piteous plight. Finally, Eurymachus is far superior to the usual Restoration villain, the melodramatic Machiavel.[18] He is the noblest of the suitors and is even gracious and courtly in his early wooing of Penelope. Though his designs are evil, he achieves heroic stature enough to be the analogue of the father of Chimène.

Lee and Otway at their best may equal or surpass Rowe's characterization here (Addison does not even come close), but Rowe is superior to them in his control of language. James R. Sutherland has said, "No living Englishman could write blank verse more beautifully than Mr. Rowe" (*Three Plays*, p. 27). Admittedly, in his earlier plays and even in this one, Rowe often strains to achieve heroic and passionate diction, and his greatest weakness lies in the self-conscious ejaculations and tropes of his amorous dialogues; but the same is true of Lee, Otway, and Addison. In *Ulysses*, however, Rowe captures and controls the language of the higher passions of indignation and disdain as never before in his tragedies of suffering innocence (but see *The Fair Penitent*). Contrast Artemisa's stiff and stilted speech, "Be fix'd, my soul" (*Works*, I, 14), with Penelope's smoother, more natural yet more powerful answers to the suitors in Act I. In the former Rowe strains for a metaphor and then contorts it from "active sparks" of "ethereal energy" to "a busy restless principle" with an "appetite" that is "clogged" by the "dull mass" of a woman's body; in the latter Rowe reaches for no metaphor but relies simply on the concrete details of Penelope's suffering, the suitor's riot and violence, and the slaughter of them all which is the price to win her (p. 14 ff).

Rowe is at his best in the rhetoric of complaint—not amorous but metaphysical. Observe his progress in these passages:

Artaxerxes.　　　　'Tis past, 'tis past;　　　　　　*[Lying down]*
　　　And all those fires that lighted up my soul,
　　　Glory and bright ambition languish now,
　　　And leave me dark and gloomy as the grave.
　　　Oh thou soft dying sweetness!—shall I rage
　　　And curse myself? Curse ev'n the Gods?—Oh no:
　　　I am the slave of fate, and bow beneath
　　　The load that presses me; am sunk to earth,
　　　And ne'er shall rise again: here will I sit
　　　And gaze till I am nothing. (*Works*, I, 74)

Arpasia. A little longer yet, be strong, my heart,
   A little longer let the busy spirits
   Keep on their cheerful round.—It wo'not be;
   Love, sorrow, and the sting of vile reproach,
   Succeeding one another in their course,
   Like drops of eating water on the marble,
   At length have worn my boasted courage down:
   I will indulge the woman in my soul,
   And give a loose to tears and to impatience;
   Death is at last my due, and I will have it. (*Works*, I, 134 f)

Penelope. Here sit thee down then, humbly in the dust,
   Here sit, a poor forlorn, abandon'd woman;
   Cast not thy eyes up to yon azure firmament,
   Nor hope relief from thence, the Gods are pitiless,
   Or busy in their heav'n and thou not worth their care;
   And oh! oh! cast 'em not on earth, to seek
   For succour from the faithless race of man;
   But as thou art forsaken and alone,
   Hope not for help, where there is none to help thee,
   But think—'tis desolation all about thee. (*Works*, II, 37)

The second seems to me better than the first, partly because its opening
lines capture something of the rhythms of its source in the opening lines
of *Samson Agonistes*, and partly because its metaphor of "drops of
eating water on the marble" seems less strained than the fires and loads
of the first. Metrically, the passages are fairly regular, but the feminine
endings of the second, rather than weakening the *passage*, as critics so
often assert, appropriately reflect the weakening of the *speaker*. The
third passage seems to me better than the others, however, precisely
because of its lack of imagery and its metrical irregularity. Here Rowe
does not strain for the sublime trope. He lets the plain language of despair do its own work and lets the emotion spill out into alexandrines
to create the effect of loss of control in still-controlled but varied
rhythms. The much more pervasive and yet not obtrusive alliteration
and assonance lend a musical resonance to the passage lacking in the
others. Even the expletives "oh! oh!" are functional, as Penelope looks
at the men who she feels have betrayed her and now hold her on either
side. Finally, the repetitive feminine ending "thee" in the last two lines

serves the same function as the feminine endings of the second passage—
to reflect a weakening—but serves it better, I think, in the repetition
itself, which gives the illusion of a polysyllabic rhyme and has something of the effect of Robert Frost's famous repetition in the last lines
of "Stopping by Woods on a Snowy Evening"—a surrendering, a letting
go.

Penelope's complaint is one of the best in Restoration tragedy and
Rowe's best writing up to that time. For both pathos and control it surpasses the uncontrolled tirades of Lee and Otway and the cold accents
of Addison. Only the complaints of some of Dryden's heroes are better.
And what makes Rowe's complaint so good, I think, is primarily his dis-
carding of the technique of Lee and Otway—the grasp for the sublime,
shocking, or sensational image. Rowe is generally at his best when he
eschews the local metaphor and relies for imagistic power on the accumulation of unobtrusive motifs, like *peace* in *Tamerlane*, *secrecy* here
in *Ulysses*, and *bread* and *bequest* later in *Jane Shore* and *Lady Jane
Gray*, respectively.

Besides its better language, what finally makes *Ulysses* Rowe's best
dramatic theodicy to that date is the structure. He handles exposition
and scene variation much better, and instead of finishing his subplot
at the end of the fourth act, as he does in the two earlier plays, here he
dovetails it with the main at the last moment to create tight structural
unity and a blend of form and theme. Emerging from the subplot, so to
speak, Telemachus comes forth to utter his last complaint in the midst
of triumph, adding a poignancy that is absent from the vain threats and
haughty exits of Artemisa and Bajazet. The familiar closing assertion
that the gods are just at last is balanced nicely against the suffering
which is man's "common lot." By sustaining that tension to the end,
Rowe achieves the least contrived and most aesthetically convincing
yet of his justifications of the ways of God to men.

NOTES TO CHAPTER II

1. See Landon C. Burns, Jr., ed., *Tamerlane, a Tragedy*, p. 6 ff, to which I am indebted throughout this opening section.

2. For the most educated guesses, see James R. Sutherland, ed., *Three Plays*, by Nicholas Rowe, p. 339; Willard Thorp, "A Key to Rowe's *Tamerlane*," p. 124 ff; and Donald B. Clark, "Nicholas Rowe," p. 65 and n.

3. Loftis exaggerates the case, I think. To say that the play represents Whig wish-fulfillment or "war-inspired Francophobia" seems an instance of the intentional fallacy. Also, Rowe is not so much of a Whig constitutionalist or antiabsolutist to deny the "right divine" of kings (Prologue, p. 83; see also I, p. 95).

4. For similar contemporary analogies, see Sir Richard Steele, *The Christian Hero*, who compares Louis XIV to a satanic "Foe" and William III to a "Glorious instrument of Providence" sent for Louis' destruction (p. 82 ff); and Jonathan Swift, "Ode to the King on his Irish Expedition and the Success of his Arms in General," in *The Poems of Jonathan Swift*, ed. Harold Williams, I, 4 ff, who compares William to Tamerlane and Louis to a *"Restless Tyrant"* (not explicitly Bajazet, but implicitly so),

Sent by just Heaven to threaten Earth
With War, and Pestilence, and Dearth. (st. 7)

5. Clark, p. 147. As Clark shows, Rowe had a copy of this edition in his library. See *A Catalogue of the Library of N. Rowe*, fol. 73.

6. For a reflection of this favorable portrayal contemporary to Rowe, see Sir William Temple, "Of Heroic Virtue," in *Five Miscellaneous Essays*, ed. Monk, p. 135 ff. Cf. Clark, "Source and Characterization," p. 146, and Alfred Schwarz, "The Literary Career of Nicholas Rowe," p. 97 f. See Rowe's *Catalogue*, oct. 377, for an edition of Temple's *Miscellanies, Second Part* (1690), which contained Temple's essay.

7. See especially Irving Ribner, *The English History Play in the Age of Shakespeare*, ch. iv, and C. A. Patrides, *The Phoenix and the Ladder*, passim.

8. Despair was traditionally associated with sloth, with *acedia* and *tristitia*. See especially Kilbee C. Brittain, "The Sin of Despair in Renaissance English Literature," passim, and D. C. Allen, *The Harmonious Vision*, p. 76.

9. The influence of Milton on Rowe has been suggested throughout, as has that of the Book of Job. Whiting has already shown explicit references to Milton, and explicit references to Job and to Plato can be found in *Jane Shore* and *Lady Jane Gray*, respectively (see chs. iii, v). In other words, I am not trying to suggest a vague tradition behind Rowe but a clear one, to which his works are implicitly—if not explicitly—related.

10. Flora H. Loughead, *Dictionary of Given Names with Origins and Meanings*. Whether Rowe knew the meaning of the word is undeterminable, and ultimately inconsequential, since the imagery he surrounds Selima with is certainly that of peace. However, the sale catalogue of his library (q.v.), with its numerous entries of books dealing with the Near East, suggests that he had more than a superficial knowledge of the culture and history of that region.

11. *Homer's* Iliad *and* Odyssey, ed. Maynard Mack et al., vols. VII–X of *The Twickenham Edition of the Poems of Alexander Pope*, VII, cxciii ff, ccxviii. Cf. George Dimock, "Crime and Punishment in the *Odyssey*," who shows that the original is, of course, a theodicy as well.

12. Pope uses the theodicean metaphor of trial to explain suffering innocence: "The age was not enlightened enough to know that calamity is often a proof of virtue, and a tryal not a punishment" (XIX.434n). Such suffering also reinforces our "certain hopes of a future state," a "time of retribution" which "will amply recompense the good man for all his calamities, or as *Milton* expresses, *Will justify the ways of God to men*" (XX.249n).

13. For their friendship, see Norman Ault, *New Light on Pope*, p. 128 ff. Also, it appears that before he died Rowe made some contribution, however small, to Pope's Homer: see Pope's acknowledgment in *Twickenham Edition*, VII, 23, and X, 443.

14. Stanford suggests that the source of Rowe's testing of Penelope is Teiresias' advice to Ulysses "to offer Penelope to some rich adulterer"—presumably as a trial (ch. ix, n. 12). Obviously, Rowe is merely expanding what is already in Homer, but the expansion was a brilliant stroke for the dramatic conflict of the play.

15. Jean Racine, *Andromaque* (1667), in *Œuvres de J. Racine*, ed. Paul Mesnard, I, 1 ff. Cf. Landon C. Burns, Jr., "The Tragedies of Nicholas Rowe," p. 170, who also sees a relationship between Penelope and Andromaque. The popularity of Racine's play in England can be inferred from the fact that it was translated for the English stage twice: anonymously as *Andromache* in 1675, and by Ambrose Philips as *The Distrest Mother* in 1712, the latter being "by all odds the most popular and successful translation of a French tragedy ever produced," according to Dorothea (Canfield) Fisher, *Corneille and Racine in England*, p. 140. Of course, Rowe's *Ulysses* predates Philips' play, but John Crowne wrote in the Preface to *Andromache* that even then Racine's play was "much esteemed in France and here, too, by some English, who are admirers of the French Wit" (as quoted in Fisher, p. 89). Certainly Rowe was a direct descendant of those admirers, as is attested by the catalogue of his library (q.v.) with its large number of French works, and by his later work in editing, translating, and even contributing to the works of Boileau, Quillet, and La Bruyère. Besides the remarkable similarity in tragic conflict, however, the strongest implication that Rowe was imitating Racine's play lies, paradoxically, in the fact that the trial of Telemachus is remarkably similar to that of Corneille's Rodrigue in *Le Cid* (see Donald B. Clark, "Nicholas Rowe," p. 145 ff, who clearly establishes the relationship between the two plays through a series of parallels). It appears that Rowe attempted to incorporate into his adaptation of one of the world's greatest classical epics the major conflicts in two of France's greatest classical tragedies.

16. Rowe's addition of the trial of Telemachus to the story of Ulysses' return can probably be attributed, at least in part, to the amazing popularity of François de la Mothe-Fénelon's *Les Aventures de Télémaque, fils d'Ulysse* (1699), which, by the time Rowe wrote *Ulysses*, had been published at least five times in French (see Alexander Cioranescu, *Bibliographie de la littérature française du dix-septième siècle*, II, s.v. Fénelon) and at least four times in English translation (see *The Catalogue of the British Museum*). Rowe certainly would have found Fénelon's didacticism agreeable, particularly his insistence throughout on the primacy of trust in Providence. And, if Rowe borrowed anything directly from him beyond the interest in Telemachus, it was probably the theme of the education of this neo-Ulysses, the heir not only to Ulysses' throne but also to the Odyssean pattern of suffering which represents the trial of virtue and faith. Moreover, Fénelon involved Telemachus in two love-affairs: an illicit one with Eucharis, one of Calypso's nymphs, which threatens his manhood and his soul (Book VI); and a licit one with Antiope, which he must defer, however, until his father's business is accomplished (Book XVII). Perhaps these affairs suggested to Rowe Telemachus' affair with Semanthe.

17. SA 377 f, 491. Cf. Anne Davidson Ferry, *Milton and the Miltonic Dryden*, pt. 2, ch. i, for a very fine analysis of the theme of secrecy in *Samson Agonistes*, an analysis to which I am indebted throughout this section. Perhaps Rowe himself, influenced so

much by Milton in his earlier plays, *Tamerlane* (see above) and *The Fair Penitent* (see ch. iv), was indebted to *Samson Agonistes*, as well as to *The Odyssey*, for this theme.

18. See Mark D. Horne, "The Villain in Restoration Tragedy," for an interesting study of the triteness of this figure, which becomes almost a pure abstraction.

III Protagonist as Saint

The Royal Convert and
Lady Jane Gray

N ROWE's *Tamerlane* we have seen that the "trial" of the Christians, Moneses and Arpasia, culminates in their death. Arpasia's prayer to the "holy martyrs," along with Moneses' faith in the certainty of an afterlife, places their suffering in the context of Christian martyrdom. Though they are not persecuted primarily for their religion (albeit Bajazet hates Christians), their story demonstrates that even in the face of torture and death the Christian dares meet his trial with trust in Providence. While the Arpasia-Moneses episode does not dominate *Tamerlane*, in *The Royal Convert* (1707) and *Lady Jane Gray* (1715) Rowe concentrates on the theme of Christian martyrdom as the extreme trial of the innocent—as the trial of the saint. Although the victims in *The Royal Convert* are reprieved at the last moment, the particular nature of their suffering—not only for their love but also for their faith— links the tragedy with *Lady Jane Gray*, and both can justly be called martyr plays. Significantly, though the historical backgrounds for both plays can be found in several sources, those same backgrounds are thoroughly treated in the great Protestant martyrology of the English Renaissance, John Foxe's *Book of Martyrs*, of which Rowe possessed a copy.[1]° That Rowe used Foxe as one of his sources is probable—but impossible to prove. What is more important is that the periods of history whence Rowe drew these plays—the Saxon conquest of Christian Britain and the English Reformation—were periods of religious persecution and martyrdom. Moreover, though the protagonists of *The Royal Convert* are fictional characters, Lady Jane Gray was in fact one of Protestant England's most illustrious martyrs.

°Notes to this chapter begin on page 105.

It is instructive, then, to view these plays in the light of the Renaissance concept of the function of hagiography. Foxe prefixed to the *Book of Martyrs* an essay entitled, "The Utility of this *Story*," in which he delineates that function, the primary aspect of which is the following: if men profit by reading "prophane" history, Foxe argues, "how much more then is it meet for Christians to conserve in remembrance the Lives, Acts, and Doings, not of bloody Warriors, but of mild and constant Martyrs of Christ, which serve not so much to delight the ear, as to garnish the life, to frame it with examples of great profit, and to encourage men to all kind of Christian godliness? As first, by reading thereof we may learn a lively testimony of Gods mighty working in the life of man, contrary to the opinion of *Atheists*, and all the whole Nest of *Epicures*. For like as one said of *Harpalus* in times past, that his doings gave a lively testimony against God, because he being so wicked a man, escaped so long unpunished; so contrariwise in these men we have a much more assured and plain witness of God, both in whose Lives and Deaths appeared such manifest Declarations of Gods divine working" (sig. a5^r).

Thus, according to Foxe, the primary function of hagiography is theodicean: to teach the workings of Providence and to answer thereby the problem of suffering innocence, raised with new urgency in this troublesome age of renascence and reformation by the doubting atheists and neo-Epicureans. In *Tudor Books of Saints and Martyrs*, Helen C. White quotes Eusebius, the first great Church historian and hagiographer, as saying that the events in his *Ecclesiastical History* evince " 'a vindication of the divine Word, in whom the faith of Christians centers' " (p. 12). According to White, all the martyr stories told in the Middle Ages were seen as episodes in "the divine epic" (p. 17); in Foxe's book, however, an even greater emphasis is put on Providence, especially in miraculous occurrences (p. 115). Most of Foxe's marvels, she continues, are "miracles of Providence" and of "retribution" (p. 165): "The sixteenth-century attack on the miraculous spared retribution, and many who scoffed at the happy chances of the *Golden Legend* [Caxton's extremely popular translation of Jacobus de Voragine's colossal medieval martyrology, *Legenda Aurea*] would have a grim satisfaction in Providence's avenging of innocent blood and bringing the persecutors of the saints to poetic justice" (p. 115). White's terms are already quite familiar to us in our study of Rowe and the Christian tragedy of suffering innocence.

The way that the lessons of martyrologies are to be taught, accord-

ing to Foxe, is by the "example" of the martyrs, who themselves did
the "dance" of Christ (sig. a5ʳ). The same, of course, is true of martyr
plays from the Middle Ages through the Renaissance. In the Restoration, the Preface to John Dryden's *Tyrannick Love, or The Royal Martyr*
(acted 1669), reiterates the concept of teaching "the precepts of our
religion" by example, by dramatic representations of "patterns of
piety": "By the harmony of words we [dramatists] elevate the mind to
a sense of devotion, as our solemn music, which is inarticulate poesy,
does in churches; and by the lively images of piety, adorned by action,
through the senses allure the soul; which while it is charmed in a silent
joy of what it sees and hears, is struck at the same time with a secret
veneration of things celestial, and is wound up insensibly into the practice of that which it admires" (*Essays*, I, 138 f). Here affective and formal theories exist side by side. Whatever the affective mechanics, the
overall designs are "images" or "patterns," like Foxe's "dance," which
are intended to instruct the audience not merely in Christian ethics
but in "things celestial," in Christian metaphysics. At least up to the
time of Rowe, then, martyr stories and plays by their very nature were
designed to portray not merely the pious lives of saints but metaphysical reality itself.

As in Foxe, the metaphysical reality portrayed in Dryden's *Tyrannick Love* is the Divine Providence Which Saint Catharine so ably defends and Which manifests Its care in the miraculous events of the play.
The same metaphysical reality is portrayed in Rowe's two martyr plays,
and his theme remains trust in the care and ultimate justice of that
Providence, even in the face of martyrdom. And while *The Royal
Convert*—in its overbearing rhetoric and contrivances—is inferior to
Tyrannick Love, Lady Jane Gray—in its muted rhetoric and simplicity—
is superior. It images forth better than any of Rowe's previous tragedies
of suffering innocence a universe that is meaningful despite even the
death of the virtuous and the triumph of the wicked.

i

As in *Tamerlane*, the motif of *peace* pervades *The Royal Convert*
(*Works*, II, 69 ff) and thus provides an approach to the meaning of the
play. Although King Hengist of Kent and the Saxon Princess Rodogune
are betrothed as a pledge of alliance among the Saxons against the
Britons, each is secretly in love with someone else: he with the British
Princess Ethelinda, whom he has kidnapped but who is secretly married
to his younger brother Aribert; and she with Aribert himself. Both Hen-

gist and Rodogune lose their *peace of mind* in pursuit of their uncontrollable—and, they discover to their dismay, illicit—desires. As a consequence even the peace of the country is threatened, in the destruction of the alliance and the strife among the Saxons which ensue. Aribert and Ethelinda, on the other hand, despite the shattering of their bridal peace by these raging intruders, find *peace of mind* in their reliance on "The great o'er ruling author of our beings" (V.ii, p. 123), and they are rewarded for their constancy with a peace on earth in which their ascendance to the throne signifies the crowning of virtue. [2]

Hengist, whose "nature" is described as "warm," "fierce," and "prone to sudden passions" (II, p. 94), is "curst within" by his lust for Ethelinda (I, p. 83) and, despite the fact he is a king, lacks "that peace / Which ev'ry slave enjoys." For he must marry Rodogune or endanger his country's peace:

> But Kings must wed
> (Curse on the hard condition of their royalty!)
> That sordid slaves may sweat and eat in peace. (II, p. 85)

And yet to marry Rodogune and lose Ethelinda would be "to reign in hell" and "never know one hour of peace again" (I, p. 83). Thus, the "medley war within" and "sickness of soul" (p. 81) which he suffers involve a conflict between his private passion and his public responsibility as king, a responsibility that requires him to be the "common victim of the state" (p. 84) and the "nursing-father" of his people (p. 80).[3] Hengist and his cunning minister Seofrid devise a stratagem to save the alliance: Prince Aribert will marry Rodogune and will become the "pledge of peace" (p. 84). Yet ironically, he to whom Hengist turns for peace becomes the cause of his complete frustration, for Ethelinda turns out to be Aribert's secret bride. Ostensibly because Aribert has broken a solemn childhood vow never to become or to marry a Christian, but really because of jealous rage, Hengist sentences him to death. Hengist's language evinces his lack of peace as he bids "ten thousand thousand horrors" come, for they "fit the present fury" of his "soul":

> The stings of love and rage are fix'd within,
> And drive me on to madness. Earthquakes, whirlwinds,
> A general wreck of nature now would please me. (III, p. 106)

The subsequent identification of his "inborn tempest" with an external tempest suggests the far-reaching ramifications of Hengist's rage. As the King's soul is disordered, so is his kingdom: at this very moment Rodogune begins to plot the rescue of Aribert and the overthrow of Hengist by her brother and his band of Saxons, and Aribert's faithful lieutenant Oswald escapes to the Britons to enlist their aid in rescuing his master. Furthermore, nature itself seems really headed toward a "general wreck." The restraining bond of "nature" (p. 100) between brothers is overcome as Hengist prepares to carry out his sentence. When he learns that Ethelinda's destination is the Briton's camp, he threatens to "shake / Their Island to the centre" to get her back (IV, p. 112). Nor does the breach of nature stop there. When Hengist demands again the return of Ethelinda, Aribert reproaches him in terms common to Western, and particularly Christian, tragedy:

Rage, and the violence of lawless passion,
Have blinded your clear reason; wherefore else
This frantic wild demand! What! should I yield,
Give up my love, my wife, my *Ethelinda*,
To an incestuous brother's dire embrace?

But Hengist contemptuously boasts that he is not awed "with that fantom, incest." "Lawless passion" has perverted reason and nature, and only the arrival of Rodogune and the Saxons frustrates his evil designs.

Since the gods thus refuse him "their better blessings" (V.i, p. 118), the defeated King disdains the "worthless crown" he has lost and determines to "rest in sullen peace." The key word "sullen" connotes both apathy and despair and indicates no real peace of mind at all. And when Seofrid in desperation informs him that Ethelinda is to be killed by Rodogune, Hengist's "medley" of warring passions returns (p. 118 f). Instead of securing the throne as Seofrid had intended, however, Hengist purposes to let "fighting fools contend in vain" for empire, while he escapes to his castle, where, contemning "idle rules," he will "riot" in incestuous lust with Ethelinda (p. 121). Ironically, with Seofrid crying, "What know'st thou not the King?" (V.ii, p. 125), a soldier deals Hengist his mortal wound as he comes in pursuit of his designs. Thus this King who has rejected his public responsibility is himself the victim of the ensuing anarchy. Furthermore, though he does not succeed in his incestuous intent, he rejects the admonition of the "fair teacher" Ethelinda to repent and to "deprecate the wrath divine," concluding, "The Gods

and I have done with one another" (p. 126). Remaining to the end
"fierce, untam'd, disdainful" (p. 127), he curses the gods and his brother
and dies. The implication is that he goes to suffer more than just an internal hell. Such is the reward—"gnashing fiends beneath, and pains
eternal" (I, p. 77)—clearly promised in the play for "man's injustice"
and unbounded "passions."

Despite her haughty pride, Rodogune also loses her peace of mind in
her passion for Aribert. Her hopes in him of both love and empire are
"blasted" (III, p. 104) by his sudden declaration of his marriage, and
"ten thousand racking passions" are released to plague her. Yet she
approaches Aribert in his prison to offer him freedom, empire, and herself, for despite his marriage, she can find no rest without him (IV, p.
109). Expecting to find him similarly distraught at the thought of death,
however, she finds him instead patiently resolved, with a "face of triumph, not of mourning" (p. 107). "Has death so little in it?" she asks,
utterly piqued. For she cannot comprehend the martyr's resolution.[4]
Most of all, she cannot brook his refusal of her offer (p. 108 f). The fury
of a woman scorned breaks out in storm imagery that recalls Hengist's
passion and the threat of internal and external chaos:

> Blast me, ye lightnings, strike me to the centre,
> Drive, drive me down, down to the depths beneath;
> Let me not live, nor think—let me not think,
> For I have been despis'd. (p. 109 f)

She surrenders herself to the passion of "revenge" and vows to make
Ethelinda the "victim" of her "offended love" (p. 112).

Nevertheless, when she returns to rescue Aribert from Hengist,
Rodogune seems to have conquered her passions momentarily and to
act with genuine magnanimity, for, "No matter what ensues," she
breaks Aribert's "bonds" and bids him forget her and "Fly far away,"
presumably to Ethelinda (p. 114). When the recaptured Ethelinda appears in the same room and rushes into Aribert's arms, however, Rodogune's jealous rage explodes, and she exclaims, "Hence, bear her hence.
/ My peace is lost for ever—but she dies" (p. 116). Rodogune bitterly
grants Aribert's wish to die with her and vows to "tear" him from her
"remembrance" and "be at ease for ever" (p. 117). But she is unable
to free herself from her passion, and as she comes to put them to death,

she must struggle to put her heart "at peace" (V.ii, p. 123). Finally, she is denied the "sullen pleasure" of her rage (p. 124)—one is reminded of the "sullen peace" Hengist seeks—by the arrival of Hengist and the Britons. Though she considers it "vain to rave and curse" her "fortune" (p. 126), she spitefully does curse the race of man and impotently prays that "woman" be allowed to

> Subdue mankind beneath her haughty scorn,
> And smile to see the proud oppressor mourn. (p. 127 f)

But in so cursing Aribert she rejects his offer of mercy (which itself belies her judgment of man as "proud oppressor") and dooms herself to the total loss of peace concomitant to despair.

Contrasted to the madness of uncontrolled passion which consumes Hengist and Rodogune is the inner peace attained by Aribert and Ethelinda, despite their loss of bridal peace and happiness. In the opening scene of the play Aribert describes to Oswald the joys of his and Ethelinda's love, joys comparable to "*Elysium*" or "the first Paradise, / When nature was not yet deform'd by winter" (I, p. 76). But their paradise is doomed from the start not to last in a fallen world, a world that *is* "deform'd by winter." Ethelinda has already described to Aribert the Christian vision of the human condition:

> I heard her with an eloquence divine,
> Reason of holy and mysterious truths;
> Of Heav'n's most righteous doom, of man's injustice;
> Of laws to curb the will, and bind the passions;
> Of life, of death, and immortality;
> Of gnashing fiends beneath, and pains eternal;
> Of starry thrones, and endless joys above.

The passage is not just a gratuitous review of Christian doctrine, for its relevance to the entire play is obvious merely from the injustice and unbounded passion we have already observed. Aribert is soon to learn that, given such a world, the only "endless joys" are those "above."

When Hengist asks him to share half the burden of his sorrow, Aribert unhesitatingly offers to bear "all" of it and to be "greatly tried" (II, p. 85). With Hengist's request that he marry Rodogune, however,

Aribert has only begun to be "tried," and yet he precipitately concludes that he is "lost for ever" (p. 89). Cursing the "Fantastic cruelty of hood-wink'd chance," he yearns for the comfort of his Ethelinda, "that dear one, / That gently us'd to breathe the sounds of peace" on his "tempes-tuous soul." Ironically, at that moment Seofrid drags in Hengist's cap-tive, Ethelinda herself. The amazed Aribert rashly suggests that they should "resolve to die together" to "Defy the malice" of their "fate" and "preserve the sacred bond" of their marriage "inviolable" (p. 90). Then, in an instant, he even more rashly concludes that to die is "in vain," for the bond is "broke already" through incest,

> And envious hell, with its more potent malice,
> Has ruin'd and deform'd the beauteous work of heav'n.

Even though Ethelinda assures him that the "horrid incest" has not taken place, Aribert still concludes that "this bad world is leagu'd with hell against her" (p. 90 f) and that they "are doom'd to death," since Seofrid has overheard their secret. He goes into a "rash" and "frantic rage," desperately trying to buy a respite with Seofrid's murder (p. 91).

Ethelinda's response to her plight is in sharp contrast to Aribert's. As he had offered to bear all of Hengist's sorrow, so she asks to suffer all manner of pains, except the "pollution" of incest (p. 90):

> Let me know
> All miseries beside, each kind of sorrow,
> And prove me with variety of pains,
> Whips, racks, and flames: For I was born to suffer:
> And when the measure of my woes is full,
> That power in whom I trust will set me free.

Unlike Aribert, however, Ethelinda does not forget in the first moment of trial this faith and resolution of the martyr. Nor does she, like Aribert, blame her condition on "hoodwink'd chance" or the "malice" of "cruel fate," nor conclude that the "malice" of hell is "more potent" than Heaven. Instead she calls on "gracious Heaven," which till now has de-fended her chastity, to guard her from hell and "its blackest crime." When Aribert is about to kill Seofrid for their momentary safeties, Ethelinda beseeches him, "Trust 'em to Heaven" (p. 91). Ethelinda is an example, then, not only to the audience (like other saints in martyro-logies, in miracle and martyr plays), but also to her *royal convert*. She is an "angel" who instructs him in the "way to everlasting happiness" (I, p. 79), and the focus of the play is on the development of his trust in Providence. Now in Act II, Ethelinda brings peace to the distracted, doubting soul of Aribert, as she introduces the theodicean argument of the play. She has a vision of angels who "succour truth and innocence below" (p. 94):

> Hell trembles at the sight, and hides its head
> In utmost darkness, while on earth each heart,
> Like mine, is fill'd with peace and joy unutterable.

Such inner peace, what Milton calls a "paradise within" (*PL* XII.587), is the result of "hope and never-failing faith" in the "holy pow'r" (p. 95). It enables the Christian to "triumph o'er the world," despite his temporary paradise lost. Aribert is "touch'd with the sacred theme" and sees himself a vision of "the guardian-angels of the good," who "pity what we suffer here below" and make the saintly Ethelinda (and himself) "their common care" (p. 95 f).

The rest of the play shows Aribert vacillating between trust and distrust in Providence. Finally, condemned to die with Ethelinda for both his love and his faith, very much like Milton's Adam (*PL* XI.527 ff), he plaintively asks if Heaven has "decreed" that "none shall pass the golden gates above, / But those who sorrow here" to purge their "inborn stains away" (p. 123). Ethelinda's theodicean answer combines the traditional metaphor of trial with the traditional concept of the Happy Death (see *PL* XI.530 ff):

> The great o'er ruling author of our beings,
> Deals with his creature man in various ways,
> Gracious and good in all: some feel the rod,
> And own, like us, the Father's chast'ning hand.
> Sev'n times, like gold, they pass the purging flame,
> And are at last refin'd; while gently some
> Tread all the paths of life without a rub,
> With honour, health, with friends and plenty bless'd,
> Their years roll round in innocence and ease.
> Hoary at length, and in a good old age,
> They go declining to the grave in peace,
> And change their pleasures here for joys above.

Aribert still complains. He has not asked for the blessed life but only for "life and *Ethelinda.*" Yet, "Heav'n thought that too much," he murmurs. Ethelinda also sorely feels the loss of that much happiness: she has admitted that Aribert's image "intercepts" her "journey to the stars" (p. 122). Yet she answers that since they have been denied their paradise on earth, they should seek

> That wond'rous bliss which Heav'n reserves in store,
> Well to reward us for our losses here;
> That bliss which Heav'n and only Heav'n can give. (p. 123)

That promised bliss—and the inner peace of those who patiently expect it—is immediately juxtaposed to Rodogune's suffering ("still I am doom'd to suffer"), as it has all along been contrasted to the general lack of peace in the world. Strengthened by Ethelinda's instructions, Aribert boasts to Rodogune in the face of tortures,

> You shall behold how a Prince ought to die,
> And what a Christian dares to suffer. (p. 124)

But now, since Rowe is never content to allow his protagonists the simple trial of merely dying, Aribert is submitted to the severest trial of all. He must watch Ethelinda die first: "And can my eyes endure it!" To Rodogune, then to the "saints and angels" (p. 125), Aribert pleads for Ethelinda, seemingly in vain. In contrast, as she meets her trial "arm'd and equal to the combat" like the true Christian hero, the constant Ethelinda would give Aribert the final lesson of example and "lead" him on "in the triumphant way" (p. 124):

> Be constant to the last, be fix'd my *Aribert.*
> 'Tis but a short, short passage to the stars. (p. 125)

In the midst of this triumph of the martyr, Aribert and Ethelinda are saved, strangely enough, by the arrival of the brother who has come bent on their destruction but whose ironic death leaves them King and Queen of Kent and victors over Rodogune and her rebelling Saxons. Thus the play ends in perfect poetic justice, and every indication is that such justice is the work of Providence. The crowning of Aribert and

Ethelinda seems a reward for constancy in their trial, and Aribert attributes their final peace on earth to Heaven's influence:

> A day of comfort seems to dawn upon us,
> And Heav'n at length is gracious to our wishes. (p. 127)

The punishment of the wicked, too, implies the Hand of Heaven, for it is remarkably appropriate. Seofrid, who to save his master would sacrifice Aribert, loses his master in rescuing Aribert. Hengist is killed in the pursuit of hell's "blackest crime" (a circumstance considered by the theologians to be an instance of particular Providence), and the chaos he has caused consumes him. In her extreme pride and passion, Rodogune has attempted to take vengeance into her own hands: "The Gods are just at length," she exults to Aribert and Ethelinda as she prepares to murder them (p. 124), and she appears to be ironically right, for justice is ultimately served and her jealous rage thwarted. All her hopes of love and empire are destroyed as she sullenly banishes herself from the race of man.

Moreover, the play has all along asked Rowe's primary question, whether the gods care. Ethelinda has insisted throughout that they do, but even Aribert at first blames either "hoodwink'd chance" or the "malice" of fate for his loss of paradisal peace. On the other hand, Seofrid at first appears to believe in Providence, for he tells Aribert and Ethelinda, "Whatever Gods there be, their care you are" (II, p. 94), and he asserts that "the ruling Gods are over all, / And order as they please their world below" (III, p. 97). When Hengist's intention to rape Ethelinda destroys Seofrid's plan for him to regain the throne, however, Seofrid (like Mirza, Bajazet, and Eurymachus before him) declares the "restless racking care" of statesmen "in vain" and swears allegiance to the "Blind goddess chance" (V.i, p. 122):

> henceforth I follow thee.
> The politicians of the world may talk,
> May make a mighty bustle with their foresight,
> Their schemes and arts, their wisdom is thy slave.

Rodogune doubts whether there are really gods "who rule o'er love and jealousy" (IV, p. 117), and she blames whatever gods there are for dealing so "unjustly with their creatures" as to deny them pleasures and make them suffer (p. 108). She seems to see the gods as merely vengeful

and otherwise scornful "of the world below" (p. 118), and her final
prayer to the "partial goddess" Nature that woman be allowed to "Subdue mankind beneath her haughty scorn" is an indication that she thinks
the deities as perverse and spiteful as she. Hengist also sees the Saxon
gods as vengeful: he offers Aribert as "a royal victim" to "glut the vengeance of our angry Gods" (III, p. 105). Furthermore, in Epicurean
fashion (which is the pervading fashion of all these comments), he
blames "the meddling hand of chance" for causing the chaos in which
he finds himself (V.i, p. 119).

But Ethelinda's faith in the "great o'er ruling author of our beings,"
who "Deals with his creature man in various ways, / Gracious and good
in all," is vindicated. Hengist says in Act II that "or love, / Or some divinity, more strong than love, / Forbids my bliss" (II, p. 88). He appears
to be right, for in the next moment Ethelinda maintains that "gracious
Heaven" has defended her up to that point from the "pollution" which
Hengist's "bliss" would entail (p. 90). The implication is that "Heaven"
continues to defend her throughout the play. Aribert has speculated
that "the ruling hand of Heaven," working "thus unseen by second
causes," has ordained Seofrid "for its instrument of good" (p. 92), and
despite his machinations and his final allegiance to the "Blind goddess
chance," Seofrid does appear to have been Heaven's instrument, for it
is he who provokes Hengist to rescue Aribert and Ethelinda from Rodogune. Though the outcome is counter to Seofrid's and Hengist's separate
designs, it appears to evince the design of Providence.

And so we must conclude, I think, that "the ruling hand of Heaven
is in it" and "at length *is* gracious" to its faithful (italics mine). Their
virtue literally crowned, Aribert and Ethelinda become the monarchs
of a new *"Britain"* which "takes its pledge of peace" from their union
of Saxon and Briton. "Nor are those pious hopes of peace in vain,"
prophesies Ethelinda, for that "pledge" will be fulfilled when again
"Auspicious Heav'n" shall "smile" and "bless" the *"British* Isle" of
Rowe's Queen Anne with the "eternal UNION" of the Union Act of
1707.[5] The inner peace of Aribert and Ethelinda's Christian faith, then,
has received an external manifestation in the peace of the land, a manifestation that is emblematic of the ultimate reward of Providence for
those who, with the peace of mind of the saint and resolution of the
martyr, trust in Its care. Thus the play has portrayed not only "patterns
of piety" in the trusting royal couple but also "things celestial" in the
care of that Providence, the metaphysical reality which corresponds to
their faith.

ii

The Tragedy of Lady Jane Gray (*Works*, II, 187 ff) is Rowe's last play and his final examination of the problem of suffering innocence. Its subject is an historical martyr, and it dramatizes her acceptance of the crown of England in a gallant attempt to save her country and its incipient Protestantism from "Bloody" Mary's succession at the death of the Boy King, Edward VI. When her attempt fails, Lady Jane no less gallantly accepts defeat and eventual martyrdom. Rowe summarizes her story thus in the Epilogue:

> The destin'd saint, unfortunately brave,
> Sunk with those altars which she strove to save.
> Greatly she dar'd to prop the juster side,
> As greatly with her adverse fate comply'd,
> Did all that Heaven could ask, resign'd, and died. (p. 248)

Himself a staunch Protestant, Rowe exaggerates even the pro-Protestant accounts of her story in Foxe's *Book of Martyrs* and Bishop Burnet's *History of the Reformation*.[6] In nearly every scene he depicts the "horrors" of a return of Papism to England, and John C. Loftis plausibly maintains that the religious element of the play was designed as anti-Jacobite propaganda during the revolution of 1715.[7] Perhaps also, as the Dedication and the Epilogue suggest, the play was intended to be an elaborate compliment to the contemporary "patroness and defender of our holy faith" (p. 189), the Princess of Wales, Caroline of Ansbach, who had refused to abandon Protestantism for Roman Catholicism and the hand of Archduke Charles of Austria, pretender to the Spanish throne.[8]

The religious dimension in *Lady Jane Gray* transcends topical motivation, however, as Loftis unfortunately does not point out. For Rowe's last play crowns his attempt at dramatic theodicy. Lady Jane is the suffering innocent par excellence, who never loses trust in Divine Providence and who acts with complete submission to God's will throughout. This "beauteous saint"—"a heroine, a martyr, and a queen" (Prologue)—is held up as "our great example" (Epilogue) to emulate. She is Rowe's finest embodiment of that "suff'ring virtue" which is tried and is not found wanting. And despite her suffering and that of England to follow her death, the play ends with the promise of ultimate providential justice for both Lady Jane and her country.

Throughout the play Lady Jane, Henry VIII's grandniece, is portrayed as a "saint" indeed, whose *only* motivation for becoming queen is literally to be Defender of the Faith—to preserve English Protestantism from the impending ravages of Catholic Mary, Henry VIII's daughter and next heir after Edward.[9] From the moment of her advent on the stage Lady Jane is preoccupied with the fate of England if Edward dies: she complains to her beloved,

> Oh, *Guilford*! what remains for wretched *England*,
> When he, our guardian angel, shall forsake us?
> For whose dear sake, Heav'n spar'd a guilty land,
> And scatter'd not its plagues while *Edward* reign'd. (I, p. 201)

She envisions "the wan King of Terrors," Death, stalking the land, while "universal ruin gathers round" and all England awaits an apocalyptic doom (p. 202), for the return of Rome portends the reign of Antichrist which is to precede "the fatal hour." Edward's dying words to Lady Jane are a prayer that England's "holy altars" be "undefil'd" and its people saved "from the yoke of *Rome*" (II, p. 205), and he beseeches her, to whom he has been joined throughout their young lives by a "sacred union" and a "wondrous sympathy" (p. 204), to "be good to *England*" (p. 205). But she does not yet know what shall be asked of her in order to do so. Until now, despite the fact that she loves him, Lady Jane has refused at such a solemn time to hear "th'ungrateful theme" of Guilford's suit for her hand (I, p. 202). Yet at the very moment of Edward's death their parents, out of policy and "the common int'rest," "ordain" their immediate marriage (II, p. 205). In obedience to her mother's "command" (p. 206) and to avoid offending Guilford, Lady Jane reconciles herself to the marriage, though she is unaware of the ambitious designs of Guilford's father, the powerful Duke of Northumberland.[10] Yet (as if Rowe wished to secure her absolutely from any imputation of political opportunism) she offers Guilford nothing but "sighs" and "tears" (p. 206 f) and exacts a pledge from him to join her on their wedding night not in bliss but in mourning. Only then does she plight him her troth, submitting not only to her parents' will but to the will of God:

> Whatever Providence allots for each,
> Be that the common portion of us both.

Thus Rowe creates a saintly Lady Jane, vulnerable to appeals from religion, country, parents, and husband, and all the details of the climactic third act are artfully calculated to show her gradually overwhelmed by such appeals, until she attempts to fill the void left by Edward herself. In the ominous Tower, while Edward's deathbed will, disinheriting Mary and Elizabeth, is secretly receiving its sanction from the council, Guilford cryptically informs Lady Jane that from her "healing hand" the "Lords o'th'Council" expect "a cure / For *England*'s loss in *Edward*" (III, p. 217). At this moment her mother, the Duchess of Suffolk (who herself abdicates her claim to the throne) enters to declare Lady Jane queen by "Heav'n's decree" and Edward's last will, made "on the verge of Heav'n, in sight of angels"—as if to give it a religious sanction. Northumberland proclaims her the savior of England's threatened faith,

> By whose bright zeal, by whose victorious faith,
> Guarded and fenc'd around, our pure religion,
> That lamp of truth which shines upon our altars,
> Shall lift its golden head, and flourish long. (p. 218)

Lady Jane is skeptical, however, that the dying King had the authority to "Bequeath his crown" to her or to "give away a people for a legacy" (p. 219), but Northumberland sweeps her scruples aside and begs her not to aid the cause of Mary by failing to be "*England*'s better angel" (p. 222). The phrase "better angel" picks up Lady Jane's earlier reference to Edward as England's "guardian angel," and it appears to be her providential *vocation* to fulfill that role. The crescendo of emotional appeals finally climaxes in typical Restoration fashion, but Rowe has handled it convincingly. Overcome by pleas to save her "country," "religion," "friends," "father," "Mother," and "Husband," in a genuine spirit of Christian self-sacrifice Lady Jane capitulates:

> Take me, crown me,
> Invest me with this royal wretchedness;
> Let me not know one happy minute more;
> Let all my sleepless nights be spent in care,
> My days be vex'd with tumults and alarms;
> If only I can save you, if my fate
> Has mark'd me out to be the public victim,
> I take the lot with joy. Yes, I will die

For that eternal truth my faith is fix'd on,
And that dear native land which gave me birth. (p. 223)

Thus she magnanimously (and beautifully) accepts her role with but
one prayer:

All that I ask, is, tho' my fortune frown,
And bury me beneath this fatal crown;
Let that one good be added to my doom,
To save this land from tyranny and *Rome*. (p. 223 f)

Her sacrifice leads only to martyrdom, however, and she will not only
be buried beneath her crown, but her one request will go unanswered.
For Princess Mary's cause gains the popular support; Northumberland's
dwindling armies are defeated in the field, and Lady Jane is left to face
the conquering Catholics virtually alone.

In the early scenes of the play Rowe has well prepared us for Lady
Jane's reversal of fortune. When Suffolk expresses reservations about his
daughter's "hasty" marriage, Northumberland counsels him to "Doubt
not any thing," for "good Heav'n," which "mixes still a comfort with
afflictions," has given them a "blessing" in their children to "wipe
away" their "tears for dying *Edward*" (II, p. 203). A moment later, however, convinced that Heaven has given him "too much" in his new
bride, Guilford in effect expresses the converse of his father's statement
in a semiserious but ironically true prophecy of his and Lady Jane's fate:

And by the common course of things below,
Where each delight is temper'd with affliction,
Some evil terrible and unforseen
Must sure ensue, to poise the scale against
This vast profusion of exceeding pleasure. (p. 208)

The world the play describes, then, is one which contains an equal mix-
ture of good and evil—a world where, as the Duchess puts it,

Ev'ry state
Allotted to the race of man below,
Is, in proportion, doom'd to taste some sorrow. (III, p. 220)

And with regard to royalty she adds,

> Nor is the golden wreath on a King's brow
> Exempt from care.

Accordingly, throughout the play Rowe stresses the uncertainty of fortune in this life. After falling out with his best friend, the Earl of Pembroke, over the love of Lady Jane, Guilford complains, "How cross the ways of life lie!" (I, p. 200). No man has "that piercing foresight" to see "Where all this mazy error will have end," he says; instead, "There is but one end certain, that is—Death," and "ev'n that certainty is still uncertain," for we know not which path leads to it. Guilford concludes, therefore, that "blind divining" is "in vain." When Northumberland sends for Lady Jane, upon whom all his plans depend, despite his previous public assertion of Heaven's "blessing," he too speaks in soliloquy of the uncertainty of human affairs:

> What trivial influences hold dominion
> O'er wise men's counsels, and the fate of empire?
> The greatest schemes that human wit can forge,
> Or bold ambition dares to put in practice,
> Depend upon our husbanding a moment,
> And the light lasting of a woman's will;
> As if the Lord of nature should delight
> To hang this pond'rous globe upon a hair,
> And bid it dance before a breath of wind. (I, p. 197)

Thus Northumberland consigns the world not to a benevolent deity but to an Epicurean "Lord of nature" who mockingly "delights" in the desperate contingency of human events.

But Northumberland's image of "this pond'rous globe" hanging "upon a hair" is a perversion of the traditional image of the world depending on a golden chain, an image which originates in Homer (*Iliad* VIII.19) and which was interpreted by Robert Burton as that "golden chain, which reacheth down from heaven to earth, by which every creature is annexed, and depends on his Creator."[11] The contingency in human affairs of which Northumberland speaks, then, does not mean, in the Christian vision, that the world is subject *only* to the caprice of fortune or to the "trivial influences" of a human will. For the world literally de-pends on Divine Providence, and its several events conform to that divine pattern traditionally called the History of Salvation, a pattern in which the human will can participate by submitting itself to the will of God. To depend solely on "human wit," however, or on the "husbanding" of a "moment" is, as Saint Paul would say, "foolishness with God" (1 Cor. 3:19).

Despite Northumberland's own lack of faith in what he asserts to him, Suffolk "trusts" in this Providence, this "good Heav'n," when his soul presages ill at the marriage of Lady Jane and Guilford (II, p. 203). And when Guilford discovers Northumberland's intentions to have Pembroke murdered for conspiring with Gardiner, though he knows that Pembroke will rush to join forces with Mary to bring about his downfall, he frees him nevertheless, placing his trust in a Heaven that governs with care:

> There is a Power,
> Who sits above the stars; in him I trust:
> All that I have, his bounteous hand bestow'd:
> And he that gave it, can preserve it to me.
> If his o'er-ruling will ordains my ruin,
> What is there more but to fall down before him,
> And humbly yield obedience! (IV, p. 230)

Lady Jane herself has said to Guilford earlier, in lines that epitomize the Christian attitude toward fate, fortune, and chance,

> Trust our fate
> To him whose gracious wisdom guides our ways,
> And makes what we think evil turn to good. (II, p. 208)

Nor does Lady Jane lose her trust in Providence when, largely because of opposition to Northumberland (IV, p. 225), her cause is defeated in the field and her erstwhile supporters in the council desert her to declare for Princess Mary (p. 231).[12] As she enters the Tower room reading Socrates' argument for the immortality of the soul in *"Plato's Phaedon"* (p. 230),[13] she encounters Guilford and asks if it be not time to "explore hereafter, / And seek some better sure abiding place." While they await their inevitable capture by the advancing armies of Sussex, Lady Jane exhorts Guilford not to fight but to summon his "nobler courage" and, along with her, to meet this "adverse fate" with "patience" and "souls secure of death" (p. 233 f), for their "hearts have now another part to play" and "must be steel'd with some uncommon fortitude" so that they "may tread the paths of horror" and, despite "fortune" and their "foes," "Ev'n in the hour of death be more than conq'rors" (p. 235). The part which they must play, of course, is that of the Christian martyr, and once again Rowe places the metaphor of trial at the center of his theodicy when Lady Jane exhorts Guilford, "Be thyself, / For see the trial comes!" (p. 234). In "A Prologue to *Lady Jane Gray*, Sent by an unknown Hand," Alexander Pope, as in his translation of the *Odyssey*, points to the function of such trials as Lady Jane's: "Great souls shine brightest by misfortunes shown."[14]

Guilford needs Lady Jane to "teach" him what "energy divine / Inspires" her with "such unshaken courage" (p. 235), for like Aribert in *The Royal Convert* and Arpasia in *Tamerlane*, he momentarily fears that death means annihilation. Lady Jane allays his fears with the diurnal and vernal analogies that have always provided man the hope of his own resurrection from the dead:

Behold the universal works of nature,
Where life still springs from death. To us the sun
Dies ev'ry night, and ev'ry morn revives:
The flow'rs, which Winter's icy hand destroy'd,
Lift their fair heads, and live again in Spring. (p. 236)

So, like Ethelinda, Lady Jane points out the "triumphant way" of Christian endurance, and her example seems to embody the lessons of martyrstories noted by Foxe in the Preface to the *Book of Martyrs*—especially, those lessons of "patience," the "hope of heavenly Comfort," and "true Christian fortitude," or "the right way to conquer, which standeth not in the power of man, but in hope of the Resurrection to come" (sig. a5ʳ).

Lady Jane and Guilford must still prove the *Scire mori* of which the epigraph to the play speaks (p. 187). After nine months in prison, they are to be executed,[15] and they meet their summons with "patience" (V, p. 237). Allowed to see her before the execution (and for the first time since their incarceration), Guilford comes upon Lady Jane as she kneels in preparation for martyrdom. "With a pleasing, sober chearfulness," she has spent the night in prayer and has "fix'd" her "hopes" upon a "rock unfailing." But the sight of Guilford "breaks the settled quiet" of her "soul" and wakens her "vanquish'd passions" once again (p. 241 f). Moreover, at this moment Pembroke arrives with news of a reprieve. Guilford blesses Queen Mary for sparing his wife, and Lady

Jane, though "Life and the world are hardly worth" her "care," becomes "reconcil'd" to them both (p. 242). The Dudleys' new hopes are
shattered, however, by Gardiner's condition wrung from the Queen
that they first, as Lady Jane puts it, "turn apostate" (p. 243), and Guilford bemoans the transience of those "hopes," which "like the spring,
with all its flow'rs," are "In one poor minute gone" (p. 244). With such
flowers, the recurring imagery of spring implies, may die Guilford's
hope of resurrection. Once again, however, Lady Jane instructs him,
climaxing the play's theme of the uncertainty of things mundane:

> Such is this foolish world, and such the certainty
> Of all the boasted blessings it bestows:
> Then *Guilford*, let us have no more to do with it;
> Think only how to leave it as we ought;
> But trust no more, and be deceived no more.

Her words, and the play itself, embody the traditional Christian lesson,
sic transit gloria mundi.

As Aribert responded to Ethelinda, so now does Guilford respond
to Lady Jane and her "divine example." He refuses Gardiner's condition
and goes to his death, relying on the hope of an afterlife and a reunion
with his wife, and calling on the support of Heaven (p. 244 f). While
he is led out to his death, Lady Jane swoons, complaining, "Can nature
bear this stroke?" (p. 245). It is the "killing stroke" of her trial, the
greatest threat to her fortitude, yet she regains composure, speaks of
the coming "peace" and the end to all her sorrows, and manifests her
continued trust in the "good and gracious hand of Providence." To her
handmaid she bequeaths a book which contains "the law of everlasting
truth" and which was her "support" when "all help else forsook" her
(p. 246). The book is, of course, the Bible,[16] and one cannot help viewing
Lady Jane's bequest in the light of the other important bequest in the
play, that of King Edward. In a world where the fate of crowns and
kingdoms is uncertain, Lady Jane bequeaths the record of the testament
of Divine Providence, upon Which alone can man completely rely.

Lady Jane's last words are the final testament to her trust in Providence. She utters the prayer not only of the English Protestants of her
day but of all Christians who endure the trial of the innocent: "Thou,
gracious Heav'n, / Hear and defend at length thy suffering people."
Earlier she has said that Heaven "disallows" her "weakness" but "to
some dear selected hero's hand / Reserves the glory" of England's "de-

liverance" (IV, p. 235 f), and now she prays for a "monarch of the royal blood" to "save" England "from the rage of *Rome*," to reign long, and to alleviate the problem of succession by leaving a son to "guard that faith for which I die to-day" (V, p. 246). Considering the contemporary political overtones and allusions of these passages and of the Dedication, Prologue, and Epilogue, we are led to infer that her final prayer is completely fulfilled only with the Glorious Revolution of 1688 and the subsequent defeat of the Jacobite Revolution of 1715—events which marked the end (at least so Rowe thought) of any claim by Catholics to the throne of England. In other words, Lady Jane's "too weak a hand" is replaced by William III's "great hand," which was "doom'd" by "the secret laws of fate" (read *Providence*) to "end the hopes of *Rome*'s tyrannic reign" (Prologue), and the "hero" and his "son" whom she seems to prophesy in her final prayer are George I and George Augustus, the Hanoverians brought to England at the death of Queen Anne to keep the crown out of the hands of the Catholic Stuarts and forever Protestant. The play insists, then, that though she herself fails, Lady Jane's faith in Providence and Its ultimate justice is historically vindicated, and as a great *martyr* to that faith, she stands herself a *witness* to its truth.

Pembroke's final comment is the play's (and Rowe's) summary statement of theodicy. In response to Gardiner's condemnation of the Dudleys for "heresy and treason" and his prediction of their "everlasting punishment hereafter" (V, p. 247), Pembroke asks who can probe "The secret purposes of Heaven"—that *mystery of things* at the heart of Judeo-Christian theodicy and the art which reflects it, from *Job* to *King Lear* to *Paradise Lost*. Pembroke continues, expanding the play's promise of providential justice for a nation to include the promise of such justice for the Dudleys and other individuals like them who "follow faithfully truth's sacred light," for they, "Tho' suff'ring here, shall from their sorrows cease, / Rest with the saints, and dwell in endless peace."

It is appropriate that Pembroke should speak these words, because he has learned, as Rowe must have hoped his audiences would, from the example of these Christian martyrs. When we first meet Pembroke, he is so insanely jealous in his love for Lady Jane that he cannot "with temper" (II, p. 210) even discuss the subject with his rival, his best friend Guilford. In contrast to Guilford's "gentle temper" (I, p. 199), formed with "passions mix'd in due proportion," his passions disdain "reason and her laws" and,

> Like all thou canst imagine wild and furious,
> Now[17] drive me headlong on, now whirl me back,
> And hurry my unstable flitting soul
> To ev'ry mad extreme.

In other words, like Hengist and Rodogune in *The Royal Convert*, Pembroke is in danger of internal chaos. As Pembroke and Guilford part at the end of this uneasy encounter, Pembroke asks only that they "contend, as friends and brave men ought, / With openness and justice to each other." Thus when he later learns of Guilford's sudden betrothal to Lady Jane, he immediately accuses him of having "betray'd" him, a fault which he can "ne'er forgive" (II, p. 211). He turns, much like Rowe's Semanthe in *Ulysses*, "to deadly and remorseless hate" (p. 212). In this "rage" and "despair" at his loss of "peace of mind" and "paradise," Pembroke betrays his friends to Gardiner and Princess Mary, repudiating the "cursed *Dudley*'s race" for their "mock'ry" of him and asking only for "vengeance" (III, p. 213 ff).[18]

Yet Pembroke is finally vanquished by Guilford's virtue. When Guilford has him arrested, Pembroke is at first defiant and spiteful, and Guilford answers him that he has come "In tenderness of friendship to preserve" him "from destruction" (IV, p. 226). But Pembroke scorns to "receive a grace" from the man he still suspects of ambition and vanity and fear of his "vengeance" (p. 227). Finally Guilford is compelled by his friend's suspicions to reveal his own father's planned vengeance against Pembroke for conspiring with Gardiner and the Catholics. Pembroke is awestruck by Guilford's "honest heart" (p. 229), and he undergoes a kind of conversion:

>   Thy virtues flash,
> They break at once on my astonish'd soul;
> As if the curtains of the dark were drawn
> To let in day at midnight.

Guilford's Christian temperance, mercy, and love have thus redeemed the soul of his friend (much as Semanthe's is redeemed) from hatred and revenge, and Pembroke is finally and fully converted, not just to Guilford's friendship but to his Christian virtue. To repay Guilford for

saving his life and to make "amends" for the harm he has done Lady
Jane and her "cause" (V, p. 242), Pembroke obtains a pardon for them
from Queen Mary, begs Lady Jane's forgiveness, and in the spirit of
Christian charity promises to "deserve" their "thanks" by offering himself as the pledge of their future happiness (p. 242 f).

When he first enters with the pardon, Pembroke's heart "Exults
and labours with the joy it bears" and with the joy of Christian virtue:

> 'Tis mercy! mercy,
> The mark of Heav'n impress'd on human kind;
> Mercy, that glads the world, deals joy around;
> Mercy, that smooths the dreadful brow of power,
> And makes dominion light; mercy, that saves,
> Binds up the broken heart, and heals despair. (p. 238)

Mercy has healed Pembroke's own despair and is the answer, along with
trust, to that most sinister of sins. The Machiavellian Gardiner, however, one of those "*Romish* priests" who teach their followers "To mas-
sacre a nation, and believe it / An act well-pleasing to the Lord of
Mercy" (I, p. 196), dismisses mercy for expediency (V, p. 238 f).[19] When
he vows to countermand the repeal, Pembroke retorts,

> Thy narrow soul
> Knows not the god-like glory of forgiving;
> Nor can thy cold, thy ruthless heart conceive,
> How large the power, how fix'd the empire is,
> Which benefits confer on generous minds:
> Goodness prevails upon the stubborn foes,
> And conquers more than ever *Caesar's* sword did. (p. 239)

Pembroke pointedly asks the "Churchman" Gardiner, "Is not the sacred purpose of our faith / Peace and good-will to man?" (p. 239 f). And
despite the frustration of Pembroke's endeavor and the final execution
of the Dudleys, "Peace and good-will" are reaffirmed as the weapons
of the kind of heroism which "conquers more than ever *Caesar's* sword
did" and which, as Foxe has pointed out, is the lesson of the martyr's
death. Rowe has focused on this Christian heroism from his first dramatic theodicy, and to the last he offers it as the exemplary behavior
of suffering innocents. Lady Jane's acknowledgment that Heaven "disallows" her "weakness" to be an effective agent does not deny the fact

that she has indeed been God's Champion, a brilliant exemplar of Christian heroism and virtue, and that her endurance is as magnanimous as the deeds of the heroes of old, including Tamerlane and Ulysses. Such endurance is what Milton in a similar contrast calls "the better fortitude / Of Patience and Heroic Martyrdom" (*PL* IX.31 f). The anguished Pembroke's final comment reiterates, as we have seen, the promise of ultimate reward for such Christian heroes, who place their trust in Providence:

> Those, who, with honest hearts, pursue the right,
> And follow faithfully truth's sacred light,
> Tho' suff'ring here, shall from their sorrows cease,
> Rest with the saints, and dwell in endless peace.

iii

As his last play, *Lady Jane Gray* nicely caps Rowe's attempt at dramatic theodicy, for it is one of his best plays, one of the best of the period, and perhaps the best martyr play of the English Renaissance and Restoration —a genre not often attempted because of the great difficulties in portraying saints. Rowe's play succeeds first of all, I think, because he has found, in his martyr plays and *Jane Shore*, an excellent medium in the English history play, where the story and the characters have a dimension of veracity and interest that is often lacking in the exotic settings of his early plays and of Restoration heroic tragedy in general. His success with the medium in *The Royal Convert* is frustrated because he tries to retain too many of the other features of heroic tragedy: bombastic language, extreme hauteur, and conflicts between love and honor that suffer an incredible number of reversals. Moreover, the trial of martydom is dragged out over far too many scenes. In *Lady Jane Gray*, however, Rowe succeeds not only with the medium but also with plot, language, and characterization.

As in our own time (*Becket, A Man for All Seasons, Mary Queen of Scots*, for instance), an historical setting serves well the purposes of a martyr play, for it relieves the stress on spiritual conflict by means of the political conflict. In the first three acts of *Lady Jane Gray* the conflict is between Rome and England, Mary and Jane, and the question is whether Jane will accept the challenge. On the other hand, what keeps this play (as well as those on Becket, More, and Mary Stuart) from being mere chronicle or mere propaganda is the spiritual dimension of even the political conflict. The question is not whether Lady Jane will take the throne for chauvinistic reasons but for a genuine religious one. In other words, before this martyr play asks whether Lady Jane will keep her faith through her trial, it asks whether she will defend her faith against Antichrist. Rowe nowhere more effectively establishes the atmosphere of the play through setting than in Lady Jane's moving speech on the Tower:

> Why came we hither?
> Why was I drawn to this unlucky place,
> This *Tow'r*, so often stain'd with royal blood?
> Here the Fourth *Edward's* helpless sons were murder'd,
> And pious *Henry* fell by ruthless *Gloster*:
> Is this the place allotted for rejoicing?
> The bow'r adorn'd to keep our nuptial feast in?
> Methinks suspicion and distrust dwell here,
> Staring with meagre forms thro' grated windows;
> Death lurks within, and unrelenting punishment;
> Without, grim danger, fear, and fiercest pow'r
> Sit on the rude old tow'rs, and *Gothic* battlements;
> While horror overlooks the dreadful wall,
> And frowns on all around. (III, p. 216 f)

Rowe calls up the real and allegorical ghosts that haunt this central symbol of the blood relationship between English history and martyrdom.

Besides the public, political conflict, Rowe also adds to his martyr play the private conflict between Guilford and Pembroke. As in *Ulysses*, the private balances the public and reflects on it. Guilford's loyalty and self-sacrifice mirror Lady Jane's, while Pembroke's rage and vengeance mirror those of Gardiner and the Catholic cause. Moreover, there is grave irony in the fact that as the satisfaction of one love serves to save England, the frustration of the other serves to destroy it. Thus in the first three acts Rowe plays off the upward movement of England's public fortunes against the downward movement of Pembroke's private ones, a contrapuntal arrangement that is ironic and foreboding of final reversal. And again, as in *Ulysses*, Rowe brings together plot and subplot at the final moment. Even if mercy does not triumph in the public realm, it does in the private in Pembroke's final attempt to redeem the friend who had redeemed his friendship. Appropriately, Pembroke prophesies private victory for those who find their *paradise within*, that which has replaced Pembroke's first "lost paradise" of Lady Jane's love

(III, p. 216) and his short-lived "paradise new-born" of her and Guilford's reprieve (V, p. 238).

The language of *Lady Jane Gray* shows Rowe at his best. With regard to figurative language, Rowe is again not very good with amorous
tropes (Guilford's) and perhaps his images of the ravages of Rome are a
bit heavy-handed (though not in contrast to the imagery of Lee, Otway,
and Banks). Rowe may again be better at the gradual building of motif
than at the local metaphor. For example, especially through his allegorical imagery of Religion, Antichrist, Death, and Horror, Rowe establishes well a sense of apocalyptic doom. Better yet, he achieves an
excellent effect by building up imagery of defenses of the faith to the
point of Northumberland's image of "our pure religion" "Guarded and
fenc'd around" by Lady Jane's "bright zeal" and "victorious faith" (III,
p. 218), then whittling the fences down to the "spot / To which our
narrow empire now is shrunk" and which Guilford vainly sets himself to
"guard" (IV, p. 233). Rowe also establishes well the imagery of *contemptus mundi*, not only in Northumberland's and Guilford's metaphysical musings in Act I but also in Lady Jane's persistent rejection of
"all those unsubstantial empty forms" of kingship (IV, p. 232) and of
"all the boasted blessings" the "foolish world" can give (V, p. 244). With
this pattern of imagery that of bequests is nicely interwoven, until Lady
Jane leaves to her woman the only thing of real worth in this world.

Rowe is occasionally very successful even with a local metaphor, as
in Northumberland's image of the world hanging "upon a hair" (I, p.
197), or in the play upon the image of Jane as the moon (p. 201). Rowe's
best local metaphors in the play are those analogies for resurrection
that close the fourth act:

> Behold the universal works of nature,
> Where life still springs from death. To us the sun
> Dies ev'ry night, and ev'ry morn revives:
> The flow'rs, which Winter's icy hand destroy'd,
> Lift their fair heads, and live again in Spring. (p. 236)

Perhaps the metaphors work so well because, instead of being mere
local coloring as are too many of the metaphors of Restoration tragedy,
they are archetypal images of resurrection and immortality and, like
Rowe's other, subdued patterns of imagery, have thematic significance.
But the lines are also well-written. Before its proper ending the second
line comes to an abrupt halt on the word "death," and thanks to a

spondee, a heavy accent marks the key words of the line—and of the passage: "life," "still," "springs," and "death." "Springs" is a pun, and both senses animate the succeeding lines. In the next line and a half, Rowe enjambs us into another spondee which emphasizes the first word, "Dies," and then he pulls up short through assonance (repeating the *i* sound), a dental (*t*), and a definite caesura, all on the word "night." Yet the second half of the line moves out of "night" into "morn," as the line —and the world—"revives." Thus "life still springs from death." Even the repeated assonance in "revives" is betrayed by the voiced fricatives. In the next two lines, the pattern is roughly the same. The first ends with the heavily dental "hand destroy'd," but the entire effect of the halting (and of "Winter") is overthrown when the words of the next line spring forth as out of the ground. Rowe emphasizes the first four monosyllables, especially the initial "Lift," in a handsome marriage of metrics and sense. Finally, he links "Lift" alliteratively (and metaphorically) with "live" and repeats "Spring" in the terminal position, suggesting not only the eternal cycle of life but the triumph of life over death, of creation over destruction, and the perpetual spring of the human soul in heaven.

What is best about the language is linked with what is best about the entire play—Rowe's characterization. The dialogue in the play seems especially suited to character: to the shifting moods of Northumberland as he manipulates others; to the shifting passions of Pembroke in his encounters with Guilford; and particularly to the toughness of Lady Jane. With a few exceptions, Rowe never lets dialogue get too long. Just as we expect a tedious tirade, he has another character enter to cut short the exchange. This general terseness sets characters in bold relief and keeps the action fast-paced. It also allows for less declamation and consequently less straining. As a result, we get crisp yet complex characters like Northumberland and Pembroke and even Gardiner, who despite himself cannot help describing—and admiring—Lady Jane's constancy, courage, and charm at her trial, and who pleads with her almost pathetically to recant.

Lady Jane is one of Rowe's finest heroines. Contrary to prevailing opinion of her as totally maudlin, after mourning for the death of Edward she eschews tears, "tender thoughts, and soft endearments" to summon the "uncommon fortitude" of the martyr (IV, p. 235).[20] In contrast to Guilford's amorous dilations, her responses to him are brief and clipped throughout. She cuts short his courtship in Act I, demands his continence on their wedding night in Act II, and asks very pointed ques-

tions of him and the others in Act III, demanding to know how she has
the *right* to be queen. In Act IV she bears her defeat with a spirit which
outshines that of all the other characters, as she utters aphoristic yet
untrite answers to the problem of suffering innocence. In Act V, her
language reflects the "settled quiet" of her "soul" (p. 241) as she controls her joy at pardon and in the next instant her disappointment at
its repeal. Again she toughly staves off Guilford's assaults on her tender
feelings, sustains the "killing stroke" of their parting (p. 245), and caps
her refusal "To barter truth for life" with these wonderful closing lines
to Gardiner:

> *Gardiner.* Wo't thou then die?
>   Thy blood be on thy head.
>
> *Lady Jane Gray.* My blood be where it falls; let the earth hide it;
>   And may it never rise, or call for vengeance:
>   Oh, that it were the last shall fall a victim
>   To zeal's inhuman wrath!

Her final act of magnanimity is the final triumph in the play of the New
Law over the Old. It is the answer, in a setting colored with the blood
of martyrs, to the cry, "Blood for blood." And her plea has a special
poignancy as one views the course not only of Renaissance English history but of all human history up to present Northern Ireland.

    By focusing on the strength of this teen-age girl in his last dramatic
theodicy, Rowe more powerfully than ever before asserts man's never-
failing ability to endure and to hope in the face of what appears apocalyptic "doom" and "universal ruin." The play concludes with the atmosphere of doom, for poetic justice is not even distributed to the
wicked, and England is left in the hands of Gardiner and "Bloody"
Mary. Thus the striking, tragic impact of the ending. Yet there is the
sense that against overwhelming odds here stood the noblest Christian
of them all, whose defeat is, paradoxically, a glorious triumph of the
human spirit. And to a Christian audience the triumph is even greater.
For they would believe not only that Lady Jane shall "rest with the
saints, and dwell in endless peace," but that her prophecies of ultimate
vindication are historically fulfilled (to the satisfaction of the demands
for poetic justice of La Mesnardière and Dryden, if not of Rymer,
Dennis, and Gildon). Thus Rowe concluded where he began, dramatically asserting that, even in the most *trying* afflictions and adversities, at

last "The Gods are great and just." Man must only, like Lady Jane, place complete trust in Providence, in "him whose gracious wisdom guides our ways, / And makes what we think evil turn to good."

NOTES TO CHAPTER III

1. *Book of Martyrs* was the popular title of Foxe's *Acts and Monuments*, of which Rowe possessed a copy of the ninth edition (1684), the one I have used (see *A Catalogue of the Library of N. Rowe*, fol. 85).

2. As a gloss on the concept of *peace of mind* and its importance in this play, I offer these words from Isaac Barrow's sermon "Of Contentment": "Contentedness [is] the virtue, which, of all other, doth most render this world acceptable, and constituteth a kind of temporal heaven; which he that hath, is thereby *ipso facto* in good measure happy, whatever other things he may seem to want; which he that wanteth, doth, however otherwise he be furnished, become miserable, and carrieth a kind of hell within him" (*The Theological Works*, III, 1). In order to achieve contentedness, Barrow continues, "We should with faith and hope rely and wait on God" (p. 13), for "the effect of . . . reposing ourselves for the future on God's providence would be perfect content and peace, according to that of the Prophet [Isa. 26:3], *Thou wilt keep him in perfect peace, whose mind is stayed on thee; because he trusteth in thee*" (p. 71). Indeed, Barrow's entire sermon could be used as a gloss on all of Rowe's plays, and on the Christian tragedy of suffering innocence in general, for he discusses the central theodicean themes of complaint and despair versus submission to the will of God, the acceptance of life as a trial (with its opportunity for Champions), and the patient expectation of justice, if only hereafter. Cf. Geoffrey Marshall, *Restoration Serious Drama*, pp. 43, 65, and passim, who sees the importance of this motif of peace in Restoration tragedy but again divorces it from all but the most nominal Christian metaphysics.

3. The play thus negatively provides an implicit definition of an ideal Christian monarch, a definition which is fulfilled in the play's closing panegyric on Queen Anne, whose "reign" is graced by "ev'ry virtue" but mostly by "peaceful arts" and who provides the *nursing* care of a "mother's love" to her country (V.ii, p. 128). Hengist's comments on kingship, particularly in the imagery of slaves, victims, sleep, and peace, seem reminiscent of Henry V's famous soliloquy in Act IV of Shakespeare's play.

4. Cf. Corneille, *Polyeucte*, IV.iii, where Pauline's feminine appeal is similarly rebuffed by Polyeucte, and where she is totally incapable of understanding the resolution of the martyr (until she herself is miraculously converted at the end of the play). Several critics have noted the resemblance between the two plays, especially in this scene and in Aribert's threat to trample on the pagan altars (cf. *Polyeucte*, II.vi, III.ii), but Paul Borgwardt appears to have been the first to have worked out the comparison (The Royal Convert *von Nicholas Rowe 1707*, p. 42 ff).

5. See Alfred Jackson, "Rowe's Historical Tragedies," p. 307, who argues the obvious topical motivation behind *The Royal Convert*, "the Union of England and Scotland."

6. Rowe mentions three sources in his Preface: Burnet; John Banks, *The Innocent Usurper*; and Edmund Smith's notes for a play on the theme. (See Donald B. Clark, "Nicholas Rowe," p. 240 ff, for a thorough study of these sources.) But Foxe's account is more detailed than any of these, even Burnet's, in its inclusion of various letters and discourses of the Lady Jane (III, 11 ff). Though he does not record it, Rowe may well owe a debt to Foxe.

7. *The Politics of Drama in Augustan England*, p. 79 f. For the background of "the Fifteen" see Charles Petrie, *The Jacobite Movement: The First Phase, 1688-1716*, especially chs. vii and viii.

8. In the Dedication Rowe praises Caroline for refusing the "first Crown of *Europe* . . . in obedience to the dictates of reason and conscience, for the sake of true religion, and for the honour of God" (p. 190). In the Epilogue Rowe writes that "For truth" and the British people "the heroine" Caroline "declines, / Austria's proud eagles, and the Indian mines," Spain's American colonies (p. 248). See Ruby L. Arkell, *Caroline of Ansbach*, ch. i.

9. Cf. Banks, *The Innocent Usurper*, who portrays Lady Jane as accepting the crown only after the self-centered histrionics of Gilford and Northumberland convince her that she must do so to save them from suicide or beheading (III, p. 26). All along Banks' Lady Jane knows she is a usurper, and Rowe seems, on the contrary, to paint her in as favorable a light as possible, perhaps in conscious opposition to Banks.

10. Rowe does not stress Northumberland's ambition, and he treats his cowardly reversal of allegiance from Jane to Mary sympathetically (IV, p. 232), though he does reveal Northumberland's sinister machinations toward Pembroke throughout. But see J. D. Mackie, *The Earlier Tudors, 1485-1558*, p. 478 ff, for a summary of Edward VI's reign and Northumberland's lust for unlimited "auctoritye."

11. *The Anatomy of Melancholy*, ed. Holbrook Jackson, III, 17 (III.1.1.2). Cf. Milton, *Paradise Lost*, when Satan speaks of "Heaven and Earth" being "link'd in a golden Chain" (II.1004 f), and when the narrator describes the new universe thus: "hanging in a golden Chain, / This pendant world" (vs. 1051 f). In his note to this passage Merritt Hughes says, "The conception runs through literature from Plato's *Theaetetus* (153 C) to Chaucer's *Knight's Tale* (I-A-2987-93)." Swift also employs the image in "Prometheus" (1724):

> There is a *Chain* let down from *Jove*,
> But fasten'd to his Throne above;
> So strong, that from the lower End,
> They say, all human Things depend:
> This *Chain*, as Antient Poets hold,   .
> When *Jove* was Young, was made of Gold. (vs. 31 ff, *Poems*, I, 345)

12. Northumberland was hated for his "traitor father" Edmund Dudley's alleged treason against Henry, for his own virtual murder of his rival protector, Somerset, and now for his attempted coup d'état (see IV, p. 224 f). See Mackie, pp. 267 and 478 ff, for accounts of Edmund Dudley's "treason" and Northumberland's rivalry with Somerset throughout the reign of Edward VI, and p. 528 f, for the story of the council's desertion of Lady Jane.

13. See Clark, "Nicholas Rowe," p. 257 ff, for a comparison of this play with Addison's *Cato* (1713), which has a similar scene.

14. Rowe, *Works*, II, 249. For Pope's authorship see Norman Ault, *New Light on Pope*, p. 138 ff, though the prologue is listed as a poem of doubtful authorship in Pope's *Minor Poems*, ed. Ault and John Butt, *Twickenham Edition*, VI, 415.

15. Probably for the illusion of some unity of time, Rowe does not specify the dates of the Dudleys' incarceration or their trial, but they were in prison from July 1553 till the following February and were tried in the meantime in November, as Rowe would well have known from either Foxe or Burnet. Though they were sentenced to death, it appeared that Queen Mary was going to be lenient, until the nearly successful Wyatt conspiracy (with which they had nothing to do) provoked her harshness, or rather that of Gardiner, her Lord Chancellor and Catholic Bishop of Winchester. See Mackie, p. 535 ff.

16. If the evidence in the text that this book is the Bible is insufficient, Rowe's audience would have known from the historical accounts of Lady Jane's death that she sent to

a sister her Greek Testament with a letter which contains the lessons of *contemptus mundi* and *memento mori*, plus a discourse on the meaning of her martyrdom. See Foxe, III, 28 f.

17. Reading from 1720 collected edition, *The Dramatick Works of Nicholas Rowe, Esq.*

18. It is natural for Pembroke to feel this way, for he sees Northumberland's flattery of him and of his suit for Lady Jane's hand (I, p. 197 f) and Guilford's subsequent attainment of that hand as obviously politically contrived, though Guilford himself is innocent of his father's machinations.

19. Like Foxe and Burnet (q.v.), Rowe presents Gardiner, and not Queen Mary, as the villain of the piece. See V, p. 238 ff, and the Preface, p. 192.

20. See Pope's "Prologue," where he says that in Lady Jane, Rowe atones "for characters here drawn before" who sigh "through ev'ry page" and languish on the stage (p. 249). Pope praises Rowe for his portrayal of Lady Jane's "gen'rous scorn" and "patient courage," "brave contempt of life" and "mind unchang'd, superior to a crown."

Two

The Trial of
the Sinner

IV Protagonist as Penitent (with Reluctance)

The Fair Penitent

he Fair Penitent and Jane Shore are Nicholas Rowe's best-known and, by common consent, his best plays. In them he turns from the problem of suffering innocence to the problem of penitence, that is, from the trial of the innocent to the trial of the sinner. Accordingly, while his theme remains trust in Providence as the only antidote to despair, he shifts the emphasis from God's justice to His mercy and from man's need for patience and endurance to his need for repentance and atonement. In other words, despite the fact that these plays have been examined in the past almost entirely on affective grounds, they are not merely vehicles for pathos. Nor are they merely gilded pills of ethical didacticism. To paraphrase Dennis, their morality would be a jest were it not for their metaphysic. These plays are Christian tragedies because in their formal design they mirror a universe controlled by a God Who cares, Who tries His creatures and eventually rewards and punishes—a God Who in Rowe's other plays answers prayers for justice and Who now answers prayers for mercy.

The emphasis on divine mercy in The Fair Penitent (1703) is especially apparent in Rowe's variations on his source, Massinger and Field's The Fatal Dowry (acted ca. 1619). Comparisons between these plays have been common in Rowe criticism, but no critic has compared them thematically; yet only such a comparison reveals the significance of the variations. Both plays focus on problems of justice and mercy. The Fatal Dowry begins and ends with Charalois (Rowe's Altamont) pleading before an official court of justice: first for the release of his deceased father's estate (not to mention his father's corpse) from the hands of creditors; and finally for his own life in a trial for the murder of his wife Beaumelle (Calista) and her lover Novall (Lothario), whom he has taken in adultery. Moreover, the central scene of the play is an improvised kangaroo court for the trial of Beaumelle by Charalois and her father Rochfort (Sciolto). In accordance with strict justice, Rochfort finds her guilty of adultery and sentences her to death; Charalois complies with the verdict, executing her summarily. But strict justice had likewise in the play's opening trial demanded payment of Charalois' father's debts, yet Rochfort, out of pity for Charalois, had paid them. Now at Beaumelle's trial, when nature most demands such pity from a father and a husband, it is denied. The implication seems to be that Rochfort and Charalois have missed the lesson of the scriptural parallel of the woman taken in adultery (John 8:1 ff) and have cast the first—and last—stone. As a result, by the end of the play Rochfort becomes a broken, guilt-ridden man, and Charalois, though he wins the mercy of the court in his trial for murder, ironically is murdered by an avenger of Novall. As he dies, he justifies what has happened to him:

> what's falne upon me,
> Is by Heavens will, because I made my selfe
> A Judge in my owne cause without their [the judges'] warrant;
> But he that lets me know thus much in death,
> With all good men forgive mee.[1]°

Thus the poetic justice is providential and embodies a lesson familiar in Elizabethan domestic and revenge tragedy: that just vengeance is the prerogative of God and His divinely established authority. The play insists, furthermore, that justice should be tempered with mercy on earth, as it is in heaven. Significantly, Charalois dies praying for the mercy which he and Rochfort refused the penitent Beaumelle—the mercy that Heaven guarantees to all repentant sinners.

Rowe's major variation on Massinger's play, then, is to shift the focus from Charalois (Altamont) to Beaumelle (Calista), from the avenger to the penitent. Consequently, while *The Fair Penitent* still deals with the relationship between justice and mercy, the emphasis shifts from the former to the latter. Moreover, instead of an avenger, Altamont is made a forgiver, and his forgiveness, together with that of Sciolto, is the human analogue to—and testament of—divine forgiveness for the finally penitent Calista.

°Notes to this chapter begin on page 143.

i

Like the relationship between Rowe and Massinger, that between Rowe and Thomas Otway, one of his acknowledged masters,[2] has often been assumed but rarely analyzed, except on such technical grounds as characterization and creation of pathos.[3] There is an important thematic similarity between *The Fair Penitent* and *The Orphan* (1680), however, which should not go unobserved. As David Walker has ably demonstrated in his unpublished dissertation on Otway, *The Orphan* metaphorically recapitulates the Fall of man.[4] Acasto has retired from the court in an attempt to create an idyllic existence—implicitly another Eden—but his attempt fails, for the problem lies not in institutions but in the flawed nature of man, as the deceit between persons so close as twin brothers attests. After their unintentional incest, Monimia and Polydor prepare to leave Acasto's retreat like Adam and Eve departing out of Paradise,[5] and as in *Paradise Lost*, the really crucial question is how they (and Castalio) will respond to their fall from innocence. Unlike Adam and Eve, they despair.

Whether Rowe garnered the idea from Otway or not—the plays *are* very similar in setting, characterization (Acasto and Sciolto, especially), pathos, and particularly in their concentration on the response to sin—*The Fair Penitent* (*Works*, I, 151 ff) has a similar relationship to the story of the Fall, for that story is constantly echoed to provide a framework for the actions of the play. By means of such a framework, the play, like Otway's, implies that ours is a fallen world and that attempts to achieve perfect happiness here are in vain. The scene opens in Sciolto's "*garden*" on Altamont and Calista's wedding day (I, p. 158). Altamont enters praying that "No mourning, no misfortunes" happen on this "sacred" day, for after terrible misfortunes, his "better stars" at last have shone, and "Heav'n" has rewarded his "virtue," bidding "*Sciolto's* bounty be its proxy" (p. 159). As a kind of heavenly agent, then, Sciolto is the "author" of Altamont's "happiness," who bids his days "be blest with peace and plenty" and who "satisfies" his soul "with love and beauty." Altamont even compares Sciolto directly to the Creator:

> Thus Heav'n from nothing rais'd his fair creation,
> And then with wond'rous joy beheld its beauty,
> Well pleas'd to see the excellence he gave. (p. 160)

Moreover, the following paean by Altamont suggests, in both diction

and content, a relationship between Sciolto and himself metaphorically
more than familial:

> Oh great *Sciolto*! oh my more than father!
> Let me not live, but at thy very name
> My eager heart springs up, and leaps with joy.
> When I forget the vast, vast debt I owe thee,
> Forget! (but 'tis impossible) then let me
> Forget the use and privilege of reason,
> Be driven from the commerce of mankind,
> To wander in the desart among brutes,
> To bear the various fury of the seasons,
> The night's unwholesome dew and noon-day's heat,
> To be the scorn of earth, and curse of Heav'n! (p. 158 f)

The sacredness of the father's "name," the "vast debt" owed by the
son, and the Cain-like banishment, all seem to me to imply a Father-son
relationship patterned after that between Adamic man and God.

Indeed, despite Calista's ominously chilling trothplight kiss (p.
160), Altamont thinks that he has found an Edenic "peace." At the end
of the first   discovered Calista's incriminating let-
                    ont at the wedding as being "satisfied
                    Calista "the perfect workmanship of
                    t the new bridegroom enters bidding
                    hat "all" his "succeeding days" will be
                    my hours be good and joyful" (II.i, p.
                    theirs a "fatal marriage" wrought by
                    oth," and even after Horatio has ac-
                    Altamont asserts in blind assurance,

> n, or good fortune,
> vealth and honour?
> peace and pleasure,
> rms.

                    his call for Hymeneal music is met
                    love and plaintive despair, mag-
                    the entire city and prays that he
                    st" (II.i, p. 173)—as if it were pos-

Later, however, echoing Calista's talk of a "sullen influence, a foe to both," which has mismatched her and Altamont, Sciolto chides her for being "Perverse and sullen all this day of joy" (III, p. 178); he has observed her,

> like some malignant planet,
> Foe to the harvest, and the healthy year,
> Who scouls adverse, and lours upon the world;
> When all the other stars, with gentle aspect,
> Propitious shine, and meaning good to man.

So it is as if a "sullen influence" or a "malignant planet"—some "foe"— has entered the propitious conjunction of stars which in the opening act had seemed to Altamont and Sciolto to dominate the world. This "foe" is spoken of in other associations. When Horatio and Altamont come to blows over Horatio's indictment of Calista, Lavinia rushes in and demands, "What busy, medling fiend, what foe to goodness, / Could kindle such a discord?" (p. 186). The connection of "busy, medling fiend" with the word "foe" implies a specific connotation—the "Foe" of medieval literature—and suggests that there is a snake (or some kind of satanic figure) in Sciolto's garden. Accordingly, Lothario sneaks into the garden on the morning of the wedding and reveals "the theft" that has already spoiled the marriage (I, p. 161)—and Sciolto and Altamont's dreams of perfection. Ironically, as if in mockery of their illusions, Rowe has Lothario describe his fornication with Calista as "perfect happiness" (p. 162). Horatio makes the analogy between Lothario and Satan —and indeed, that between the play and the story of the Fall—fully explicit. Standing out in relief to the integrating, circular movement of the Hymeneal dance, Horatio scrutinizes Calista and observes the "starts of guilt" which show through her "specious face of innocence and beauty" (II.i, p. 173). He exclaims when she leaves,

> With such smooth looks, and many a gentle word,
> The first fair she beguil'd her easy lord;
> Too blind with love and beauty to beware,
> He fell unthinking in the fatal snare;
> Nor could believe that such a heav'nly face
> Had bargain'd with the devil, to damn her wretched race.

In the very next scene, as if on cue, the devilish Lothario reenters and is surprised by Horatio, who defends the honor of his friend's bride and powerfully inveighs against Lothario and the "tribe" of neo-Epicurean libertines (II.ii, p. 175), whose hedonism "spurns at sacred order" and leads to moral anarchy. But even in this confrontation, the analogy to the story of the Fall seems to remain, however subdued. Piqued at being discovered by Horatio for the second time (the first occurring in the garden when Lothario drops Calista's letter), Lothario calls him his "evil genius" (p. 174). There is a faint suggestion that, indeed, Horatio *is* emblematically an interfering "genius," or angel—that he is something like the devilish Lothario's Gabriel—for a series of parallels appears to establish an allusive referent for the scene in Satan's encounter with Gabriel in Book IV of *Paradise Lost*. In terms that seem to echo, howbeit obliquely, the discovery of the satanic toad at the ear of Eve, Horatio describes in retrospect his first discovery of Lothario: at that moment, Horatio says to him,

> Thou fled'st! and guilt was on thee, like a thief,
> A pilferer descried in some dark corner,
> Who there had lodg'd with mischievous intent
> To rob and ravage at the hour of rest,
> And do a midnight murder on the sleepers.[6]

In their encounter Lothario and Horatio square off somewhat like Milton's angelic champions, each vaunting his challenge; Lothario is as proud and contemptuous as Satan, and Horatio, like Gabriel, continually exposes the speciousness of his arguments. Finally, when Lothario defiantly vows to act "like birds . . . / That haunt in woods, in meads, and flow'ry *gardens*" and to "Rifle the sweets, and taste the choicest *fruits*, / Yet scorn to ask the *lordly* owner's leave" (p. 176, italics mine), Horatio, somewhat like Gabriel, warns him to stay out of *this* garden (they are standing in the street that runs by it):

> But henceforth, boy, I warn thee shun my walks;
> If in the bounds of yon forbidden place
> Again thou'rt found, expect a punishment,
> Such as great souls, impatient of an injury,
> Exact from those who wrong 'em much. (p. 176 f)[7]

As in *Paradise Lost*, these mighty opposites nearly come to blows, but the conflict is interrupted and left inconclusive, to be fought by other combatants on other grounds (the garden itself).

The allusive parallel here, as elsewhere, is admittedly very elusive. Of course, there is no direct one-to-one relationship between Milton and Rowe (after all, Calista has already sinned), but it is to Rowe's credit that he does not make this play a transparent allegory (compare *Tamerlane* and countless other contemporary tragedies which unsubtly play off the greatest poem and favorite analogue of the period). Nevertheless, Horatio's speech directly—and the other distant echoes indirectly— serve, I think, to place the action of *The Fair Penitent* in a context which suggests that what is going on is a reiteration of the Fall of man, despite Sciolto and Altamont's paradisal expectations. Having clung to those expectations at the expense of his lifelong friendship with Horatio only to have his bride deny him the "peace" and "pleasure" he had supposed her "dowry," Altamont, like the Adam Horatio has compared him to, has fallen "unthinking in the fatal snare." At the opening of Act IV, he enters Sciolto's garden (the very setting implies the significance of the action: here was the false paradise born and here it and the "fiend" that disturbed it will die), and he epitomizes the condition of the human soul as it vacillates from delusions of paradise to despair:

> WITH what unequal tempers are we form'd?
> One day the soul, supine with ease and fulness,
> Revels secure, and fondly tells herself,
> The hour of evil can return no more;
> The next, the spirits pall'd, and sick of riot,
> Turn all to discord, and we hate our beings,
> Curse the past joy, and think it folly all,
> And bitterness, and anguish. (p. 188 f)

"I have lost my peace," he concludes (p. 190), and in a moment his false paradise is gone forever, for he discovers Calista and Lothario together and overhears her admission of guilt. After he has avenged himself and killed Lothario, Altamont complains in profound anguish that Calista has heaped "Curses and sorrows" on him and left him "more than murdered" (p. 191). Sciolto himself, having banished Calista forever, concludes in despair, "Oh *Altamont!* what a vast scheme of joy / Has this one day destroy'd!" (p. 194). Destroyed is Sciolto's paradise, because he was unable for even one day to shut out, as he has tried to do, "losses and disappointments, cares and poverty, / The rich man's insolence,

and great man's scorn" (II.i, p. 172)—in short, the evils of the world. As
in Otway's *The Orphan*, evil cannot be escaped, and attempts to do so
end in disaster. That night when all Genoa is in chaos, Sciolto says of
Calista,

> Amidst the general wreck, see where she stands,
> Like *Helen*, in the night when *Troy* was sack'd,
> Spectatress of the mischief which she made. (V, p. 201)

The analogy to Helen works, like the one to Eve, as a referent by which
it is implied that Calista has recapitulated, on a lesser scale, the "mischief" of her ancestral prototypes.

Complaining, "Hadst thou been honest, thou hadst been a cheru-
bin" (p. 202), Sciolto asks Calista why she has cursed him and spoiled his
happiness. Her answer is a perfectly appropriate rebuff to Sciolto's deluded expectations and inhuman demands:

> Because my soul was rudely drawn from yours;
> A poor imperfect copy of my father,
> Where goodness, and the strength of manly virtue,
> Was thinly planted, and the idle void
> Fill'd up with light belief, and easy fondness;
> It was, because I lov'd, and was a woman.

The answer is brilliantly in character for the proud Calista, who refuses
to lose her "great spirit" (p. 201) before a father who had wanted a son
(see I, p. 159) and who has been implacably righteous and demanding
toward the daughter he got instead. But Calista's answer takes on its full
meaning when she later says,

> Now think, thou curst *Calista*, now behold
> The desolation, horror, blood and ruin,
> Thy crimes and fatal folly spread around,
> That loudly cry for vengeance on thy head;
> Yet Heav'n, who knows our weak imperfect natures,
> How blind with passions, and how prone to evil,
> Makes not too strict inquiry for offences,
> But is aton'd by penitence and pray'r. (p. 204)

The Prologue has announced Rowe's design to "still let Nature be his care" and not to "paint all things fair, / But shew you men and women as they are," for "Few to perfection ever found the way" (p. 156).[8] The "Nature" of man is fallen, the play insists, and thus "a poor imperfect copy" of the heavenly father—"weak," "prone to evil," and emphatically not cherubic, as Sciolto would have it. Therefore, the Fall of man repeats itself, as in Otway's play, in each generation, despite man's efforts to avoid it, to create a false paradise, to "fondly" tell himself, "The hour of evil can return no more."

ii

As Calista stands amidst the desolation she has wrought, the full ramifications of Horatio's early complaint are realized: "Oh, that the ruin were but all thy own!" (I, p. 166). Calista has truly brought "ruin" to her husband, her family, and all of Genoa, and not so much because of her original sin but because of her indignation at Lothario, on the one hand, and her attempt to conceal her sin, on the other. She admits to Lothario that only "indignation" for his "unmanly insolence and scorn" urged her, out of "desperation," to marry Altamont and thus "wound" herself "to be reveng'd" on him (IV, p. 190). As Horatio points out to her, she has thereby not only given "her honour to a wretch" but compounded her sin by hypocritically plighting "to a noble youth her faith" (III, p. 181). In so doing, Calista also attempts to conceal her sin. To Lothario Lucilla describes her as seeking "some melancholy shade, / To hide her sorrows from the prying world" (I, p. 164). To Lucilla Calista announces her desire to

> hide me,
> From the base world, from malice, and from shame;
> For 'tis the solemn counsel of my soul,
> Never to live with public loss of honor. (II.i, p. 169)

As her bridegroom approaches, she prepares to conceal from him her "soul's accesses" by "dissembling," so that his "hostile husband's eyes" cannot explore "The warring passions, and tumultuous thoughts" that "rage within" (p. 170 f). When Sciolto chastises Calista for being "Perverse and sullen," he suspects that "some sullen thought that shuns the light, / Lurks underneath that sadness" in her "visage" (III, p. 178 f). Later Calista denies Horatio's accusations and tears the evidence against her—the letter to Lothario—to "atoms" (p. 192), a metaphor which suggests the havoc she is wreaking. Then, denying Horatio's allegations, she

turns Altamont against him and destroys their friendship. Finally, by
stubbornly insisting in her indignation to see Lothario once again, she
not only gets him killed but destroys her husband's and her father's
happiness, catapults the whole city of Genoa into civil chaos, and causes
her father to provoke his own death.

But try as she may in her indignation and shame to conceal her sin,
the action of the play demonstrates, in accordance with the Judeo-
Christian, the Classical, and the English dramatic traditions, that Calista's sin will find her out.[9] In his sermon, "Concealment of Sin no Secur-
ity to the Sinner," Rowe's contemporary divine, Robert South, discusses
several ways in which sin is revealed. "God *sometimes* takes the Work
of *Vengeance* upon himself," he writes, and "repays the Sinner, by some
notable Judgment from Heaven." For example, he continues, sometimes God "strangely blasts him in his Name, Family, or Estate, so that
all about him stand amazed at the Blow" (*Forty-Eight Sermons*, IV, 172).
The ruin of her "Name," her "Family," and her "Estate" by the end of
the play is, I submit, just such a judgment upon Calista, for the world of
the play seems governed by such a Providence. Unlike Rowe's *Ulysses*,
The Fair Penitent does not present a providential deity on the stage.
There are several indications throughout the play, however, of the presence of Providence. For instance, Sciolto's "bounty" is said to be
Heaven's "proxy," and as Altamont says,

> By Heav'n, he found my fortunes so abandon'd,
> That nothing but a miracle could raise 'em. (I, p. 159)

Lucilla prays to the "sacred Powers, whose gracious providence / Is
watchful for our good," that she be kept from Calista's anguish (II.i, p.
170). When Lavinia and Horatio are banished, Lavinia places all her
trust in a God Who provides for His creatures: in words reminiscent of
the Sermon on the Mount and especially the analogy of "the lilies of the
field" (Matt. 6:28 f), she says,

> The holy Pow'r, who clothes the senseless earth,
> With woods, with fruits, with flow'rs and verdant grass,
> Whose bounteous hand feeds the whole brute creation,
> Knows all our wants, and has enough to give us. (IV, p. 185)

Horatio and Sciolto both insist that Heaven rewards virtue: Horatio
says of "The brave" that "Heav'n and men are judges of their actions"

(II.ii, p. 174); more explicitly, Sciolto says of "gracious Heav'n" that It has "endless blessings still in store, / For virtue, and for filial piety" (V, p. 207). Heaven evidently punishes vice, too, for when Lothario crosses swords with Altamont, he says defiantly, "Earth, Heav'n, and fair *Calista* judge the combat" (IV, p. 191). We can only assume when he is killed that, in accordance with the traditional trial by combat, Heaven has indeed passed Its judgment.

With the presence of Providence suggested so often in the play, we must also assume, it seems to me, that such accidents as Lothario's loss of the letter and Altamont's overhearing of Calista's admission of guilt are to be interpreted as providential. Bishop South writes, "There is sometimes a strange, providential Concurrence of *unusual, unlikely Accidents*, for the Discovery of Great Sins" (p. 162). Even "dumb, inanimate Things"—like letters—"are sometimes unaccountably enabled to clamour and depose against the guilty Wretch; so that, to the Amazement of the World, he is drawn forth into *publick View*, out of all his lurking Holes, and *Pavilions* of *Darkness*" (p. 156 f). Henry H. Adams describes throughout his study of Elizabethan domestic tragedy any number of such "accidents," as does Charles H. Peake in his similar study of eighteenth-century domestic tragedy—although the latter, while he labels the lost letter in Susanna Centlivre's *The Perjur'd Husband* (1700) an instance of providential intervention (p. 190), dismisses the same device in *The Fair Penitent* as "theatrical method" (p. 209). But then, Peake sees no evidence at all of particular Providence in the play, nor does he think Rowe places Calista's sin in a theological context (p. 209 f).[10] Such a reading denies the evidence already mentioned and much more. For what makes this play the most powerful Rowe wrote is its conflict, the struggle between remorse and repentance that rages in Calista's soul, as she undergoes the very Christian trial of the sinner.

By handsomely orchestrating a series of key phrases and images first used by Horatio and Lavinia at the end of Act I and then echoed a moment later by Calista and Lucilla at the beginning of Act II, Rowe introduces us to Calista and her state of mind (p. 168 ff). Lavinia speaks of the "sound of joy" of the wedding party, while the bride herself bids Lucilla never to "disturb" her "solemn sadness with the sound of joy." Horatio, aware of the pollution of his friend's marriage, rails against "false ones," libertines, whose "Heav'n" is "variety" (or "changing"),

while Lucilla urges Calista to reject the "false *Lothario*" forever in favor
of her bridegroom, who knows not "the courtly vice of changing"—the
vice to which Calista has fallen victim. Lavinia's comparison of her own
heart to a "cottage," an hospitable "lonely dwelling" for her husband,
evokes all the benign associations of retirement, while Calista's description of the "melancholy scene" she longs to dwell in alone turns con-
tented retirement into a "retreat" of "despair." Most importantly, Lavinia asks if there can be such "false ones" as Horatio describes,

> and have they peace of mind?
> Have they in all the series of their changing
> One happy hour?

The very next instant, in perfect stage irony, Calista enters to provide
the living answer, as she exclaims, "And my dear peace of mind is lost
for ever."

Despite her white wedding gown, then, and Altamont's hopes of
"white and lucky" days,[11] Calista is shrouded in "black despair" (II.i, p.
169). She says that all her "thoughts" are "indignation, love or shame,"
and precisely these conflicting elements make up "The warring passions, and tumultuous thoughts, / That rage within" and "deform" her
"reason" (p. 171). The three elements are evident from our first glimpse
into her tortured soul, her letter to Lothario. In it she announces her
intention to marry Altamont "*in spite of*" her "*weakness*" for Lothario
(I, p. 165). The letter also reveals Calista's inner conflict between love
and shame when she ambivalently calls Lothario "*too faithless, yet too
lovely.*" Then, in the opening scene of Act II, while Calista desires to
"hide" from "shame" (p. 169), her "lab'ring" heart "swells with indignation" (p. 170) at Lothario (as well as at the idea of being "a tale for
fools"), and she longs "to discharge the burden" on him in one last inter-
view. And yet, although she insists that she has been "wrong'd enough"
to resist Lothario's charm, she admits that she would "pardon" the
"dear betrayer" (the combination of words itself indicates her ambivalence) if he should "sigh to be forgiven."

Lucilla's function during this scene is that traditional spiritual
work of mercy, admonishing the sinner. She describes Calista as "Be-
nighted in a wilderness of woe" after Lothario, "that wand'ring fire,"
has "misled" her "weary steps" (p. 169)—an *ignis fatuus* which is perhaps an allusion to the serpentine "wand'ring Fire" that misleads the
steps of Eve in *Paradise Lost* (IX.634 ff). She herself represents, as her

Dantesque name suggests, the far more reliable guiding light of grace. In language echoing homiletic admonitions to sinners, she warns Calista of "the manifest destruction, / The gaping gulf," into which she is rushing in her foolish desire to see "this faithless man again" while relying only on her "Rage" and "indignation" to preserve her from falling anew (p. 170). "Trust not to that," she implores, urging Calista to listen to her "ever-faithful" Lucilla and to embrace the "faithful" Altamont (p. 169). (By now the epithets "faithless" and "faithful" have taken on more than secular connotations.) But when Calista declares that her "genius" drives her on, Lucilla, unequal to the task, entrusts herself to the care of "gracious providence," lest she be similarly deceived. Thus trust in Providence is contrasted to a foolish trust in "indignation," and before Calista's shame and sense of guilt can be efficacious, the play seems to say, she must learn to turn to God with humility. "They that do from the bottom of their hearts acknowledge their sins, and are unfeignedly sorry for their offences," says the authorized "Homily of Repentance," "will cast off all hypocrisie, and put on true humility, and lowliness of heart" (*Certain Sermons or Homilies*, p. 346).

Having observed Calista and "mark'd the starts of guilt, / That shook her soul" (p. 173), Horatio assumes the same function as Lucilla. He will try to convince Calista of "the crime and danger" of ever seeing Lothario again and will try to "wake" any "spark of Heav'n" that remains "unquenched / Within her breast" (II.ii, p. 177). Praying that he might find the "gracious words"[12] to "softly steal upon her soul" without arousing her "tempestuous passions" (III, p. 179), Horatio approaches Calista and offers

> To sooth the secret anguish of her soul,
> To comfort that fair mourner, that forlorn one,
> And teach her steps to know the paths of peace. (p. 180)

Calista would like to learn of such a "paradise," for, she says, " 'tis sure, I long to be at rest." She does not know that Horatio is aware of her real loss of peace. He responds to her curiosity with the Scholastic ethic that "to be good is to be happy" and that "Guilt is the cause of sorrow," citing the example of "angels" and "the blest," who "Are happier than mankind, because they are better" and who, because they know no guilt, "rest in everlasting peace of mind, / And find the height of all their Heav'n is goodness." But, the implication is, since man is fallen and therefore subject to guilt, the only paradise and peace afforded him in this life is that *paradise within* which comes from virtuous activity. Thus Horatio answers Calista's desire (as well as Sciolto and Altamont's, by the way) for "paradise" and "peace of mind."

When, despite Horatio's awkward efforts to be subtly suggestive, Calista meets his admonition with indignation that some "bold parasite's officious tongue" should "dare to tax" her "with guilt" (p. 181), he is forced to name her sin explicitly (though ascribing the attribution to rumor): she is

> a false fair one,
> Who plighted to a noble youth her faith
> When she had giv'n her honour to a wretch.

Thus Calista's worst crime is not the fornication itself, which was a sin of passion as Lothario describes it (I, p. 162), but rather the hypocrisy of her pledge of "faith" and her pollution of that "nuptial band," which Horatio tells Lavinia "should be the pledge of peace" (p. 168). Because Calista and Altamont are not "one," even as the "blended waters" of "meeting rivers" (III, p. 180); because they are not "join'd by Heav'n," as Horatio so pointedly implies, a "train of wretchedness" will follow their marriage. In other words, their marriage is in direct contrast to Horatio and Lavinia's, which, as Frank Kearful has pointed out in his article, "The Nature of Tragedy in Rowe's *The Fair Penitent*" (p. 357 ff), provides the marital norm in the play, expressed especially in the sententious closing tags of each act. In the tag at the end of Act III, Lavinia's statement that for Horatio she will forsake "country, brother, friends, ev'n all I have" (p. 188), seems to me to establish positively, if Horatio's talk of "meeting rivers" is not enough, the scriptural standard for marriage: "Therefore shall a man leave his father and his mother, and shall cleave unto his wife: and they shall be one flesh" (Gen. 2:24, etc.). As the concluding moral of the play indicates, Calista's violation of this sacred union is one of Horatio's—and the play's—chief concerns:

> By such examples are we taught to prove,
> The sorrows that attend unlawful love;
> Death, or some worse misfortunes, soon divide
> The injur'd bridegroom from his guilty bride:
> If you would have the nuptial union last,
> Let virtue be the bond that ties it fast. (V, p. 207)

It is important for those who would dismiss this tag as obnoxious moralizing to see at least that the didacticism is based upon a sacramental definition of marriage and that the poetic justice practiced on Calista and promised for those who abuse the "nuptial union" is, in the universe this play images, a divine judgment.

Prompted by Calista's bold contempt and indignation, Horatio grows finally bold himself and insists that Calista, if her "fame" or "peace" are worth her "care," must "listen to the means are left to save 'em" (III, p. 181 f):

> 'Tis now the lucky minute of your fate.
> By me your genius speaks, by me it warns you,
> Never to see that curst *Lotario* more. (p. 182)

Just as he has been Lothario's "genius" (an "evil" one to the mind of Lothario but a good one in the world of the play), so now Horatio assumes the role of "genius" to Calista implicitly in opposition to the "genius" that she earlier says drives her on to see Lothario again (II.i, p. 170). In Rowe's obviously calculated repetition of the word, there is the intimation that Calista's opposing genii owe something to the good and bad angels of the Morality plays, who contend for the protagonist's soul. Lothario might be seen, then, as something like Calista's evil genius or bad angel (certainly her satanic tempter), who seduces her when "Fierceness and pride, the guardians of her honor, / Were charm'd to rest" (I, p. 162). Lucilla and Horatio are also something like guardians of her honor, metaphorically good or guardian angels. Horatio's command that Calista "kneel" and "in the awful face of Heav'n" vow never to see Lothario again indicates his function (albeit assumed) of heavenly agent (III, p. 182). Nevertheless, as she did Lucilla's Calista rejects Horatio's admonitions, squelching his triumphant display of the lost letter by snatching and destroying it. Finally she declares,

> I am myself the guardian of my honour,
> And wo'not bear so insolent a monitor.

In the context I have been describing, the word *guardian* takes on special connotations which serve—not so much to identify Horatio as a guardian angel—but to complete the process of identifying his function as *ad-monitor* and to focus our attention on the theological nature of Calista's struggle. A moment later, despite her indignation at Horatio and subsequently at Altamont for defending his friend; despite her railing at "the marriage chain" and "that tyrant, man," Calista reveals, however unintentionally, her awareness of the need for repentance in her threat to retire to a "cloister" to learn "religious hardships," to "fast, and freeze at midnight hours of pray'r." What she says in petulant spite is ironically the only appropriate course of action.

Calista does not yet repent, however. Ignoring the warnings of Lucilla and Horatio, she keeps her rendezvous with Lothario in what is the central scene of the play. "They that do truly repent," says the "Homily of Repentance," "must be clean altered and changed, they must become new creatures, they must be no more the same that they were before." Such an alteration is called "amendment of life," and it is one of the four necessary parts of repentance (p. 346). In Christian literature proof of such purpose of amendment usually takes the form of the trial of the sinner in the same temptation to which he has earlier succumbed. Milton's *Samson Agonistes* is a perfect example, where Samson's climactic encounter with Dalila tests his incipient repentance against the uxoriousness to which he has twice fallen prey. Like Samson, Rowe's Calista must prove that she has learned "so much of Adder's wisdom" to "fence" her ear against Lothario's "sorceries" (SA 936 f), and not to let, as Lucilla has warned, the "deceiver love" overcome her once more. Only then can she progress, as Samson does, toward placing her trust "in the living God" and despairing "not of his final pardon / Whose ear is ever open" (SA 1140, 1171 f).

The severity of Calista's trial is emphasized by Rowe's portrayal of her tempter in such attractive colors that, as Frank Kearful and others have pointed out, many of Rowe's eighteenth-century critics, including Doctor Johnson, questioned either Rowe's morality or his artistic judgment—or both.[13] Kearful rightly shows, however, that "such attacks fail to do justice to the complexity of . . . Rowe's moral awareness"—and religious awareness, I would add. He continues, "Precisely because evil so often is more obviously attractive than goodness is Rowe's characterization appropriate—and moral" (p. 354).[14] Indeed, Rowe's practice is in accord with that of Spenser (the Bower of Bliss), Marlowe (Helen of Troy), Shakespeare (Iago or Cleopatra), Milton (Satan or Dalila), Otway (Don John[15]), and the Christian tradition in general. The appeal and popularity of the gay Lothario is thus not a mark of Rowe's failure but of his great success.

Now on the one hand, the appeal of Lothario is a mitigating factor in the imputability of Calista's guilt, for he is truly a seductive devil and has taken her in an hour of weakness (I, p. 162). As a final mitigating factor, Rowe has Lothario report that Calista, at their next meeting after the seduction,

> Call'd ev'ry saint and blessed angel down,
> To witness for her that she was my wife.

Thus, "Heav'n, who knows our weak imperfect natures, / How blind with passions, and how prone to evil," would not make "too strict inquiry" for her "offence" with Lothario (though the pollution of her marriage is a different story). On the other hand, by the time of her meeting with him in Act IV, Calista is fully aware of Lothario's intentions, as is the audience, which has heard him gloat to Rossano and tease and toy with Lucilla. So Calista would have no excuse for falling again. Yet, as she has admitted to Lucilla, she still loves him. This moment is the trial, as Rowe has said so often before, the climax of Calista's war of passions, indignation, love, and shame. And she passes the test. In words that recall and reinforce her earlier talk of retiring to a "cloister," she meets Lothario with resignation and the kind of "Adder's wisdom" Samson learned:

> Seek not to sooth me with thy false endearments,
> To charm me with thy softness: 'tis in vain;
> Thou canst no more betray, nor I be ruin'd.
> The hours of folly, and of fond delight,
> Are wasted all and fled; those that remain
> Are doom'd to weeping, anguish, and repentance. (p. 189)

She shuts her ears to his sensual reminiscing on their sin, bidding "That guilty night" be concealed forever since it gave her up to "shame" and "sorrow" (p. 189 f). Lothario's specious arguments that they continue their affair in adultery Calista meets with indignation and disdain. Though for a moment she thinks how happy she might have been with him, she finally and fully sees him for what he is—a libertine rake—and out of this awareness, not merely out of indignation, she makes her final rejection:

> But wherefore nam'd I happiness with thee?
> It is for thee, for thee, that I am curst;

For thee, my secret soul each hour arraigns me,
Calls me to answer for my virtue stain'd,
My honour lost to thee; for thee it haunts me,
With stern *Sciolto* vowing vengeance on me;
With *Altamont* complaining for his wrongs. (p. 190 f)[16]

While by no means a complete conversion to repentance, Calista's
rejection does seem to open the way for grace (if she will only accept it).
In the subsequent "combat" which Lothario calls on "Earth, Heav'n,
and fair *Calista*" to judge, Altamont must be seen as the champion of
the cause of men, God, and Calista's soul. His role as a kind of champion
is underlined when Lothario says, "thy genius is the stronger" (p. 191),
for Rowe has weighted the word "genius" with angelic connotations.
Altamont's defeat of Lothario, then, not only represents the just punishment of the libertine but also suggests a providential approbation of
Calista's resistance to her tempter. And yet, because she has, against the
warnings of her good genii, stubbornly insisted on seeing Lothario
again, she pays a terrible price for her triumph: her lover is killed and
the ruin of her "Name," her "Family," and her "Estate" has begun.

iii

The shock of Lothario's death and of her exposure impels the proud
Calista not to contrition but to despair. She cannot bear to have her
"shame" revealed or to be "forgiv'n," "Daily to be reproach'd" or "to
be outdone" by Altamont's virtue (p. 191 ff). So she first tries in vain to
kill herself, then longs for a "grave beneath," to be "sunk to the bottom
low" (p. 192). When her outraged father learns the truth, Calista, completely mortified, begs him for the "mercy" of death (p. 193). Such a
plea is ironic, because Calista should be asking for mercy, but not that
of a summary execution. Once again, as in Rowe's other tragedies—and
Christian tragedies in general—the conflict is ultimately between trust in
Providence and despair. The depth of Calista's despair is indicated by
her desire to "curse / The chearful day, men, earth, and heaven," and
even Sciolto "For being author of a wretch" like her—a desire reminiscent of and as spiritually deadly as the temptation of Job to "curse God,
and die" (2:9). Again in her spite and self-pity Calista vows to "fly" to a
"dismal" and desperate retreat. Yet again her description of the retreat
is ambiguous, since it also depicts a penitential sequestration. She talks
of "Fasting, and tears, and hardship" without "light" or "food" or
"comfort" (p. 194). Though she is describing a suicidal despair and is

spitefully taunting Sciolto, still she declares that before her death Sciolto will see,

> At length her tears have wash'd her stains away,
> At length 'tis time her punishment should cease.

The implication of her equivocal words, then, is that her soul is torn between contrition and chagrin, and the question the play now asks, from the moment of Lothario's death, is whether Calista will die, like Lothario, indignantly recalcitrant. Her indignation is, of course, both her greatest virtue and her greatest vice, and Rowe's successful portrayal of it is what makes her the finest character he ever drew. From beginning to end Calista is magnificent in her indignant response to everything from false lovers to would-be monitors to tyrannic husbands and fathers to pedant "gownmen" (V, p. 200). The tragedy is that such a great spirit has been derailed, and the audience anxiously attends her end: whether indignation will lead ultimately to salvation or damnation; whether such a spirit can ever bear to be "forgiv'n." This is Calista's final trial.

With only a few recent exceptions, critics have long maintained that the title of this play is a misnomer, that Calista is not "penitent" at all.[17] They argue that she completely rejects penitence in Act V. In his very fine article "The Tradition of the Formal Meditation in Rowe's *The Fair Penitent*," however, Lindley Wyman has shown us that the opening of the act is not "melodramatic," as most critics insist, but that the trappings of the scene—especially the skull and the book[18]—are traditional devices for provoking a meditation on death that leads to penitence. Wyman points out that Calista's rejection of the artificial penitential book (and, I might add, of the "pageantry" and "farce" of the skull and bones) is not a rejection of penitence but a measure of the depth of remorse which Calista feels, a depth beyond that which such a book can reach (p. 416): as Calista says,

> I have more real anguish in my heart,
> Than all their pedant discipline e'er knew. (p. 201)

Calista has not yet turned remorse into repentance, however. She is still on the brink of despair, as the act's opening song attests, with its phantasmagorical rendition of a demonic temptation to suicide (similar to that endured by Aribert in *The Royal Convert*). Indignation, love, and

shame still divide her soul: her persistent ambivalence toward Lothario
is reflected in the epithet "dear perfidious" (p. 202),[19] and she meets
Sciolto's "fatal indignation" by mustering her own haughty spirit.
When he asks if she has "dar'd to meditate on death" and "consider'd
what may happen after it"—how her "account may stand, and what to
answer"—Calista responds that she has "turn'd" her "eyes inward" and
has found such "foul offence" that she longs for death as "the end of
shame and sorrow" and as a "place of rest."[20] Thus her shame, like Samson's at first, tends to self-loathing, a course of action, according to Milton, which is diametrically opposed to Christian patience and righteousness (see SA 503n). In one of the play's (and Rowe's) most poignant
passages, Calista says in her despair,

> Death is the privilege of human nature,
> And life without it were not worth our taking;
> Thither the poor, the pris'ner, and the mourner,
> Fly for relief, and lay their burdens down. (p. 203)

As we have seen before in this study, according to the Christian vision,
death is indeed rest—for the just. What is lacking in Calista's attitude
is again couched in her very words, in the faint echo of that famous description of the Christian's proper refuge from suffering and sin: "Come
unto me, all ye that labour and are heavy laden, and I will give you rest"
(Mat. 11:28). Calista must learn to look not simply to death but to
Heaven for "relief."

What finally begins to overcome Calista's desperation is her father's "pity and forgiveness," which reduce her to tears at his feet and
charm her,

> More than if angels tun'd their golden viols,
> And sung a requiem to my parting soul.

The simile is significant, because an angelic requiem to her parting soul
depends precisely upon the "pity and forgiveness" she must contritely
seek from both her earthly and heavenly fathers. Yet even when she
does consider how her "account may stand" with Heaven, her contrition
is marred by her indignation at stern man, who, unlike Heaven, cannot
be appeased with "penitence and pray'r" (p. 204), that "Cheap recompence" which "here" would "not be receiv'd," for here,

> Nothing but blood can make the expiation,
> And cleanse the soul from inbred, deep pollution.

She looks up and painfully sees Altamont, "another injur'd wretch" who she thinks has come "To call for justice." The precise point of the scene —and ultimately of the play—is that he has not, and it is his "gentler virtue" (p. 205)—his merciful forgiveness—that finally vanquishes Calista's pride.

According to Charles H. Peake, the purpose of Calista's speech on Heaven's understanding of human weakness is "to contrast what she believes is God's justice with that of men, and in so doing, to point to the great injustice in the double standard of morality" (p. 209). Indeed, throughout the play the plucky Calista has inveighed against man's tyranny over woman, especially in her fine soliloquy, "How hard is the condition of our sex," in which she pictures the tyranny of the husband succeeding to the tyranny of the father (III, p. 179). In the light of her enforced marriage, Calista's resentment is somewhat justified (although she does admit that no amount of forcing could have made her marry Altamont). Moreover, Sciolto is portrayed as a tyrant of strict justice toward his daughter. When Horatio thinks of showing Calista's lost letter to Sciolto, he hesitates, commenting, "It follows that his justice dooms her dead" (I, p. 166). Calista's soliloquy just mentioned is a reaction to Sciolto's vindictive threat to deny his "fond" parent's love if she "E'er stain" her "honour" (III, p. 179) and to cast her off,

> as one whose impious hands
> Had rent asunder Nature's nearest ties,
> Which once divided never join again.

In the face of such a threat, it is no wonder that Calista would want to conceal her sin. After it is discovered and Lothario slain, she confuses her father's voice with the vindictive "voice of thunder" (IV, p. 192). Although Bonamy Dobrée considers this comparison bathetic (*Restoration Tragedy*, p. 156), it is, on the contrary, psychologically, artistically —and theologically—appropriate. As Adams and Peake show throughout their studies (and as we have seen throughout this study), such thunder was considered in both theater and *theatrum mundi* a sign of divine justice. The confusion of her father's voice with divine thunder implies that Calista's guilty conscience fears not only her father's but also God's retribution. Furthermore, Sciolto has in the opening scene already been characterized as a heavenly agent (his "bounty" is Heaven's "proxy") and a Creator-like figure. In a play in which the story of the Fall is an informing metaphor, Sciolto's voice is perhaps supposed to faintly remind us of God's calling for Adam and Eve while they vainly try to hide (Gen. 3:8 ff), as Calista has tried to do.

Sciolto's immediate reaction to Calista's sin is the "rash revenge" of killing her (p. 193), and even when Altamont restrains him from that "crime," he vows still to "have justice done": he warns Calista,

> Hope not to bear away thy crimes unpunish'd,
> I will see justice executed on thee,
> Ev'n to a *Roman* strictness; and thou, nature,
> Or whatsoe'er thou art that plead'st within me,
> Be still, thy tender strugglings are in vain.

After he banishes her to "some dark cell" where "death and hell detested rule maintain," he exclaims to Altamont, "Oh damn her! damn her!" (p. 195). He has assumed the role of a vindictive deity dooming his offenders to hell, and he rushes out of those gates he had opened even to his enemies to "sacrifice to justice" Lothario's entire "race" in the name of his and Altamont's vengeance. His vindictiveness brings Sciolto to Calista in Act V, where he maintains that her honesty is "a gem long lost, / Beyond redemption gone" (p. 202) and praises her prideful desire to die as

> worthy of that spirit
> That dwelt in ancient *Latian* breasts, when *Rome*
> Was mistress of the world.

Finally, the "stubborn virtue" of his "*Roman* strictness" prevails over a father's tenderness, and after hesitating while "Thrice justice urg'd" it, he now presents her with a dagger. Though he allows himself a moment to subdue the "rigid judge" and indulge his tenderness, still he concludes that she "must die," and he bids his last farewell (p. 203 f).

It is this strict justice that Calista contrasts to Heaven's and thus she expects nothing from Altamont but "upbraiding." Altamont answers her, however, "Falsly, falsly / Dost thou accuse me," for he does not now come "To call for justice" but to forgive. His first response to Calista's sin has indeed been revenge, for he attacks Lothario, saying, "vengeance is the only good is left" (IV, p. 191), though he is acting in the role of something like a heavenly Champion. Howbeit, immediately afterwards he restrains Sciolto from the "crime" of "rash revenge" and declares that his own soul now "kindles not with anger or revenge" (p. 195). Instead, he eschews "the temper of *Italian* husbands" and (in sharp contrast to Sciolto and Massinger's Charalois) accepts his "infamy with patience, / As holy men do punishments from Heav'n" (V, p. 204). Juxtaposed to vengeance and vindictive human justice, then—to a *"Roman"* (or even Old Testament) "strictness"—are the Christian virtues of mercy and forgiveness, and the play represents on one level the transmutation of the Old Law into the New, where man learns to patiently leave vengeance to Heaven and, in emulation of Heaven, to temper his justice with mercy. Calista has not sinned "Beyond redemption."

The theme of mercy is introduced in the opening scene of the play, when Horatio describes, in a passage reminiscent of Rowe's *Tamerlane*, how Altamont redeemed his father's body from the "hard creditors" and "sentence of the cruel law" by selling himself

> to slaves who ne'er knew mercy,
> Sour, unrelenting money-loving villains,
> Who laugh at human nature and forgiveness,
> And are like fiends the factors of destruction. (I, p. 159)

But Sciolto's "bounty" toward Altamont which redeems him from his father's debts is the "proxy" for Heaven's own mercy. Rowe thus extracts the salient point of Massinger's first two acts—Rochfort's mercy in the face of demands for strict justice—and he makes explicit the providential nature of that mercy. Furthermore, mercy is the controlling motif for the subplot concerning Altamont's quarrel with Horatio, in which, ironically, Altamont defends Calista's false honor and banishes his true friend (after all, his name is Horatio). To Lavinia Horatio declares that the cause of the quarrel is

> such a sin to friendship, as Heav'n's mercy,
> That strives with man's untoward, monstrous wickedness,
> Unweary'd with forgiving, scarce could pardon. (III, p. 186)

The point is, of course, that Heaven "could" and would pardon it—or
any sin, no matter how heinous—provided that the sinner is contrite
and does not despair. Like Calista's speech in Act V, Horatio's speech
here emphasizes the disparity between human and divine mercy.
Heaven is "unweary'd with forgiving," while Horatio, as we see in Act
IV, is implacably unforgiving—at first. Considering himself ordinarily
"patient" (contrast his with Altamont's later "patience"!) and "willing
to forgive," Horatio maintains that too great an injury has been offered
him to relent (p. 197). But Lavinia reminds him of their need to emulate
Heaven's mercy toward them in their recent escape from Lothario's
friends:

> Oh, let us bless the mercy that preserv'd us,
> That gracious pow'r that sav'd us for each other;
> And, to adorn the sacrifice of praise,
> Offer forgiveness too; be thou like Heav'n,
> And put away th'offences of thy friend,
> Far, far from thy remembrance. (p. 196)

Lavinia's speech echoes a familiar theme from the Sermon on the
Mount: "Be ye therefore merciful, as your Father also is merciful"
(Luke 6:36). The echo further serves, in conjunction with similar echoes
of the same topos, to invoke the entire Sermon and its central doctrine
of mercy and forgiveness.

Horatio is slow to heed Lavinia's advice, however. When Altamont
confesses that he has "wrong'd" him and describes how "Heav'n has
well aveng'd it," Horatio considers it "weakness to be touch'd" (p. 197
f). Yet, while Altamont refuses to ask Horatio "To pity or forgive" and
instead applauds his attitude as "just" (p. 198), still he correctly brands
that attitude "insolence of hate," just as Lavinia has called it a "sullen
gloomy hate" (p. 197). To this "just" attitude Rowe contrasts Altamont's
own loving, forgiving spirit, his "yielding softness" which would forgive
Horatio for a similar offense. Only after Altamont collapses from the
"blows" first Calista and now Horatio (not to mention Lothario) have
dealt him does Horatio respond to Lavinia's constant appeal and finally
forgive Altamont. Reciprocally, Horatio begs forgiveness of the other
two for his "stubborn, unrelenting heart" and offers to "bear" Altamont's "sorrows" himself (p. 199). In his recovery, Altamont almost
seems to have returned from the dead ("I thought that nothing could
have stay'd my soul, / That long ere this her flight had reach'd the

stars"), in order that he might "set all right" with his friend—the kind of squaring of accounts Jesus talks about in the Sermon on the Mount (Matt. 5:23 f)—and, with Horatio's and "Heav'n's forgiveness" on his "soul," die in peace and "be at ease for ever." It is as though the friend's forgiveness is the earthly sign (or *proxy*) of Heaven's, for Altamont had not mentioned Heaven's forgiveness until Horatio forgave him. Thus the pathos of this scene is not a merely gratuitous evocation of the emotions of the audience (such an evocation may well not succeed, especially with our modern "sensibilities") but a functional element of the drama itself, as in many so-called "pathetic" tragedies. For, as Dryden says, pity is "the noblest and most god-like of moral virtues" (*Essays*, I, 245); as Lucilla says in this play, "pity" distinguishes "manhood" from "the brutes" (I, p. 163); and such tragedies as those of Dryden and Otway and Rowe, particularly *All for Love, Venice Preserved,* and the "she-tragedies," attempt to show the conquest of such men as Antony, Priuli, and Horatio by this chief virtue of Christianity, without which all the rest, however heroic, are as tinkling cymbals.

Rowe develops the theme of mercy in the subplot thus to underscore its importance in the main. At the first sign of Altamont's mercy toward her—when he prevents her suicide and admits that despite her sin he still loves her—Calista exclaims in chagrin, "Think'st thou I mean to live? to be forgiv'n?" (IV, p. 192). Even when he defends her from her father's wrath, she refuses to be "indebted" to his "pity" or "oblig'd" to his "virtue" (p. 193). Finally in Act V, Altamont actually goes so far as to "mourn" with her for her "loss" in Lothario, accepting the fact that "fate" had not made her his (p. 204). Calista's pride and indignation are at last overwhelmed, her humiliation turned to humility:

> Oh, *Altamont!* 'tis hard for souls like mine,
> Haughty and fierce, to yield they've done amiss;
> But oh! behold my proud, disdainful heart,
> Bends to thy gentler virtue. (p. 205)

She *has* lived to be forgiven after all, for now, as her heart is "bent" toward Altamont's "gentler virtue" of mercy, she seems to gain what the "Homily of Repentance" calls "contrition of the heart" (p. 342). She finally comes to see, furthermore, that "Such are the graces that adorn" Altamont that she might have been "blest" with him and "died in peace"; in other words, that where she found only "destruction" with the gay Lothario, with the not so gay but virtuous Altamont she would have found happiness and peace of mind, such as this world can afford.

Altamont believes that they could still be happy together, but the consequences of Calista's compounding and concealing of her sin are not yet over. Sciolto having received the mortal wound "he seem'd to wish for" in his despair (p. 206), Calista backslides and in a similarly desperate and "fatal rashness" stabs herself. Altamont is prevented from following suit by Horatio, who exclaims,

> Some foe to man,
> Has breath'd on ev'ry breast contagious fury,
> And epidemic madness.

Whether "foe to man" refers specifically to Satan or obliquely to the satanic Lothario, certainly the presence of evil in the world and in human nature has been manifested to a horrifying degree. Yet it seems that Altamont's victory over Calista has not been in vain, for she humbly and penitently begs Sciolto to "forgive" and "bless" her before she dies. No longer the "rigid judge," Sciolto has finally, and at great cost, learned to dispense to his own daughter the mercy he had earlier shown Altamont and to view human imperfection as Heaven does. At last he judges Calista equitably in the light of the human trial and her performance within it:

> Thou hast rashly ventur'd in a stormy sea,
> Where life, fame, virtue, all were wreck'd and lost;
> But sure thou'st borne thy part in all the anguish,
> And smarted with the pain; then rest in peace,
> . . . .
> And may'st thou find with Heav'n the same forgiveness,
> As with thy father here.—Die, and be happy.

Calista's anguish, then, has been her expiation, and she is released from her trial. Charmed with these "Celestial sounds" (as if it were her "father" *there*—in heaven—speaking), Calista's "soul" at last attains "Peace," and she dies praying, "Mercy, Heav'n!" (p. 207). Ever since Lavinia's comparison of the distraught Horatio to a "sick man" lifting up his "hands and eyes for mercy" as he "thinks upon his audit" (I, p. 167), such a prayer has been the standard in the play for the proper

Christian *ars moriendi*, a standard which Calista, who has "dar'd to meditate on death" and upon her "account," has finally met "when the trial comes" (p. 202).

As if to assure us that Calista will "find with Heav'n the same forgiveness" as Sciolto grants, Rowe has Altamont say,

> Hadst thou a thousand faults,
> What heart so hard, what virtue so severe,
> But at that beauty must of force relented,
> Melted to pity, love, and to forgiveness.

Furthermore, in a speech that recalls the opening scene of the play and Sciolto's role as Heaven's agent in rewarding Altamont's "piety," the dying Sciolto prays to "gracious Heav'n," which has "endless blessings still in store, / For virtue, and for filial piety," to "multiply" Its "mercies" on Altamont. Whether the failing Altamont will receive these "mercies" on earth is irrelevant, for the lesson of the scene is, as it has been throughout the play—and throughout Rowe's tragedies—trust in Providence.

In *The Fair Penitent*, then, human forgiveness is both imitative and emblematic of the mercy promised by Providence to all repentant sinners. Rowe seems to be saying that in a world where the Fall is being continually reconfirmed, sinful man must place his trust in divine mercy and must attempt to emulate that mercy in his dealings with his fellow sinners: to paraphrase Lavinia, "Let us bless the mercy that preserves us, and to adorn the sacrifice of praise, offer forgiveness too; let us be like Heav'n." Such human mercy, as in Horatio's forgiveness of Altamont, Altamont's forgiveness of Calista, and especially Sciolto's dying words to Calista, becomes a sign of divine mercy. And Calista's final plea, "Mercy, Heav'n," becomes at once a mark of her complete repentance and of its efficacy. Calamitous as the ending of the play is, the final note is one of hope and reconciliation. Calista's atonement—that is, etymologically, her *at-onement* with her father and her husband—signifies her *at-onement* with God, by virtue of *the* Atonement, which Altamont's love and spirit of self-sacrifice recall. For the one thing that does achieve perfection amidst all the imperfections of the fallen world of the play is Altamont's love, rooted in Christian *charitas* and reminiscent of Christ's sacrifice to appease the vindictive wrath of the Old Testament Jehovah: interposing between Sciolto and Calista, Altamont proclaims,

Stay thee, *Sciolto*, thou rash father, stay,
Or turn the point on me, and thro' my breast
Cut out the bloody passage to *Calista*;
So shall my love be perfect, while for her
I die, for whom alone I wish'd to live. (IV, p. 192)

Altamont's meekness, so long the butt of criticism, is really that of
Christ, and it is the leaven of his forgiveness that raises Calista's soul to
humility and mediates her way from the "dark abode" of despair and
hell to the "Celestial sounds" and "Peace" of the "Heav'n" upon which
she finally calls (V, p. 206 f). Significantly, the "last dear object" of
Calista's eyes as she sighs her soul toward heaven is the Christ-like Altamont, of whom she begs "pity" (p. 207).

Thus, like *Tamerlane*, by means of the typological imagery that
runs throughout—from the story of the Fall, to the good and bad genii,
to Sciolto's Jehovah-like wrath, to Altamont's Christ-like love—*The Fair
Penitent* reaches back through the traditions of Renaissance drama to its
roots in medieval drama. Like his predecessors Marlowe, Shakespeare,
Milton, and Otway, Rowe has transferred the portrayal of the trial of
the sinner from allegory and religious ritual to psychologically realistic,
if still richly emblematic, drama. And his heroine—unlike Faustus, Macbeth, Satan, Acasto's children, or her own Lothario, and very much like
Adam and Eve and Samson—finally eschews despair and avails herself of
the means of grace, provided by a God Whose care for His lost sheep,
according to the vision that informs the play, tempers His justice with
mercy.

iv

The Fair Penitent is Rowe's most popular play today (witness the criticism) not because its allusions and typological imagery work so well and
not because its language is his best—that of *Jane Shore* is better—but,
I suspect, because its conflict and characters are the most engaging. Not
that the language is bad. Rowe has his usual lapses in "softer" dialogue
(between Horatio, Lavinia, and Altamont), but Calista's soliloquies in
Acts III and V are excellent, not only in their powerful expression of
the double standard but in the quality of the lines themselves. Let us
examine them closely:

How hard is the condition of our sex,
Thro' ev'ry state of life the slaves of man?

In all the dear delightful days of youth,
A rigid father dictates to our wills,
And deals out pleasure with a scanty hand:
To his, the tyrant husband's reign succeeds;
Proud with opinion of superior reason,
He holds domestic bus'ness and devotion
All we are capable to know, and shuts us,
Like cloister'd idiots, from the world's acquaintance,
And all the joys of freedom. Wherefore are we
Born with high souls, but to assert ourselves,
Shake off this vile obedience they exact,
And claim an equal empire o'er the world? (p. 179)

Now think, thou curst *Calista*, now behold
The desolation, horror, blood and ruin,
Thy crimes and fatal folly spread around,
That loudly cry for vengeance on thy head;
Yet Heav'n, who knows our weak imperfect natures,
How blind with passions, and how prone to evil,
Makes not too strict inquiry for offences,
But is aton'd by penitence and pray'r;
Cheap recompence! here 'twould not be receiv'd,
Nothing but blood can make the expiation,
And cleanse the soul from inbred, deep pollution. (p. 204)

The alliteration of *d*'s in the opening of the first speech is a perfect vehicle for Calista's exploding indignation at the tyranny of fathers, an
indignation that continues to explode in the alliteration of *p*'s, emphasized by the initial trochee, as the tyranny of the husband is introduced
("Proud with opinion of superior reason"). The explosion culminates in
the wonderfully indignant phrase "cloister'd idiots." Finally, the passage concludes very strongly with its masculine endings and two stressed
initial words, "Born" and "Shake," the first of which is enjambed. And
Calista's imperious temper is reflected in her very choice of metaphor
(however justified it may be). She speaks as haughtily as Rowe's Artemisa and Rodogune, yet here Rowe controls the rhetoric, as he does in
Ulysses.

In the second speech Rowe uses rhythms and sound effects well to
signify Calista's three moods. The masculine endings and the alliteration of *k* sounds suggest her wrath and self-loathing in the first four

lines. But Rowe softens the next four with three feminine endings, alliteration of *h* and *w* sounds, assonance of *oo* sounds, and easy elisions, all of which seem to mute the continuing plosives and bring us to rest calmly on the phrase, "penitence and pray'r." The lulling effect of the lines is then immediately shattered by the sudden spondees of the next line and by the initial trochee and unmitigated plosives of the next two. Of course, as in almost any passage of poetry, it is the sense which finally tells us how to read the lines, but I think in both these passages Rowe has provided the necessary equipment to make them effective vehicles of powerful expression.

There are other good speeches in the play, but most of them are in dialogue, which is difficult to discuss apart from character. The conflict of this play works so well, I think, not only because Rowe has excellently portrayed Calista's great spirit in travail but because he has structured the play in a series of dynamic encounters whose dialogue is crisp, lively, often powerful, and always perfectly in character. The first encounter is between Lothario and Lucilla, when the libertine's insouciance and insolence are beautifully displayed in his mockery of the pious servant, whom he sees as a treat for a "keeping cardinal" (I, p. 164), and of her undone mistress, whom he perversely calls "the fair inconstant."

The second important encounter is that between the jubilant and probably somewhat inebriated Altamont and the cold, disdainful Calista, who answers his amorous entreaties and jocund overtures with a wintry blast:

> Some sullen influence, a foe to both,
> Has wrought this fatal marriage to undo us. (II.i, p. 171)

One must imagine the looks on their faces as Sciolto exuberantly takes one in each arm and caresses them, as the song of unrequited love is sung, and as Horatio stares across at Calista (p. 172). It is a fine piece of stagecraft.

The third encounter is between Horatio and Lothario, when the brave but unsophisticated warrior is pitted against the brazen cavalier rake. Lothario's flouting of Horatio's warnings and flaunting of his triumph over Calista provoke Horatio into this excellent invective against libertines:

> A skipping, dancing, worthless tribe you are,
> Fit only for yourselves: You herd together;

And when the circling glass warms your vain hearts,
You talk of beauties that you never saw,
And fancy raptures that you never knew. (II.ii, p. 175)

With apparent assuredness, he concludes,

Rather than make you blest, they would die virgins,
And stop the propagation of mankind. (p. 176)

Horatio's indignation is thus well portrayed and articulated—as well as
his naivety, we might at first be tempted to say, for, of course, he is
wrong. But Rowe has created Horatio more complex than a tragic
braggart-soldier. Even while he denies to Lothario the possibility that
Calista has fallen, we know he is plagued within, for earlier his own
"heart forebodes it must be true" (II.i, p. 173). He is merely defending
the honor of his friend, to the point of dying for it if necessary. The verbal duel ends with dialogue which epitomizes the thematic and stylistic
essence of the scene: Horatio enjoins Lothario from the garden upon the
threat of death,

Or something worse; an injur'd husband's vengeance
Shall print a thousand wounds, tear thy fine form,
And scatter thee to all the winds of Heav'n. (II.ii, p. 177)

In other words, Horatio's arm will deliver that "vengeance" upon the
fashionable, courtly figure cut by this impudent Don Juan—who taunt-
ingly retorts,

Is then my way in *Genoa* prescrib'd,
By a dependent on the wretched *Altamont*,
A talking Sir, that brawls for him in taverns,
And vouches for his valor's reputation?

This is dialogue perfectly in character—and vice versa.

The fourth encounter is the best in the play, that between Horatio
and Calista. Again Horatio's lack of sophistication betrays him, and his
bumbling "gracious words" (III, p. 179) soon give way to the roughest
plain-dealing. For Calista simply destroys him. Instead of falling on her
knees in contrition as he had expected, she calls him "spy," "parasite,"
and "ruffian" (p. 180 f), and she decries his "ambiguous shuffling phrase"

(p. 181). In his last attempt to be diplomatic, Horatio sincerely but almost comically compares himself to a husband who risks his life to save his "tender wife" and "little fondlings" from a burning house. Calista's response is a scathing rebuke not only to Horatio's accusations but to his ineptness:

> Is this! is this the famous friend of *Altamont*,
> For noble worth, and deeds of arms renown'd?
> Is this! this tale-bearing, officious fellow,
> That watches for intelligence from eyes;
> This wretched *Argus* of a jealous husband,
> That fills his easy ears with monstrous tales,
> And makes him toss, and rave, and wreak at length
> Bloody revenge on his defenceless wife;
> Who guiltless dies, because her fool ran mad?

After this speech, the tearing of the letter is simply the coup de grace and the verbal dissection of Altamont ("Go fawn upon him," p. 183) nearly anticlimactic.

The climactic encounter of the play is that between Lothario and Calista. Throughout, Lothario is smooth and seductive as he tries to kindle her passion anew, and he is brilliantly impudent in his mock complaint to heaven:

> She calls me false, ev'n she, the faithless she,
> Who day and night, whom Heav'n and earth have heard
> Sighing to vow, and tenderly protest,
> Ten thousand times, she would be only mine,
> And yet behold, she has giv'n herself away,
> Fled from my arms, and wedded to another,
> Ev'n to the man whom most I hate on earth. (IV, p. 190)

And Calista answers his mockery and his loose and easy temptation to adultery in perfect character:

> How didst thou dare to think that I would live
> A slave to base desires, and brutal pleasures,
> To be a wretched wanton for thy leisure,
> To toy, and waste an hour of idle time with?
> My soul disdains thee for so mean a thought.

Even Lothario must retreat from this powerful squelch of the greatest of male tyrants in the play—one who threatens to make her a far greater slave than either father or husband.

The last major encounter of the play really extends over the remainder of Act IV and throughout Act V. It is the encounter among Calista, Sciolto, and Altamont: the avenger and the forgiver on either side of the distraught sinner who defiantly rails at both of them and thrice tries desperately to kill herself or be killed before she finally succeeds. Rowe sustains the quality of dialogue till the end, as she disdains to be forgiven by the one or to be a "triumph" for the other (IV, p. 193). She not only violently rejects the trappings of penance but she dares the "ghosts, fantastic forms of night" to ascend and "match the present horror," the *real* horror of Lothario's corpse (V, p. 201). Even as she is nearly overcome by her father's forgiveness, she rouses herself to rail at his vindictive justice. She finally really yields only as her very life is ebbing. Rowe created no other character whose dialogue so perfectly expresses passion and greatness of soul. Neither did any other playwright of his time, not even Dryden.

The quality of the play, then, lies not only in Rowe's adept handling of theme and typological imagery but in his portrayal of profound psychological conflict mainly through the dialogue of a series of encounters which serve very well indeed to give us excellent, unforgettable characters—Calista and Lothario, at least, if not also Horatio.[21] The encounters between Horatio, Altamont, and Lavinia do not work as well, but they are still good by Restoration standards. The play as a whole—in coherence of structure, in patterns of imagery, in characterization, and in dialogue—surpasses even Otway's *Venice Preserved*, I think (where both language and coherence go awry after the third act), to become second only to Dryden's *All for Love* among the best of Restoration tragedy.

NOTES TO CHAPTER IV

1. *The Fatal Dowry*, ed. T. A. Dunn, V.ii.384 ff.
2. See the Dedication and the Prologue to *The Ambitious Stepmother*, in *Works*, I, 5, 7.
3. See, e.g., Malcolm Goldstein, ed., *The Fair Penitent*, by Nicholas Rowe, p. xx.
4. "Moral Vision in the Drama of Thomas Otway," ch. iv. Cf. John M. Wallace, "Dryden and History: A Problem in Allegorical Reading," p. 284.
5. IV.447 ff, in *The Works of Thomas Otway*, ed. J. C. Ghosh, II, 67.

6. Cf. *PL* IV.797 ff, especially these words of Ithuriel and Gabriel to Satan, who has been compared to a "Thief" (IV.192) and who is discovered in the dark corner of Adam and Eve's bower:

> Why satst thou like an enemy in wait
> Here watching at the head of these that sleep?
> . . . .
> Imploy'd it seems to violate sleep, and those
> Whose dwelling God hath planted here in bliss? (vss. 825 f, 883 f)

7. Cf. *PL* IV.962 ff:

> But mark what I arede thee now, avaunt;
> Fly thither whence thou fledd'st: if from this hour
> Within these hallow'd limits thou appear,
> Back to th'infernal pit I drag thee chain'd.

Following George Whiting's lead ("Rowe's Debt to *Paradise Lost*"), I have tried to show throughout this study that Rowe's themes and imagery are very similar to Milton's. As Whiting has shown, nowhere is Rowe's debt more explicit than in *Tamerlane*. Since *The Fair Penitent* was the next play he wrote, it should not be surprising to find Milton's influence still strong, if less explicit.

8. Most critics have wrenched this statement out of context, interpreting it to refer to Rowe's "domestic" characterization. On the contrary, Rowe is justifying his portrayal of "some frail vicious characters" by appealing to "Nature"—in this instance, human nature. Such an appeal is *not* "naturalism," as Frank Kearful asserts ("The Nature of Tragedy in Rowe's *The Fair Penitent*," p. 352).

9. The proverb "Be sure your sin will find you out" is found in Num. 32:23 and is echoed in Job 34:22; it also finds expression in the pagan writings of Theocritus, Cato, Seneca, etc. See *The Home Book of Proverbs, Maxims, and Familiar Phrases*, ed. Burton Stevenson, p. 2119. The more familiar proverb is "Murder will out," but in either variation it is a constant motif in Classical and English tragedy (and even comedy) of all kinds—revenge, domestic, problem, etc. The idea is explicit throughout Henry H. Adams, *English Domestic or, Homiletic Tragedy*, and Charles H. Peake, "Domestic Tragedy in Relation to Theology."

10. Peake concludes, "Rowe's *The Fair Penitent* is in harmony with the Addisonian view that the tragic world reflect the more subtilized conception of Providence, which virtually eliminates a particular Providence" (p. 210 f). But Rowe is merely doing what some of the better Christian tragedians—Shakespeare and Dryden in particular—often do. Peake himself admits that Catherine Trotter's *The Unhappy Penitent* (1701) is a dramatic failure precisely because "the guiding hand of Providence is made so obvious that all subtlety and all interest are lost, and the interpretation of every event is made painfully explicit" (p. 180). Trotter's *The Fatal Friendship* (1698) is a better play, Peake argues, because she "attempts to shape the action in such a way as to reveal the workings of Providence without destroying the illusion of actuality," whereas in her other play "the mystery and the subtlety in the action are gone" (p. 182). One can easily show by the same criteria (among others) what makes *The Fair Penitent* a better—but no less Christian—play than either by Trotter, and a play whose theme is no less emphatically trust in Divine Providence.

11. Dougald MacMillan and Howard Mumford Jones, eds., *Plays of the Restoration and Eighteenth Century*, gloss the phrase thus: "By the Romans a fortunate day was supposed to be marked by a white stone. The equivalent of our 'red-letter' day" (p. 454).

12. Like the epithets "faithless" and "faithful," the continual epithet "gracious," as in Lucilla's "gracious providence" above, takes on a more than secular connotation and reminds us of Calista's need for—and Heaven's promise of—grace.

13. See Kearful, "The Nature of Tragedy," p. 353 f. Johnson's criticism is expressed in "The Life of Nicholas Rowe," in Rowe, *Works*, I, 3*. (The pagination being separate but not Roman, I distinguish it with an asterisk.)

14. Landon C. Burns, Jr., "The Tragedies of Nicholas Rowe," p. 109 f, further maintains that Lothario is more attractive than Altamont because we must sympathize with Calista's initial choice between them. There is some merit to this opinion, but we must remember that Calista *is* wrong and that Sciolto *is* right in the choice.

15. See Donald B. Clark, "An Eighteenth-Century Adaptation of Massinger," p. 243 ff, for a comparison between Don John and Lothario.

16. The play is, in short, like so much of the better Restoration drama—comedy as well as tragedy—antilibertine. Nowhere is this theme more powerfully enunciated than in Horatio's brilliant invective against the "false ones" in this world whose only "Heav'n" is "variety"—a heaven that turns out to be hellish bestiality:

> One lover to another still succeeds,
> Another, and another after that,
> And the last fool is welcome as the former:
> 'Till having lov'd his hour out, he gives place,
> And mingles with the herd that went before him. (I, p. 168)

17. The most recent of these interpretations was given in a paper by Annibel Jenkins, "Patience and Penitence: Love and Innocence in Dante, Rowe, and Goethe," delivered in the Comparative Literature section of the thirty-eighth annual meeting of the South Atlantic MLA in Jacksonville, Fla., November 1968. Jenkins maintains that, like Dante's Francesca and unlike Goethe's Marguerite, Rowe's Calista is unrepentant and thus an eternal martyr to secular love. See *The South Atlantic Bulletin*, 36, 9, for a précis. Cf. Goldstein, ed., *The Fair Penitent*, p. xviii f, who considers Calista's suicide the measure of her "self-loathing" and mentions no further development in the progress of her soul. Kearful, p. 360, refers to Calista's repentance as "presumed" (that is, in the title of the play) but never explicit. Astonishingly, Eugene Waith, *Ideas of Greatness*, says that "luxuriant grief" is "the sole and particular theme of the fifth act" (p. 274).

18. Donald B. Clark, "Nicholas Rowe," p. 113, notes a general similarity between Rowe's play and Edward Ravenscroft's *The Italian Husband* (1697) and mentions that the heroine Alouisia, in a similar "charnel" scene, is discovered kneeling before a table with a book and a picture of Magdalene, but he does not comment on the obvious significance of such props.

19. Dryden has Dido apply the same epithet to Aeneas (*Aeneid*, IV.439, in *The Poems of John Dryden*, ed. James Kinsley, III, 1156), and since the epigraph to the play also concerns Dido—"Quin morere, ut merita es, ferroque averti dolorem" (p. 151; *Aen.* IV.547)—we are invited to see Calista's struggle in the light of Dido's, to identify that struggle as the temptation to suicidal despair, and to fear its outcome.

20. Cf. Shakespeare's Gertrude in *Hamlet*, in *The Complete Plays and Poems of William Shakespeare*, ed. W. A. Neilson and C. J. Hill:

> O Hamlet, speak no more!
> Thou turn'st mine eyes into my very soul,
> And there I see such black and grained spots
> As will not leave their tinct. (III.iv.88 ff)

21. I am obviously in total disagreement with Eugene Hnatko, "The Failure of Eighteenth-Century Tragedy," p. 466, when he calls the play "a 'tragedy' of one-dimensional figures who do not engage the modern audience at all. . . . All the characters working within the simple moral framework are stick-figures declaiming, mere plot necessities." The statements strike me as assertive and unempirical.

V   Protagonist as Penitent (with Resignation)

The Tragedy of Jane Shore

ane Shore was one of the most famous concubines in English history, and her story was recorded and reiterated from the Renaissance through the Restoration by chronicle, lyric, drama, and ballad.[1]° When Nicholas Rowe came to treat her story, although he was obviously familiar with many of its earlier treatments,[2] he evidently turned primarily to Heywood's homiletic history play, *Edward IV*,[3] as Donald B. Clark has argued ("Nicholas Rowe," p. 210 ff), for Heywood's is the only treatment besides Rowe's in which Jane dies in the arms of her forgiving husband. What Clark does not discuss, however, and what is most germane to Rowe's play, is that Heywood's *Edward IV*, especially the second part, is a study of Christian mercy and forgiveness, a variation on a theme from the Sermon on the Mount: "Blessed are the merciful, for they shall obtain mercy" (Mat. 5:7).

The mercy of Heywood's repentant Jane toward the poor and the afflicted ultimately obtains mercy and forgiveness for her, not only from those she has comforted, but from her jailer and even those most wronged, Edward's Queen and Matthew Shore. When Shore (disguised as Flood!) is about to be unjustly executed, the Reverend Doctor Shaw echoes, albeit in an *improper* spirit, the Sermon on the Mount: "Well, Flood, forgive the world, / As thou wilt have forgiveness from the heavens."[4] Shore accepts the advice in the *proper* spirit. He asks God's forgiveness, forgives the unmerciful King Edward, and prays thus for Jane: "God forgive thee, ev'n as I forgive; / And pray thou may'st repent while thou dost live." Later the reprieved Shore brings relief to Jane even at

°Notes to this chapter begin on page 177.

the expense of his own life, and she calls his relief "grace" sent "from God" (IV.iii, p. 175). At the moment of their death together, Shore again forgives her "as freely from my soul, / As at God's hands I hope to be forgiven" (V.ii, p. 188).

That Jane will indeed obtain mercy from God is strongly suggested not only by Heywood's allusions to the Mercy-Beatitude but also by the play's emphasis on trust in Providence and by the imagery of bread which is emblematic of that Providence. When Jane is abducted while trying to save the Dutch Captain Stranguidge and his crew (with Flood among them), who have unwittingly violated the recent truce with France, Stranguidge exclaims to his men,

> What remedy! the God of heav'n helps all.
> What say ye, mates? our hope of life is dash'd.
> Now none but God, let's put our trust in him,
> And ev'ry man repent him of his sin! (II.i, p. 129)

Soon thereafter, Heywood depicts Shore's "Christian patience, at the point of death" (II.iv, p. 141), and later he shows Edward's sons preparing themselves for sleep—and death as well—by meditating on the Psalms: Edward says to Richard, "Brother, see here what David says, and so say I: / Lord! in thee will I trust, although I die" (III.v, p. 159). Jane exhibits the same trust in Providence. When she hears of her punishment from Gloucester, she accepts it as a just retribution for her adultery, saying, "God's will be done!" (IV.i, p. 164). The earthly relief— or "grace"—which she receives and attributes to Providence (IV.iii, p. 176) appears emblematic of heavenly grace. Her jailer, Brackenbury, suggests the relationship between the two: when Jane in the depth of her penitence cries, "Let my heart's deep throbbing sighs be all my bread" (p. 171), he enters *with a prayer-book, and some relief in a cloth,*" and says,

> God comfort thee, good soul!
> First take that to relieve thy body with;
> And next receive this book, wherein is food,
> Manna of Heaven to refresh thy soul! (p. 172)

Jane responds,

> Welcome, sweet prayer-book, food of my life,
> The sov'reign balm for my sick conscience!

Thou shalt be my soul's pleasure and delight,
To wipe my sins out of Jehovah's sight.

Even though she dies, then, Jane has fed on the "bread of life" (John 6:35). The implication is that her sins are forgiven and that she has gained eternal salvation.

In the light of the themes of Rowe's other plays, particularly *The Fair Penitent*, it should not be surprising that Heywood's *Edward IV* appealed to him. In *The Tragedy of Jane Shore* (1714)⁵ he artfully adapts —and greatly improves—the second part, focusing on exactly the same central concern of trust in divine mercy and employing the same kind of Biblical language and Christian symbolism. Rowe's major change is that he provides Jane with a severe trial in which she proves her repentance, atones for her sins, and is reconciled to both her husband and her God.

i

Throughout *Jane Shore* Rowe presents us with a "poor penitent" (V, p. 184), whose demeanor is in sharp contrast with that of the merry mistress she was wont to be. She was "Once a bright star that held her place on high" (I.i, p. 141), when, as Richard says,

                              all was jollity,
Feasting and mirth, light wantonness and laughter,
Piping and playing, minstrelsy and masking;
'Till life fled from us like an idle dream,
A shew of mommery without a meaning.

But now the Epicurean "revel-rout is done," as Hastings reports to Richard:

She never sees the sun, but thro' her tears,
And wakes to sigh the live-long night away.

In her first scene, Jane enters the stage in "sad and sober cheer," for "grief besets her hard" (I.ii, p. 142). At the mention of Antwerp, whither her husband had fled when she deserted him for King Edward, she reveals her "shame" to her new servant, Dumont (who is Shore himself disguised):

> Alas! at *Antwerp!*—Oh forgive my tears!
> They fall for my offences—and must fall
> Long, long, ere they shall wash my stains away. (p. 143)

When Dumont pretends that Shore is dead, Jane wishes in her grief that she "had liv'd within his guiltless arms, / And dying slept in innocence beside him!" Her best friend Alicia enters at this moment and misinterprets Jane's tears as the signs of continued grief over Edward's death. She thinks Jane would like to make that "old Time come back" which gave her so many "golden" years of "happiness" (p. 144). While Jane cannot deny Edward's incomparable charm, which might have seduced even "Impassive spirits, and angelic natures," she vows before "Heav'n and his saints" that she wishes "no hour" back again, declares that Edward's magnificence was her "curse," and tells the flattering Alicia, "Name him no more: / He was the bane and ruin of my peace." Still, Alicia would have Jane resurrect her former "charms" to curry favor with Richard, but Jane insists that her "form" has "long forgot to please" and that "The scene of beauty and delight is chang'd" (p. 145). Ironically, her form has *not* ceased to please, and Alicia implies that her own lover Hastings is captive to its charms. Jane ingenuously denies the charge and insists again, in words which seem to purposefully echo Richard's earlier speech, that she has totally rejected her sinfully frivolous past:

> Too much of love thy hapless friend has prov'd,
> Too many giddy foolish hours are gone,
> And in fantastic measures danc'd away;
> May the remaining few know only friendship.

Besides depicting Jane as thoroughly repentant, Rowe mitigates her guilt. While Hastings speaks of her "wild escapes of lawless passion," in the next breath he softens them to "the long train of frailties flesh is heir to" (I.i, p. 142). King Edward is pictured as so irresistible that even angelic perfection would succumb to him "like yielding human weakness" (sc. ii, p. 144). In an impassioned speech, "Why should I think that man will do for me," Jane also exposes the "partial justice" of the double standard by which she is judged (p. 146 f). While Jane's attitude is partly a petulance similar to Calista's in *The Fair Penitent* and while she, like Calista, is ultimately proved wrong about the implacability of *all* men, still her attack on masculine libertinism and its double standard is justified, for it is proven true not only in her own "Ruin" (p. 147) but also in Alicia's. Finally, in Act V, describing his encounter with Jane when the "royal spoiler" took her away "in triumph" (p. 176), Shore tells of her "amazement," her "burning crimson" blushes, her "shriek heart-wounding," and her tears. Bellmour responds,

> Alas! for pity! Oh! those speaking tears!
> Could they be false? Did she not suffer with you?
> And tho' the King by force possess'd her person,
> Her unconsenting heart dwelt still with you?

Nearly all the previous treatments of Jane's story had described her marriage to Shore as enforced (by her parents), but Rowe here follows Heywood's lead, where the couple is happily married and Edward must resort to the threat of force (*Edward IV*, 1.V.i). This version provides an even greater extenuation for Jane's desertion (an enforced marriage being no excuse for willful adultery), though it by no means exonerates her for the years she remained at court.

As in Heywood's play, moreover, Jane has become famous for her deeds of mercy and for using her influence with the King to help the oppressed. Her charity is stressed throughout the play, and in the words of the authorized "Homily of Repentance," such "good fruits" are the signs of "amendment of life, or a new life" (*Certain Sermons or Homilies*, p. 346). Accordingly, Alicia maintains that all Jane's "gentle deeds of mercy" shall not be forgotten but that those she has helped "Shall cry to Heav'n, and pull a blessing" on her: "The Saints and Angels have thee in their charge, / And all things shall be well" (I.ii, p. 146). When at the end of the play Bellmour presents Shore to Jane as her "better angel" (V, p. 181), we know that Alicia's prophecy has been partially fulfilled in the man whom (as Dumont) she has charitably employed and who has subsequently defended her from rape and finally brought her sustenance and forgiveness.

Yet Alicia's prophecy is profoundly ironic, because Jane is to find all things well only in death, and throughout the rest of the play the depth of her contrition is to be sorely tried. When Hastings comes to take payment for his "service" of supposed mercy in Jane's behalf (II, p. 151), she beseeches him to look elsewhere and leave her alone with her "shame" (p. 152). Hastings' incredulity at "this peevish, this fantastic change" is completely understandable, his petulance appropriate, for he has been familiar with the merry mistress, who "us'd to dance for ever, / And cast a day of gladness all around." Impatiently, he advises her to wait for a deathbed repentance (a sinful presumption on the mercy of God, according to Christian morality), and when she resists his embraces, he attempts to rape her, his very language insinuating the sensuality and "transports of increasing passion" she has vowed to forget (I.ii, p. 146):

> Come let me press thee,
> Pant on thy bosom, sink into thy arms,
> And lose myself in the luxurious fold. (II, p. 153)

While Jane acknowledges her guilt and the justice of Hastings' railing, she resists him with all her strength and proves her contrition and purpose of amendment:

> Yet let the saints be witness to this truth,
> That now, tho' late, I look with horror back,
> That I detest my wretched self, and curse
> My past polluted life. All-judging Heav'n
> Who knows my crimes, has seen my sorrow for them. (p. 152)

She chooses to "die" rather than ever "know pollution more" (p. 153). It appears that "All-judging Heav'n" has indeed seen Jane's "sorrow" —and that Jane's "gentle deeds of mercy" have *not* been forgotten, that "Saints and Angels" *are* guarding her—for when in desperation she finally calls on "*grac*ious Heav'n" for help (italics mine), Dumont appears and vanquishes Hastings. The implication, as in similar scenes of Rowe, is that Dumont's arrival is providential and that the once inconstant Jane has been rewarded for the constancy of her repentance. Accordingly, Dumont asserts that "Heaven's guard" attends her "cause" (p. 155), and he exhorts her,

> O pursue,
> Pursue the sacred counsels of your soul,
> Which urge you on to virtue; let not danger,
> Nor the incumbring world, make faint your purpose.
> Assisting Angels shall conduct your steps,
> Bring you to bliss, and crown your end with peace.

Like Calista, Jane has been proved in a test of her greatest weakness and has opened the way for Heaven's grace.

Dumont goes on to promise Jane too much, however. He assures her that she can escape to "a little peaceful refuge"—the kind of false paradise we have seen so often in Rowe—where "No serpents climb" (p. 156; Dumont is being metaphoric, but the suggestion is the same) and where "Plenty, and ease, and peace of mind shall wait you, / And make your latter days of life most happy." Jane appropriately asks, "Can there be so much happiness in store?" (p. 155). The answer that the play offers is that there cannot (except that *paradise within*), for despite Jane's penitence and her charity, despite the various mitigations of her guilt, she must still expiate her sins and make full atonement. Rowe's treatment of Jane Shore is finally as tough-minded as Heywood's, where, as Henry H. Adams puts it, "the circumstances do not extenuate her fault, for stern Christian morality demands harsh punishment for adultery" (p. 91). As Bellmour says in the concluding moral of Rowe's play,

> No common vengeance waits upon these crimes;
> When such severe repentance could not save
> From want, from shame, and an untimely grave. (V, p. 185)

Heaven has saved Jane from further "pollution," but she still must suffer the "storms" (II, p. 155) of retribution. In poetic (implicitly providential) justice, Jane is undone by those "fatal beauties" (III, p. 157) which incited a king's love and which now incite desire in Hastings and envy in Alicia. Because she has unwittingly attracted Hastings, though she is saved from his lust, her guardian Dumont is seized by the outraged Hastings as a lesson to her "not to scorn" his "power" (III, p. 159), and Alicia's "jealousy" provides a "wile" to destroy her (p. 156 f). Despite all her protestations of "holy friendship" (I.ii, p. 146), she betrays Jane and delivers her into the hands of her enemies.

But those enemies are as mistaken in their estimation of Jane, and women in general, as is Hastings. Richard considers Jane one of those "mincing minions" whose "dainty gew-gaw forms dissolve at once" when abandoned by their keepers (III, p. 158). When he calls this "puling whining harlot" before him to use her influence on Hastings (IV, p. 163), he expects the inconstancy of a "paltry piece of stuff," "A moppet made of prettiness and pride" (p. 164). Instead he is met, as was Hastings, with the constancy and fortitude of a reformed woman. At obvious risk to her life she praises Hastings' defense of the Princes despite his assault on her, asks eternal mercy and reward for him, and exhorts him, as Dumont has exhorted her, to pursue virtue:

> Go on, pursue! Assert the sacred cause:
> Stand forth, thou proxy of all-ruling providence,
> And save the friendless infants from oppression. (p. 166)

Despite Richard's command that by her "monkey gambols" she make Hastings "yield obedience" to him, Jane stands firm and, with the "grace of speech" she disclaims, eloquently vows to "plead till death the cause of injur'd innocence" (p. 166 f). Richard threatens to make her as wretched as Job:[6]

> Ha! dost thou brave me, minion! dost thou know
> How vile, how very a wretch, my pow'r can make thee?
> That I can loose fear, distress, and famine,
> To hunt thy heels, like hell-hounds, thro' the world;
> That I can place thee in such abject state,
> As help shall never find thee, where repining,
> Thou shalt sit down, and gnaw the earth for anguish,
> Groan to the pitiless winds without return,
> Howl like the midnight wolf amidst the desart,
> And curse thy life in bitterness of misery? (p. 167)

Yet Jane dauntlessly chooses to be thus wretched rather than speak "injustice" or "wrong the orphan who has none to save him." As always, Rowe makes the metaphor of trial explicit. Richard replies, " 'Tis well— we'll try the temper of your heart." It is clear that Jane's trial has only begun and that no rural cottage, no false paradise, is in store for her. Richard banishes her to Job's "dunghill."

Jane endures her trial, however, and like Milton, Rowe employs these echoes of the Book of Job to emphasize that which enables her to do so—patient trust in Providence, Whose "help" *can* "find" her, even in the most abject state. But her trial is that not of the innocent but of the sinner, and her hope is for Heaven's ultimate mercy. She bows to Heaven's "most righteous judge," owning His "justice" in Richard's "hard decree"[7] and submitting to her chastisement in a spirit of atonement:

No longer then my ripe offences spare,
But what I merit let me learn to bear.
Yet since 'tis all my wretchedness can give,
For my past crimes my forfeit life receive;
No pity for my suff'ring here I crave,
And only hope forgiveness in the grave.

In the next act Bellmour describes Jane as accepting her cruel punishment and the crowd's derision "With the gentlest patience": "Submissive, sad, and lowly" her look, "Yet silent still she pass'd and unre-
pining," except when she raised her eyes to Heaven to "beg that mercy
man denied her here" (V, p. 174). As she enters the stage the afflicted
public penitent, Jane's words (in the best speech Rowe ever wrote) ex-
pound her patient acceptance of her punishment in the resounding
Biblical tones and imagery of the Book of Job and the Psalms:[8]

Yet, yet endure, nor murmur oh my soul,
For are not thy transgressions great and numberless?
Do they not cover thee like rising floods,
And press thee like a weight of waters down?
Does not the hand of righteousness afflict thee?
And who shall plead against it? Who shall say
To power Almighty, thou hast done enough?
Or bid his dreadful rod of vengeance, stay?
Wait then with patience, till the circling hours
Shall bring the time of thy appointed rest,
And lay thee down in death. (p. 177)

Jane's "temper" has been tried and her penitence proved. Her trust in
Providence is unshaken, even though Dumont's hopes for her are shattered and her own prayers for Hastings' triumph and earthly reward
unheeded. In her patient expectation of death, justice is satisfied, and
she turns to her friend, her husband, and her God for mercy.

ii

Just as in *The Fair Penitent*, the subplot in *Jane Shore* underscores the
major themes in the play. Like King Edward and Jane, Hastings and
Alicia are illicit lovers, who sin against God, against each other, and
against Jane. And they, like Jane, must make atonement. It is Hastings'
redeeming glory that he does, and Alicia's damning shame that she does

not. The opening description of Hastings presents us with a man of admirable qualities: "Religious rev'rence" towards "*Edward*'s royal memory," "honour, honesty, and faith" (I.i,p.140)—the qualities Rowe has continually opposed to the self-interest of Machiavellian-Hobbist statesmen. "And yet," says Richard,

> this tough impracticable heart
> Is govern'd by a dainty-finger'd girl;
> Such flaws are found in the most worthy natures.

Hastings' amorousness is indeed his tragic flaw, although Richard is thinking of the wrong "girl." For Hastings is one of those "lawless libertines" Jane inveighs against (I.ii, p. 147), another Lothario, who, as Rowe very capably draws him, can dismiss an old mistress (Alicia) in cool and cruel disdain and in the next moment pursue a new one (Jane) in hot lust. In so doing, however, Hastings incurs poetic—and providential—justice. Like Lothario, he has raised the scorn of a spirit as great as his. In Calista-like indignation (and in fine poetry), Alicia rails at him,

> You triumph! do! and with gigantic pride,
> Defy impending vengeance. Heav'n shall wink;
> No more his arm shall roll the dreadful thunder,
> Nor send his lightnings forth: No more his justice
> Shall visit the presuming sons of men,
> But perjury, like thine, shall dwell in safety. (II, p. 150)

Hastings responds in mockery that if he has "beyond atonement sinn'd," he hopes for any other "plague" than Alicia's tongue. Yet underneath the mockery lie the real threat of divine vengeance and the real need for atonement in this play. And Alicia, unwittingly fulfilling her furious vow of vengeance, becomes the instrument of that justice against this nobleman, who, as Dumont says later, "stains" his "honours" by his treatment of women (p. 154). Alicia's letter to Richard, though directed against Jane in hopes of having her removed, inadvertently and ironically causes Richard ultimately to condemn Hastings to a summary execution, and Hastings finally acknowledges the justice of his punishment:

> I see the hand of Heav'n is arm'd against me,
> And, in mysterious providence, decrees
> To punish me by thy mistaking hand. (IV, p. 172)

The scene between Hastings and Alicia before his death is fraught
with language and imagery which suggest the thematic significance of
their actions, a significance which finally becomes explicit. While Hastings is about the "business" of preparing himself for death (p. 170),
Alicia bursts in upon him and owns that she has destroyed him. Incredu-
lously he asks what he could have done "so beyond the reach of pardon,
/ That nothing but my life can make atonement." When she explains
the revengeful fraud, he contemns the "merciless, wild and unforgiving
fiend" of her "Accursed jealousy" (p. 170 f), and he calls the "mischief"
which has befallen them "Heav'ns just award" for her revenge on "innocence which never wrong'd" her (p. 171). The implicit theme of mercy
(as opposed to devilish revenge) now becomes explicit. Alicia kneels
before Hastings to beg forgiveness, and her plea moves him to an admission of his own guilt and to compassion and atonement:

> Here then exchange we mutually forgiveness,
> So may the guilt of all my broken vows,
> My perjuries to thee be all forgotten,
> As here my soul acquits thee of my death.

As he leaves, his last words are a prayer for Alicia and an attempt to protect Jane's "innocence" from any further harm (p. 173). Thus in his forgiveness and compassion Hastings seems to have successfully accomplished the "business" of preparing his soul for death, and perhaps he
has merited the grace to do so by his stout defense of his country and
its rightful King. In a way, Jane's prayers for him, at least for "signal
mercies" (IV, p. 166), have been answered. His forgiveness of Alicia
augurs heavenly forgiveness for himself, for as he has said earlier to
Richard, "Good Heav'n . . . renders mercy back for mercy" (I.i, p. 142).
Alicia profits neither by Hastings' example nor by his warning,
however. Her values are revealed in her first speeches, where she says
that women's "happiness" lies in "empire," that "beauty is their sov'-
reign good," and that they long to "reign" over even a "Monarch" (I.ii,
p. 144). Accordingly, as did Jane with King Edward, she has "abandon'd
. . . all" for Hastings (II, p. 149) and has consequently lost her "peace"
of mind (p. 147), for as Catesby puts it, "The dame has been too lavish
of her feast, / And fed him till he loaths" (I.i, p. 140). In brief, she has,
like so many women in Restoration drama, played the libertine's game
and been left a "wretched bankrupt" (II, p. 149). Now her plot to re-
cover Hastings has backfired, but instead of adopting his spirit of pa-

tience and repentance, she can think only of vengeance against Richard
and Jane. Eschewing New Testament mercy, she prays to the "great
avenger" to invoke the Old Testament *lex talionis* of "blood for blood"
against Richard (IV, p. 173), and piqued that Hastings' "last thoughts"
would turn to her "rival," she applies the same principle to her:

> Shall she be blest, and I be curst, for ever!
> No; since her fatal beauty was the cause
> Of all my suff'ring, let her share my pains.

In rejecting forgiveness, then, and in embracing revenge, Alicia reaps
those particular mental and spiritual "pains" which, as her vivid description reveals, are "the torments of the last despair."

Thus the subplot not only underscores the major themes of the play,
but it presents two patterns of action that can be followed after sin—one
of humble repentance and forgiveness, leading to the mercy of atonement, and one of indignant rage and revenge, leading to the madness of
despair. The former pattern is that followed not just by Hastings but
also by Jane, and the latter that followed by Alicia, who is, throughout
the play, Jane's foil. Both women are now forlorn mistresses, but the
contrast between them is extremely significant. Therefore, Rowe brings
them together in a climactic encounter. In Act I Alicia has solemnly
vowed her undying friendship toward Jane, her "other self" (I.ii, p. 146):

> If I not hold her nearer to my soul,
> Than ev'ry other joy the world can give,
> Let poverty, deformity and shame,
> Distraction and despair seize me on earth,
> Let not my faithless ghost have peace hereafter.

By the time of Act III Alicia's vow has already been broken: her
"chang'd eyes" are now "blasted" with Jane's "beauty" (p. 156), and she
betrays her. By the time of Act V Alicia's vow has come back to plague
her: seized by "Distraction and despair," she rushes out to confront Jane
in rage and revenge.

Jane has prophesied that "Ere yet a few short days" Alicia would
behold her "poor, and kneeling / Before thy charitable door for bread"
(I.ii, p. 145). Yet she has firmly trusted that with Alicia her "wretched-

ness" would "find relief" and "shelter from the storm" (p. 146). Thus to
her she has entrusted her jewels, "all that I can call my own." When
later Jane chances upon Alicia's house in her wanderings, she cries,
"Blessed opportunity! / I'll steal a little succour from her goodness"
(V, p. 178). But she is denied entrance. When the distracted Alicia
finally appears, Jane does beg, as she has prophesied, "for charity's dear
sake, / A draught of water and a little bread" (p. 179). Alicia replies,
"I know thee not," and, in her raving, bids Jane seek her food among
the birds of prey or her bread "Where wanton hands upon the earth
have scatter'd it, / Or cast it on the waters." Having recognized Jane
at last, Alicia accuses her of Hastings' "murder" and still adamantly
refuses Jane's plea for "mercy": "Mercy! I know it not" (p. 180). At this
point her mind pathetically cracks, and she runs away screaming of the
suicide to which her vision of Hastings' ghost drives her, a vision which
shows that she completely misunderstands Hastings' parting attitude
toward her. Her refusal to be merciful has brought upon her the poetic
justice of Hastings' prophecy:

> oh! should'st thou wrong her [Jane],
> Just heaven shall double all thy woes upon thee,
> And make 'em know no end. (IV, p. 173)

As is usual in literary madness, Alicia's words make a kind of sense.
In her denial of bread the very words indicate her denial of mercy: the
"wanton hands" that have "cast" their bread "on the waters" are those
hands which do so in obedience to the mandate of Ecclesiastes, "Cast
thy bread upon the waters: for thou shalt find it after many days" (11:1).
This entire chapter of Ecclesiastes, as is obvious from the commentaries,
is an exhortation to works of mercy, or liberality. The *Assembly Annotations* glosses the first verse thus: "That is, be liberall to the poor, and
though it be as a thing ventured at sea, or cast into the water, yet it shall
bring thee profit. . . . As seed, though not presently, yet after some time it
will encrease. Worldly men think laying up the way to be rich, but God
thinks laying out to be the way."[9] Jane has been such a liberal, merciful
person, yet ironically she is denied mercy by her "other self"—a similarly sinful mistress who has not taken the path of atonement. But, as in
Heywood's *Edward IV*, this imagery of bread has further significance in
Jane Shore, for it reinforces the entire theme of mercy—what Hastings
calls "tender-hearted charity" (I.i, p. 141)—and unites it with the theme
of Providence.

From the opening act, bread is associated with charity and becomes a symbol of the Corporal Works of Mercy. Jane's description of Bellmour, her "gentle neighbor" (an appellation whose connotations reach back to the parable of the Good Samaritan), provides the play with a New Testament standard of behavior:

> ah! good *Bellmour!*
> How few, like thee, enquire the wretched out,
> And court the offices of soft humanity?
> Like thee reserve their raiment for the naked,
> Reach out their bread, to feed the crying orphan,
> Or mix their pitying tears with those that weep?

Jane has herself upheld this standard, and accordingly, in words which echo the Book of Job,[10] she justifies herself before Richard:

> Alas! my gracious Lord! what have I done
> To kindle such relentless wrath against me?
> If in the days of all my past offences,
> When most my heart was lifted with delight,
> If I withheld my morsel from the hungry,
> Forgot the widow's want, and orphan's cry;
> If I have known a good I have not shar'd,
> Nor call'd the poor to take his portion with me,
> Let my worst enemies stand forth, and now
> Deny the succour which I gave not then. (IV, p. 164)

On the other hand, Alicia and Richard have violated this standard. Alicia refuses Jane the bread of charity and totally rejects mercy, and when Jane, unwittingly betrayed by Alicia, comes to Richard and "Intreats a little bread for charity" (III, p. 158), he plans instead to use her charms in conforming Hastings to his will. Accordingly, Catesby asks Richard,

> Is not her bread
> The very means immediate to her being,
> The bounty of your hand? (IV, p. 163)

Richard does indeed threaten Jane with "fear, distress, and famine," and when she refuses to cooperate, sends her out to "rot upon a dunghill" without "comfort, food, or harbour" (p. 167). Whoever administers relief to her shall die. Thus Richard pays only lip service to the Christian duty he himself enunciates—"To cherish the distress'd" (I.i, p. 141)—and at the end of the play Shore appropriately asks Catesby, "Is Charity grown treason to your court?" (V, p. 184). One of the implications of this theme of bread and charity is, then, that on either side of the Christian standard these characters are arranged something like the sheep and the goats of Christ's Doomsday prophecy, who merit their just desert as they were charitable "unto one of the least of these my brethren" (Mat. 25:40).

The imagery of bread continues. Jane resists Richard's threats by embracing her adversity thus:

> Let me be branded for the public scorn,
> Turn'd forth, and driven to wander like a vagabond,
> Be friendless and forsaken, seek my bread
> Upon the barren wild, and desolate waste,
> Feed on my sighs, and drink my falling tears;
> Ere I consent to teach my lips injustice,
> Or wrong the orphan who has none to save him. (IV, p. 167)[11]

Although bread is denied her by her persecutors and her best friend, the implication of Jane's resistance to Richard's temptation is that "Man shall not live by bread alone" (Mat. 4:4): material bread is *not* "The very means immediate to her being." For to the Christian, bread has always signified sustenance not only material but also spiritual. In the Gospel of John, after the miracle of the loaves and fishes, the people sought Jesus because they "were filled" (6:26), yet they requested a further sign like Moses' manna from heaven. Jesus answered, "I am the bread of life: he that cometh to me shall never hunger; and he that believeth on me shall never thirst" (vs. 35). Accordingly, Jesus instituted the Eucharist and bread became one of the central symbols of Christianity, both through the constant repetition of the Communion ceremony and through the Lord's Prayer: "Give us this day our daily bread." Bread, then, is the symbol of providential care.[12] Thus when Shore comes to relieve Jane in Act V, he is "the messenger of grace and goodness" in a double sense. The material sustenance he gives her does not save her life, but the spiritual "grace and goodness"—his forgiveness—is, as in Heywood, a pledge of her eternal salvation. Like Hastings and unlike Alicia, she dies beseeching Heaven's "mercy," and the final implication of the imagery of bread is that Heaven will provide for her soul, because she has herself given bread to the needy.

iii

As the play's epigraph from the *Aeneid* indicates, Jane's "lord of former days [*coniunx pristinus*] responds to her sorrows" (VI.473, Loeb). After he has heard Bellmour's description of her suffering, Shore, like Altamont in *The Fair Penitent* and unlike Alicia in this play, overcomes the powerful last vestiges of a husband's "revenge" and "jealousy" by contemplating the severity of her punishment (V, p. 177). He concludes, "Hence with her past offences, / They are aton'd at full." The key word is "aton'd," for Jane has truly paid for her sins, and in a pattern of suffering which suggests *the* Atonement. Her open penance through the streets "from the public cross,"[13] together with the derision of the crowd, appears to be modeled on the Way of the Cross. Donald B. Clark notes the resemblance: "There are, certainly, reminiscent images drawn from the *via dolorosa* in Jane's walk of penance, bearing her candle, looking 'submissive, sad, and lowly,' 'feeble and sorely smit with pain,' her bare feet marking the flinty pavement with blood" ("Nicholas Rowe," p. 216). Moreover, Rowe's stress on the duration of "three days" (V, pp. 179, 183), Jane's desertion by her friends, and especially her betrayal and denial by one who had solemnly pledged "holy friendship" but now declares, "I know thee not"—all seem details calculated to reinforce the pattern, and they elicit this complaint, rich in typological overtones, at Alicia's door:

It was not always thus; the time has been,
When this unfriendly door, that bars my passage,
Flew wide, and almost leap'd from off its hinges
To give me entrance here; when this good house
Has pour'd forth all its dwellings to receive me;
When my approach has made a little holy-day,
And ev'ry face was dress'd in smiles to meet me:
But now 'tis otherwise; and those who bless'd me,
Now curse me to my face. (p. 178)

The typological overtones and patterns function not to make Jane a Christ figure, however, but to recall the Atonement, when Christ took man's sins upon Himself in order to redeem him. According to the doctrine of justification, Jane's atonement is efficacious because of Christ's:

she can achieve *at-onement* with God because, as Rowe's typological patterning suggests, she can participate in Christ's Atonement, which enabled Adam's descendants once again, as Christian doctrine expresses it, to become children of God and heirs of heaven. Rowe has artfully stressed Jane's oneness with Christ, the Mediator for His fellow members of the Mystical Body and the Communion of Saints.

At the end of the play Shore comes to Jane to signal the efficacy of her atonement and to grant her relief, not only physical but spiritual, for he comes to forgive and his actions take on an emblematic meaning. "To chase away despair," the temptation which is explicit in the Job imagery of Richard's earlier threat (IV, p. 161) and has been present since Hastings' first description of Jane as "pining in despair" (I.i, p. 141), Bellmour presents the undisguised Shore to Jane,

> unlike to that *Dumont* you knew,
> For now he wears your better angel's form,
> And comes to visit you with peace and pardon. (V, p. 181)

But for Jane the appearance of her husband is a "dreadful vision," because in her weakened state[14] she thinks she sees his "angry shade" (p. 182) returned to haunt her (as in Alicia's vision of Hastings' vengeful ghost). When Jane realizes that Shore is alive, "in despair" she abandons her "distracted soul to horror":

> Fall then ye mountains on my guilty head,
> Hide me, ye rocks, within your secret caverns:
> Cast thy black veil upon my shame, O night!
> And shield me with thy sable wing for ever.

Alfred Schwarz thinks that Jane's expression of "horror and shame" is "excessively rhetorical" ("Example," p. 243), but the rhetoric itself is highly significant, a continuation of the "sonorous imitation" of Biblical imagery and rhythms which Schwarz himself has noted in Jane's speech, "Yet, yet endure, nor murmur oh my soul," and which, as I have tried to indicate, runs throughout this play. The opening lines of the passage just quoted employ a common scriptural apocalyptic image (Hos. 10:8; Luke 23:30; Rev. 6:16), one exploited by Milton only a few years earlier (*PL* VI.842 f). In other words, despite Shore's assurance that he has come "To bring thee back to thy forsaken home, / With tender joy, with fond forgiving love," in the depth of her remorse, like Calista, Jane expects—nay, even implores—a Doomsday wrath:

> No, arm thy brow with vengeance; and appear
> The Minister of Heaven's enquiring justice.
> Array thyself all terrible for judgment,
> Wrath in thy eyes, and thunder in thy voice;
> Pronounce my sentence, and if yet there be
> A woe I have not felt, inflict it on me.

The point of the scene, however, is precisely that Shore is not a "Minister" of "justice" but of mercy. Instead of the Old Testament "great avenger" Alicia appeals to (IV, p. 173), Shore gradually assumes, to Jane's disturbed mind, the aspect of a risen savior:

> Art thou not ris'n by miracle from death?
> Thy shroud is fall'n from off thee, and the grave
> Was bid to give thee up, that thou might'st come
> The messenger of grace and goodness to me,
> To seal my peace, and bless me ere I go. (V, p. 182 f)

While Shore has not literally risen from the dead, though Jane might think so, the passage implies that he represents One Who has and Who guarantees forgiveness to those who repent.

Finally, Jane accepts the grace proffered by this messenger, overcomes the despair that has destroyed Alicia, and throws herself at her husband's feet:

> Oh let me then fall down beneath thy feet,
> And weep my gratitude for ever there;
> Give me your drops, ye soft descending rains,
> Give me your streams, ye never-ceasing springs,
> That my sad eyes may still supply my duty,
> And feed an everlasting flood of sorrow. (p. 183)

This ending of the play has been described as "unbearably lachrymose,"[15] and indeed it might be termed maudlin—or rather, Maudlin, for this image of Jane weeping at the feet of a risen messenger of grace in a scene of forgiveness recalls the most famous of all sinners, Mary Magdalene, who washed the feet of Christ with her tears and obtained forgiveness because of her love and her faith (Luke 7:37 ff). Jane's mistaking Shore for a risen savior adds to the association, since it was Magdalene who discovered the Risen Christ. The association is the culmination of the imagery of tears that runs throughout the play. Recent studies of the figure of Magdalene in English literature have revealed that in medieval literature "she was looked upon as the patron saint of sinners and penitents, who were urged to follow the example of her conversion and changed life."[16] Moreover, "the Magdalene was . . . a witness of divine mercy, showing mankind the importance of penitence" (p. 95). The immense popularity of the saint is evidenced not only in the voluminous literature about her but also in the facts that her feast day was declared a holiday of precept in England at the Council of Oxford in 1222 and that a religious order was named after her, the Order of Magdalene, established in 1324 primarily for reformed harlots—like Jane Shore (p. 100). Indeed, the *Catholic Dictionary* shows that this last connection still exists today: "*Magdalen.* An euphemism for a reformed and penitent prostitute, from the common notion that St. Mary Magdalen had been a harlot. Technically, the name was formerly given to members of religious congregations of penitents, and now to those in homes for the reclamation of prostitutes and other unfortunates" (ed. Donald Attwater et al., p. 318).

Magdalene's literary popularity continued into the Renaissance at least up to the time of Crashaw (and why not beyond?): "Having inherited a rich medieval Magdalenic literary tradition based on both scripture and legend, the English renaissance . . . remained rather persistently preoccupied with the saint for a hundred and fifty years [1500–1650]. In some ways Magdalene was a central figure in a Christian world view, for ordinary mortals might see in her sinfulness triumphantly transformed to sanctity a hopeful possibility for their own lives."[17] There was an "extraordinary revival of English literary interest in Magdalene between 1591 and 1650" which crossed the boundaries of religion and sect (p. 122). Furthermore, "the Magdalene theme was part of a broader mood of tearfulness in post-Tridentine literature" (p. 124). Consequently, the figure of the Weeper was adapted to other stories, for example, Thomas Churchyard's "Tragedy of Jane Shore" (p. 135). Indeed, perhaps the interest in the story of Jane Shore (as well as those of Rosamond and Lucrece) was itself inspired by the revival of interest specifically in Magdalene, especially in the late 1500s when Churchyard's and Anthony Chute's Jane Shore poems and Heywood's play were printed (see Rowan, p. 458 ff), along with the Magdalenic poems of Breton, Nashe, Lodge, and Henry Constable. Many of the works dealing with Jane Shore, and particularly Heywood's, stress her tears of penitence. Perhaps it can even be said that Heywood's Jane is properly Maudlin, although Rowe is the first to fully exploit the association. His use of this association in his characterization of Jane Shore focuses further attention on the theme of trust in providential mercy. Jane becomes another example of the appealing lesson of Magdalene—that, in the words of Saint Paul, "where sin abounded, grace did much more abound" (Rom. 5:20). Thus Shore becomes the Christ-like "messenger of grace and goodness" as he reaches down to comfort the Weeper at his feet:[18]

> I have long
> Beheld, unknown, thy mourning and repentance;
> Therefore my heart has set aside the past,
> And holds thee white, as unoffending innocence. (p. 183)

Far from being "the Minister of Heaven's enquiring justice," he is the minister of Its forgiveness, for he acts out the words of Christ, "I will have mercy, and not sacrifice: for I am not come to call the righteous, but sinners to repentance" (Mat. 9:13).

In contrast to the false "arm" of Alicia, Shore now offers Jane his true arm for support ("Lean on my arm")—a gesture which epitomizes the entire meaning of the play. For from the beginning Rowe has spun out a complex but consistent and extremely significant imagery of *hands* and *arms*—an imagery which underlines the basic themes. The images fall roughly into two categories—images of the *hand of justice* and images of the *hand of mercy*—and both hands belong ultimately to God. In an abuse of power and justice, Richard disdains the "pageant sceptre" which the council has placed in his "hand" (III, p. 160) and sees instead "The sceptre and the golden wreath of royalty" themselves as "hung" within his "reach" (I.i, p. 139). Thus he maneuvers to wrest them from the defenseless and "harmless hands" of Edward IV's infant sons into his own "abler hands" (IV, p. 165 f). Richard is also associated with the oppressive "hand of justice" (I.i, p. 141) or "of power" (sc. ii, p. 145), that "heavy hand" (IV, p. 164) which brings "calamity" on Jane with its "strong gripe" (III, p. 158), as it confiscates all the favors Edward once bestowed on her and finally turns her into the street. But Richard's evil hand, which is appropriately—and according to the Tudor myth, providentially—"blasted, dry, and wither'd" (p. 168), has merely been the unwitting instrument of the divine "hand of righteousness," which has punished Jane for her prior sins, as she humbly acknowledges (V, p. 177).

The same abuse of power and justice is shown in Hastings' "cruel hand of pow'r" (III, p. 157) which punishes Dumont's "saucy hand" (p. 159)—actually an "arm resolv'd" in the cause of virtue and Heaven in a *trial by combat* (II, p. 154)—for protecting Jane from rape and for defeating Hastings' own "failing hand." And in perfect poetic justice, Hastings, who has been described as being controlled by the "dainty-finger'd" Alicia and as receiving the "distaff" from her "with a hand as patient / As e'er did *Hercules*" (I.i, p. 140), like Hercules falls by the "weak hand" of a woman (IV, p. 170). Hastings explicitly attributes the workings of Alicia's "mistaking hand" to those of the "hand of Heaven" (p. 172). In such a way has Heaven's "arm" rolled "the dreadful thunder" (II, p. 150) which Hastings has flouted in his dealings with Alicia, Dumont, and Jane. Perhaps because he has cursed "the innovating hand" of usurpation, however, and vowed (as Richard interprets him) that he would "arm" his "hand" against it, he ultimately merits the grace to call on that Hand of Heaven for "mercy" (IV, p. 172).

In contrast to Richard's "wither'd" arm is Jane's *hand of mercy*, a hand she does not allow, despite Hastings' advice (II, p. 152), to wither in sin as it becomes "wither'd" in age, and a hand which certainly merits mercy at the Hand of Heaven. Jane's "poor hand" is always extended, like Bellmour's, in acts of charity, even to her disguised husband, whom she agrees to employ as Dumont (I.ii, p. 143). She ingenuously asks Richard, "Can my unworthy hand / Become an instrument of good to any?" (IV, p. 165), and her hands are implicitly identified with those "wanton hands," as Alicia describes them, which cast their bread upon the waters in liberality (V, p. 179). Accordingly, the charitable "bounty" of her "hand," as Alicia has predicted (I.ii, p. 146), does finally "pull a blessing" on her—the blessing of forgiveness. But Jane is first persecuted by those whose hands know no mercy: by Richard, whose anti-providential "grace" (I.i, p. 142) denies her the "bread" that is the "bounty" of his "hand" (IV, p. 163); by the "dear companions" of her "joyful days," "Whose arms were taught to grow like ivy round" her but who now desert her (V, p. 181); and by those "villainous hands" that in derision hurl filth "upon her head" (p. 174) as she traces out Christ's Way of suffering, "With no one hand to help" (p. 176). She turns to Alicia, who has pledged to be the "partner" of her bosom forever (I.ii, p. 145 ff) and on whose "friendly arm" Jane, in her search for a "charitable hand," has leaned, only to have Alicia betray her into "the great

Protector's hand" (III, p. 156 ff). To Alicia's "hand" Jane has "trusted all" her last possessions and even her very self, only to be denied and spurned in her hour of need (V, p. 179).

So Jane must ultimately turn for "succour" to her "lord of former days," who now returns her earlier offer of a "poor hand" to him disguised with his own offer of a supporting "arm" (as though he were saying, "Inasmuch as ye have done it unto one of the least of these my brethren, ye have done it unto me"). In contrast to Alicia, Shore has kept his vow to "give her help and share one fortune with her" (V, p. 175), and he declares that his "arms" are "open to receive" her (p. 182) as a true partner of his bosom. Finally, Shore's extended hand is emblematic of the *hand of mercy* of her other *Lord of former days*, the spiritual bridegroom or *Coniunx pristinus* of Jane and of the entire Church. The Hand of Heaven, then, while it chastens the former mistress, draws to Abraham's bosom the charitable "poor penitent" and bids her "speak peace" to her "sad heart" (V, p. 184).

And yet, as he was when he earlier promised an earthly retreat, Shore is again woefully mistaken when he says to Jane, "The measure of thy sorrows is compleat" and "The hand of power no more shall crush thy weakness" (p. 182). As Bellmour's moral makes clear, not even Jane's "severe repentance" could save her from "an untimely grave"— the full measure of her atonement. The relief that Shore has brought to his "poor penitent" is allowed by Providence to be only that of mind and soul, for he is captured and condemned for his corporal charity, and "this blow" completes Jane's "ruin" (p. 184). As she dies, she pathetically pleads again, "Forgive me!—but forgive me!" And Shore's final forgiveness emphasizes again the relationship between human mercy and divine:

> Be witness for me, ye celestial host,
> Such mercy and such pardon as my soul
> Accords to thee, and begs of heaven to show thee;
> May such befall me at my latest hour,
> And make my portion bless'd or curs'd for ever. (p. 184 f)

As in *The Fair Penitent* and Heywood's play, then, human forgiveness becomes emblematic of divine. Shore's words recall Hastings' early statement and thus conclude the theme of mercy in the play: "Good Heav'n . . . renders mercy back for mercy" (I.i, p. 142). The words are a paraphrase of the same Beatitude central to Heywood's play: "Blessed are the merciful, for they shall obtain mercy." And as in Heywood's, the entire thrust of Rowe's play suggests that, because she has been penitent and charitable, Jane's final plea—"Oh, mercy heaven" (p. 185) —shall not go unanswered. At the end, her own Way of the Cross, patterned as it is upon the Atonement, has brought her, deserted and derided, to her own Calvary of expiation and to a final *at-onement* with her husband and her God.

Like *Lady Jane Gray*, Rowe's *Jane Shore* fails to distribute poetic justice not only to some of the innocent but to some of the wicked as well, and that fact accounts for much of the tragic force of the ending. By Richard's edict (IV, p. 167), Shore and Bellmour must die for their charity, and despite Jane's assurance that Hastings, as "the proxy of all-ruling providence" (p. 166), shall be assisted in the cause of Edward's "friendless infants" by "Saints" and "warring angels," England is left in the cruel hands of Richard and his "inhuman villains" (V, p. 184), who have dominated so much of this play. Thus the world the play describes seems to be the world Milton describes at the end of *Paradise Lost*—"To good malignant, to bad men benign" (XII.538). On the other hand, because Shore and Bellmour have themselves been merciful, we know according to the message of the play that they shall obtain mercy, if not in this life at least in the next. Moreover, Rowe's audience would have been familiar with Richard's subsequent history and the providential interpretations—from the chronicles to Shakespeare—of his eventual overthrow. With Providence so immanent in the world of *Jane Shore*, then, it is not too much to speculate that Hastings' curse—"Remember him, the villain, righteous Heav'n / In thy great day of vengeance" (III, p. 161)— promises eventual justice for England, and that, on the more universal level of his curse and of Jane's trust in "all-ruling providence," the play promises ultimate—if only eschatological—justice for the suffering innocent.

iv

Allardyce Nicoll has said that Rowe's *Jane Shore* and *Lady Jane Gray* "are indeed by way of being masterpieces" (*A History of English Drama*, II, 100). Alfred Jackson more modestly opines, "Together with *The Fair Penitent* and *Lady Jane Gray* it [*Jane Shore*] brought Rowe from the rut of Augustan dramatists and set him in a place apart" ("Rowe's Historical Tragedies," p. 323). Surely his "*She*-Tragedies," the term which he somewhat ironically coined for such plays in the Epilogue to *Jane Shore* (p. 186), are the finest tragedies of their time—and, in my opinion, of the entire century which succeeded them. And they are better than anything Lee wrote, if not Otway. The honors for Rowe's best play must go to either *The Fair Penitent* or *Jane Shore*. Which of the two is probably a moot question. *The Fair Penitent* is more engaging, I have argued, because of its excellently portrayed conflict raging in the great soul of Calista. But in other respects, *Jane Shore* is equal or superior to the earlier play. The subplot is as carefully and as significantly related to the main, although in the earlier play the one plot is clearly subordinate to the other, and the result is greater structural unity than in *Jane Shore*. Here Hastings and Alicia almost steal the show from Jane; there could almost be said to be three protagonists (as in *Ulysses*).

Structural unity aside, Hastings and Alicia are two of the best characters Rowe ever drew, and they help shift the emphasis away from the resigned heroine (compare *Lady Jane Gray*) and give the play a much more engaging conflict than it would otherwise have. Alicia is the descendant of Calista and inherits her magnificent indignation. Rowe captures her shifts in mood brilliantly from the beginning: "Does *Hastings* undertake to plead your cause?" (I.i, p. 145), she blurts, then recovers immediately, though the passion seeps through in irony:

> But wherefore should he not? *Hastings* has eyes;
> The gentle Lord has a right tender heart,
> Melting and easy, yielding to impression,
> And catching the soft flame from each new beauty.

When Hastings answers her exploding passion with contempt, she rises up to inveigh admirably against him:

>   Dost thou in scorn
> Preach patience to my rage? And bid me tamely
> Sit like a poor contented idiot down,
> Nor dare to think thou'st wrong'd me—Ruin seize thee,
> And swift perdition overtake thy treachery! (II, p. 149)

She is as fierce as Artemisa or Rodogune, yet as with Calista Rowe has found the rhetoric to contain her outbursts of passion, from her curses to her madness. Her scene with the condemned Hastings is one of Rowe's best, where he modulates her mood from frantic self-accusation to indignant accusation of Hastings to abject remorse and finally to jealous revenge. And I think her mad scene better portrayed than that of Otway's Belvidera. Her answer to Jane is especially poignant:

> Mercy! I know it not—for I am miserable.
> I'll give thee misery, for here she dwells. (V, p. 180)

Even her allegorical description of her house, which she describes as crashing down upon her head, seems to me to succeed, despite the strain it puts on our modern sensibilities. As she runs after her deluded vision of Hastings' ghost, her parting words to Jane are an excellent pathetic touch: "But come not thou with mischief-making beauty / To interpose between us." Even in the underworld she fears that the shade of Jane's "fatal beauty" will come between her and Hastings.

Next to Lothario, Hastings is Rowe's best male character, and he is more fully developed, more complex—a blend of the libertinism of Lothario and the passion-cum-honor of Pembroke. Rowe excellently balances Alicia's tirades with Hastings' cool, libertine "indifference" (II, p. 148), culminating in his last ironic coup de grace:

> Let any other kind of plague o'ertake me,
> So I escape the fury of that tongue. (p. 150)

And in a handsome stroke of irony, Hastings' supercilious soliloquy on the wild escapes of passion in women—"How fierce a fiend is passion? With what wildness" (p. 150 f)—is juxtaposed to his own wild escapes a moment later, when, bewildered by Jane's resignation, he resorts to rape. Rowe perfectly portrays his frustration both with Jane—"Away with this perverseness,—'tis too much; / Nay, if you strive—'tis monstrous affectation" (p. 153)—and with Dumont:

> 'Tis wond'rous well! I see my saint like dame,
> You stand provided of your braves and ruffians,
> To man your cause, and bluster in your brothel. (p. 154)

The other side of Hastings is portrayed as well, I think. His spontaneous patriotism bursts forth in fine lines, where, despite his disclaimer, he finds the words to "give a scope to passion" (III, p. 162). Bonamy Dobrée (*Restoration Tragedy*, p. 156 f) does not like his speech, "The resty knaves are over-run with ease" (III, p. 160), but weak as it may be (and I am not convinced it is), it seems to be well offset by the later, "Curse on the innovating hand attempts it" (p. 161), and especially by this moving speech on the England ravaged by the War of the Roses:

Have we so soon forgot those days of ruin,
When *York* and *Lancaster* drew forth the battles;
When, like a matron, butcher'd by her sons,
And cast beside some common way a spectacle
Of horror and affright to passers by,
Our groaning country bled at every vein;
When murders, rapes, and massacres prevail'd;
When churches, palaces, and cities blaz'd;
When insolence and barbarism triumph'd,
And swept away distinction; peasants trod
Upon the necks of nobles; low were laid
The reverend crosier, and the holy mitre,
And desolation cover'd all the land;
Who can remember this, and not, like me,
Here vow to sheath a dagger in his heart,
Whose damn'd ambition would renew those horrors,
And set, once more, the scene of blood before us? (p. 161 f)

Who indeed? What price revolution? Not that Rowe was not an egalitarian: Dumont expresses well the "difference" between commoner and noble:

Yet Heaven that made me honest, made me more
Than ever King did when he made a Lord. (II, p. 154)

Still, Hastings' speech powerfully expresses the grim horrors of civil war, especially in one of Rowe's rarely excellent local metaphors, the comparison of England to "a matron, butcher'd by her sons."

In an evaluation of this play that is one of the most appreciative, Alfred Jackson calls Hastings' soliloquy on death—"Yes *Ratcliffe*, I will take thy friendly council" (IV, p. 169)—one of "the finest passages in the play" ("Rowe's Historical Tragedies," p. 318). I agree, but I would add that his entire subsequent dialogue with Alicia is excellent in its mature and measured grace. His speeches of forgiveness are perhaps Rowe's best attempts to express the softer passions, for they have about them

the soothing, paternal tone of a man grown instantly old in wisdom, as
he comforts and counsels the frantic, misguided girl he leaves behind:

> 'Tis all in vain, this rage that tears thy bosom;
> Like a poor bird that flutters in its cage,
> Thou beats thyself to death. (IV, p. 173)

Finally, as he is more noble in spirit, so is Hastings more eloquent in
rhetoric than Richard, whose diction generally betrays his baseness.
Rowe does not make the common mistake of having his villain speak
better lines than anyone else in the play. Hastings is more eloquent than
anyone else but Jane.

One has only to contrast Jane with the nearly raped Amestris to
see how far Rowe has progressed in his ability to particularize character,
while still retaining emblematic and typological resonances. And far
from being sentimental, the usual charge laid against her, Rowe's Jane
seems to me magnanimous in her liberality, her courage, and her purpose of amendment. She is not "puling" or "whining" but is as tough
in her resignation as the later Lady Jane. Her refusal to hear any more
about Edward—"Name him no more: / He was the bane and ruin of my
peace" (I.ii, p. 144)—is as stout and firm as Calista's refusal to hear any
longer Lothario's allurements. Her diatribe against the double standard
—"Why should I think that man will do for me" (I.ii, p. 146 f)—is nearly
as good as Calista's—"How hard is the condition of our sex"—even
though Jane's is a rhymed tag. In another of Rowe's good local metaphors, Jane reveals the depth not only of her contrition but also of her
self-knowledge and humility when she gently rebuffs Hastings thus:

> Cast round your eyes
> Upon the high-born beauties of the court;
> Behold, like op'ning roses, where they bloom,
> Sweet to the sense, unsully'd all, and spotless;
> There choose some worthy partner of your heart
> To fill your arms, and bless your virtuous bed;
> Nor turn your eyes this way, where sin and mis'ry,
> Like loathsome weeds, have over-run the soil,
> And the destroyer shame has laid all waste. (II, p. 152)

The metaphor of the garden unobtrusively ties the passage together, and Jane becomes implicitly the withered Rose of London, who still attracts in spite of—or perhaps because of—her gracious demurrer.

As I noted before, like Hastings, Jane finds the eloquence she disclaims to bravely answer Richard and defend the Princes. But Rowe has learned to do something else in this play other than write his best set speeches. He has learned to capture worlds of emotion and meaning in short, clipped phrases, as in Alicia's "*My* friend! my Lord" (II, p. 148 —my italics, but the line must be read with heavy ironic emphasis on that word because of Hastings' answer, "Yes, Lady, yours") or her "You triumph! do!" (p. 150). The better examples are uttered by Jane. The best line in the entire scene with Richard is this one, supposedly Sarah Siddons' most effective:[19] "Does he! does *Hastings!*" (IV, p. 165). In view of Jane's previous night, what worlds does this line speak! It is the spring which releases her magnanimous blessings upon him and her inspired defense of the Princes. Finally, at the end of the play, Jane utters the clipped, pathetic line that moved even Dr. Johnson: "Forgive me!—but forgive me!" (V, p. 184).[20] Viewed in isolation from the rhetorical pattern Rowe has established, the line loses some of its effect, but seen as the culmination of a pattern of cryptic utterances, it is supremely effective, I think. The inclusion of the word "but" is a master stroke that saves the line from a whining, pleading, "Forgive me—please forgive me." In the sense of "only" or "just" (paraphrase ruins the line), "but" is worth a thousand words between this couple which has just renewed its intimacy through such particular details as the string of pearls,[21] and it also perfectly expresses the catching in Jane's breath and voice as she is nearly overcome by emotion—and by death.

Obviously, throughout this section, and the entire study as well, it has been impossible to talk about character without talking about the language through which character is expressed. And language is the triumph of *Jane Shore*. Not that there aren't several lines Rowe should have blotted: "You knew perhaps—oh grief! oh shame!—my husband" (I.ii, p. 143), or "My tasteless tongue cleaves to the clammy roof" (V, p. 183). In general, however, as Jackson puts it, Rowe's language "flows harmoniously along" (p. 317) in what Schwarz calls "the unusually natural tone of its dialogue" ("Example," p. 240). And as James R. Sutherland puts it, in his attempt to imitate his master "Rowe catches at times the very rhythm of Shakespeare's blank verse" (p. 34). I would add that Rowe catches what, following Schwarz's lead, I have tried to suggest throughout this chapter—the very rhythms of Scripture. He culminates a process begun in Ethelinda's speeches in *The Royal Convert*—"Oh lift thy eyes up to that holy pow'r" (*Works*, II, 95) and "The great o'er ruling author of our beings" (p. 123)—a fusion of Biblical rhythms, diction, and imagery. Witness again Jane's great speech:

> Yet, yet endure, nor murmur oh my soul,
> For are not thy transgressions great and numberless?
> Do they not cover thee like rising floods,
> And press thee like a weight of waters down?
> Does not the hand of righteousness afflict thee?
> And who shall plead against it? Who shall say
> To power Almighty, thou hast done enough?
> Or bid his dreadful rod of vengeance, stay?
> Wait then with patience, till the circling hours
> Shall bring the time of thy appointed rest,
> And lay thee down in death. The hireling thus
> With labour drudges out the painful day,
> And often looks with long-expecting eyes
> To see the shadows rise, and be dismiss'd.
> And hark! methinks the roar that late pursu'd me,
> Sinks like the murmurs of a falling wind,
> And softens into silence. (V, p. 177 f)

I have already noted (n. 8) the Biblical diction, imagery, and allusions. Rowe uses to perfection the same type of rhetorical Jobish question as Ethelinda's "Does not the deep grow calm, and the rude North / Be hush'd at his command?" (p. 95). Moreover, the passage brings to perfection Rowe's early attempts at Miltonic rhythms in Arpasia's "A little longer, yet, be strong, my heart" (*Works*, I, 134). Prosodically, it is Rowe's richest passage. It is anything but regular iambic pentameter, for the first line opens with a spondee (perhaps in imitation of Jane's halting steps); the second is an alexandrine; and the third and fourth would barely stress more than three or four syllables. Yet it is excellent blank verse, with a fine enjambment, "Who shall say / To power Almighty," and a fine caesural pause on the word "death." Alliteration of *r*'s pervades the passage and provides a rich, rolling resonance. Less pervasive but also prominent are the *d*'s. Furthermore, Rowe repeats the same or similar sounds through not one but two or more lines, as in *ur-or* in 1 and 2, *-ess* in 2, 4, and 5. And there is an interesting quasi-internal rhyme between the terminal "eyes" of line 13 and the middle "rise" of the next. These are the major sound effects until we come to the most lyrical lines of the passage,

> And hark! methinks the roar that late pursu'd me,
> Sinks like the murmurs of a falling wind,
> And softens into silence.

The opening trochee of the second line sounds a strong note after which the rhythm falls off in imitation of the sense down to the soft alliteration of *s*'s reflecting silence. Again, we say the sound imitates the sense only because we know what the sense is. But the rhythms and sounds do seem calculated to bring Jane to a quiet caesural stop at the end of her reflective passage, and the repeated word "murmurs" seems to have moved from a metaphorical, internal sense in the opening line of the whole passage into a literal sense, as Jane murmurs quietly into momentary silence before she asks her next, nonmetaphysical questions.

Good ideas alone will not make a good play. Thus I have tried to show throughout this study not only the thematic continuity of Rowe's tragedies but the aesthetic quality of his language, characterization, imagery, and structure in the better ones. If it were not for these elements—the smoothness of Rowe's verse, especially in the complaints; the appropriateness of his dialogue; the vividness of his better characters, particularly his spirited women; the dovetailing of plots; and the intricate weaving of unobtrusive but very significant motifs and image patterns and allusions—Rowe's tragedies would be, as are the great majority of tragedies of his time, merely interesting objects of study for historians of various sorts. His best are, however, artistically successful plays worth reading for their aesthetic merit.

Nevertheless, good techniques alone will not make good plays, either. To claim our respect and attention, serious plays must address themselves to central human concerns, such as the problems of suffering innocence, of guilt and expiation, of the existence of a god who cares. Form must be married to theme. What is best about Rowe's imagery and allusions, for instance, is that they are functional. As I have said earlier, once we understand the significance of Rowe's patterns and actions, and once we understand the literary, theoretical, and philosophical context of his art, we can begin to fully appreciate it, to see that the parts relate to the whole. No longer, then, will the death of Cleone in

The Ambitious Stepmother, for instance, seem gratuitous or meaningless; nor the Miltonic allusions in *Tamerlane* and elsewhere; nor the props in Act V of *The Fair Penitent*; nor all the false paradises and complaints and prisons and Machiavels and attempted rapes and mysterious accidents and endings, and especially all the trials.

In this light, what ultimately makes *Jane Shore* Rowe's most polished if not his best play is its organic unity. Its parts are beautifully interwoven so that nothing is without significance. This is especially true of its imagistic and allusive texture. Without an appreciation of that texture and an understanding of the meaning it provides, the play becomes simply a meaningless melodrama. But in the fifth act especially, when one realizes the significance of Jane's language and her tears and of Shore's offer of bread and his arm, then one sees the play in all its dimensions, particularly that most often missed by readers and critics alike, the metaphysical.[22] For brilliantly concrete as it is, from details of English history and folk traditions down to the "conserves" Shore offers his lost wife (V, p. 183), *Jane Shore* is nevertheless a typological Christian tragedy. At the end Jane is a type of Magdalene and Shore a type of Christ and the play itself an image of a world where there are unmistakable *signs* of a God Who cares and Whose care is imitated and emulated by those who believe in His name. Nowhere else has Rowe woven those types and emblems and signs into so rich and integral a dramatic tapestry.

Finally, *Jane Shore* provides a fitting conclusion for the study of Rowe's tragedies not only because it is his most polished play but because it includes all his major themes. It embodies the promise of both divine mercy and divine justice. Furthermore, the "poor penitent" has actually "turn'd saint" in her charity, as the Prologue says, and like Lady Jane Gray, she becomes a kind of Champion, as she rises to defend "the cause of injur'd innocence" (IV, p. 167). In a way, then, she is all Rowe's protagonists wrapped into one, an epitome of the Christian heroism that his tragedies define: having lost paradise on earth, she finds one within and endures her trial with patience and penitence, conquering despair by submitting to the will of God and trusting in his "gracious" care. Therein, I am fully persuaded, lies the meaning of Rowe's tragedies and, it is hoped, a key to the understanding and appreciation of similar Christian tragedies from the Renaissance to the Restoration and beyond. Let us at least, however, no longer neglect or reject Rowe's tragedies out of hand, without studying their intrinsic meaning and merit.

NOTES TO CHAPTER V

1. For the most recent discussion of the various versions of her story, see D. F. Rowan, "Shore's Wife," whose facts are generally correct, although his political interpretation of the literary (as opposed to the folk) tradition concerning Jane is highly suspect in the light of the explicit religious didacticism throughout that tradition. Cf. Donald B. Clark, "Nicholas Rowe," p. 205 ff, and James R. Sutherland, ed., *Three Plays*, by Nicholas Rowe, p. 348.

2. Rowe mentions the ballads in the Prologue (*Works*, II, 137), had all the relevant chronicles in his library (see *A Catalogue of the Library of N. Rowe*, passim), and might even have been familiar with some of the lyrical treatments—at least Drayton's, since his library contained the 1610 edition of Drayton's *Poems*, which included the "Heroicall Epistles" between Jane Shore and Edward IV (*Catalogue*, oct. 341).

3. See Henry H. Adams, *English Domestic or, Homiletic Tragedy*, p. 88 ff, who places Heywood's play squarely in the tradition of Christian tragedy he is discussing.

4. 2.II.iv, in *The First and Second Parts of King Edward IV*, ed. Barron Field, p. 142. The catalogue of Rowe's library records an unnamed, undated volume of Heywood (quarto 70), perhaps one of the many early seventeeth-century editions of *Edward IV*.

5. Or, *Jane Shore: A Tragedy, Written in Imitation of Shakespeare's Style*, in *Works*, II, 131 ff. For the best discussions of Rowe's "imitation" of Shakespeare, see Sutherland, p. 33 ff, and Alfred Schwarz, "An Example of Eighteenth-Century Pathetic Tragedy: Rowe's *Jane Shore*," p. 246 f.

6. *A Review of the* Tragedy of Jane Shore (1714) calls attention to the play's many "moving and instructive" allusions to Scripture, and especially to the Book of Job, best left to the individual reader to discover (p. 10 ff). The sitting down in anguish, complaining aloud, and cursing of life all recall the imagery of Job, the topos for abject wretchedness.

7. That even the wicked could be agents of providential justice was a commonplace in the writings on Providence in Rowe's period; for example, William Sherlock writes that "bad men" are allowed to be "prosperous" often in order to "make them Instruments of the Divine Providence, in chastising the Wickedness of other men" (*A Discourse Concerning the Divine Providence*, p. 148).

8. A. Schwarz, "Example," p. 242, calls the speech "a sonorous imitation of Old Testament imagery." The diction ("transgressions," "hand of righteousness," "rod of vengeance"), the imagery ("floods," "weight of waters"), and the rhetorical questions are all found especially in the Book of Job or the Psalms, or both. The tone is that of the last chapters of Job, while the spirit is that of the penitential Psalms.

9. *Assembly Annotations* was the popular name of *Annotations upon all the Books of the Old and New Testament* (1645).

10. Especially these verses: "If I have withheld the poor from *their* desire, or have caused the eyes of the widow to fail; Or have eaten my morsel myself alone, and the fatherless hath not eaten thereof" (31:16 f). The writer of *A Review of the* Tragedy of Jane Shore was the first to record the general similarity to this particular chapter (p. 11 f).

11. For the language of this passage, cf. Gen. 4:14 and Psalm 109.

12. See Isaac Barrow, "An Exposition of the Lord's Prayer," in *The Theological Works*, VII, 416 ff, where he insists that complete reliance on Providence is the import of the petition for "daily bread." He says, for example, "We must esteem God's providence our surest estate, God's bounty our best treasure, God's fatherly care our most certain and most comfortable support" (p. 418).

13. John T. McNeill and Helena M. Gamer, *Medieval Handbooks of Penance*, p. 29 f, point out that such penance, particularly on Ash Wednesday, was common in the late Middle Ages and that the compilers of the Book of Common Prayer were in favor of this

form of penance. A. Schwarz, "Example," p. 242n, points out that Jane's penance was historical and was illustrated by Blake (see frontispiece).

14. Throughout the play Rowe has stressed Jane's failing health. Therefore, the speed with which she languishes, especially under the conditions of hunger and exposure, is not implausibly precipitate.

15. Rowan, p. 463. The poor caliber of Rowan's criticism is revealed when he says that Shore starves to death at the end of the play.

16. Helen M. Garth, *Saint Mary Magdalene in Medieval Literature*, p. 93.

17. John J. McDermott, "Mary Magdalene in English Literature from 1500–1650," p. 217.

18. Shore's action here, like that of Hastings toward Alicia earlier, resembles Adam's stooping to forgive Eve in *Paradise Lost* (X.937 ff), which itself seems patterned on Christ's archetypal forgiveness of Magdalene.

19. See Jackson, p. 320, n. 1, who quotes Arthur Penrhyn Stanley, *Historical Memorials of Westminster Abbey*, who quotes a "Dean Milman," who quotes Mrs. Siddons. Somewhere along the way the line gets misquoted as " 'Twas he, 'twas Hastings." The fault is not Jackson's, for Stanley has the misquotation (II, 32, n. 3).

20. See Jackson, p. 316, n. 5; and A. Schwarz, "Example," p. 243, where he also notes Rowe's effective use of "the short, expressive, dramatic sentence."

21. Dobrée, *Restoration Tragedy*, p. 154, does not like this line either, but A. Schwarz, "Example," p. 243, has shown that it reestablishes intimacy, and I would add that it is perfectly appropriate for a goldsmith and his wife (after all, it was in their shop that Edward sought Jane's "jewel," in Heywood, *Edward IV*, 1.III.iv) and for a play where Jane's jewels cannot secure her friendship but where her lord of former days forgives her and still calls her at the end "my heart's treasure" (V, p. 185).

22. For the most recent—and perhaps the most egregious—example of this failure, see Eugene Hnatko, "The Failure of Eighteenth-Century Tragedy," p. 464, where he calls *Jane Shore* " 'sentimental' " because "evil is not seen in a totally inclusive order but in individual actions and individual characters insofar as they fail to follow virtue by suppressing passion."

Appendix

A

CATALOGUE

OF THE

LIBRARY

OF

Nicholas Rowe, Esq;

DECEAS'D,

Late POET-LAUREAT to *His Majesty*.

BEING

A Collection of very Valuable Books
in *Old English* HISTORY, POETRY,
&c. in *Greek, Latin, French, Spanish,* &c.
neatly bound, gilt or letter'd.

Which will begin to be Sold the *Fair Way*
[the *Price* being fix'd on the first Leaf of each
Book] at *Exeter Exchange* in the *Strand,* on
Wednesday the 26th of this *August,* 1719, beginning at Nine a-Clock in the Morning.

∘∘

NB. *There's a large Collection of MSS.*

∘∘

Catalogues to be had of Mr. *Chetwood* in *Russel-street, Covent-garden,*
Mr. *Graves* at St. *James's,* Mr. *Mears* without *Temple-bar,* Mr. *Clem-
ents* in St. *Paul's* Church-yard, Mr. *Strahan* in *Cornhill,* and at the
Place of Sale.

Libri Gr. Lat. Fr. Span. &c.

FOLIO.

1	L'Oyseau *des Offices & Ordres*		1610
2	Matth. Westminster	*Francos.*	1601
3	De Antiquit. Britan. Ecclesiæ, per *Parker,*	*Hanov.*	1605
4	*Spelmanni* Glossarium	*Lond.*	1687
5	*Tho. Mori* Opera	*Lovan.*	1565
6	*Cambdeni* Anglia Normanica	*Franc.*	1602
7	_____ Britannia (sine Mappis)		
8	Pontificale		
9	*Harpsfeldi* Historia Ang. Ecclesiastica	*Duaci,*	1622
10	*Montani* Biblia Hebraica		1619
11	*Pindari* Opera	*Oxon.*	1697
12	*Galei* Scriptores, 3 vol.	*ib.*	1684, 1691
13	Matthew Paris	*Lond.*	1684
14	*Plinii* Historia Naturalis	*Bas.*	1525
15	*Seldeni* Mare Clausum	*Lond.*	1635
16	*Spondanus* Homer.	*Basil.*	
17	*Seneca* Opera		1593
18	*Spelmanni* Glossarium	*Lond.*	1626
19	_____ Concilia, 1st vol.	*ib.*	1639
20	*Mariana Istoria Espagna,* 2 *vol.*	Madr.	1678
21	*Cambdeni* Annales, 2 vol.	*Lond.*	1627
22	Rerum Britannicarum Script. Vetustioris	*Lugd.*	1587
23	*Tulii* Opera, 2d tom.	*Lond.*	1681
24	*Commentaires de Terrien*		1654
25	Richelet *Dictionaire,* 2 *vol.*		1709
26	*Memoires Royales Oeconomies* Henry le Grand		
27	Corpus Poetarum, 2 vol.		1713
28	Bayle *Dictionaire Historique,*		1702
29	*Selden's* Eadmerus		1623
30	*Whartoni* Anglia Sacra		1691

English Folio's.

31	*Ben Johnson's* Works	
32	Sir *Tho. Brown's* Works	
33	*Dee* of Spirits	
34	*Herbert's* Travels	
35	*Hale's* Origination	
36	*Keble's* Statutes	1681
37	*Prynne's* King *John*	1670
38	_____ 2d tom. and *Henry* III.	1666
39	*Pitfield* on Animals	1688
40	*Bolton's* Justice	1638
41	*Usher's* Body of Divinity	1653
42	*Sandy's* Travels	1615
43	*Selden's* Tracts	1683
44	Votes	1680
45	*Bacon's* Natural History	1651

46	Poly Chronicon	
47	Orlando Furioso	
48	*Edmond's* Cæsar	1609
49	*Guillim's* Heraldry	1638
50	*Atwood's* Fundamental Constitution	1690
51	*Morrice* on the Sacrament	1660
52	*Rycault's* Peru	1688
53	*Husband's* Collections	1646
54	*Shaftsbury's* Tryal	1681
55	Bentivolio and Urania	1660
56	*Bacon's* Henry VII.	1622
57	*Dugdale's* Origines Juridiciales	1671
58	*Minshieu's* Dictionary of 9 Languages	1626
59	*Weaver's* Funeral Monuments	1631
60	*Speed's* Chronicle	1623
61	*Phillips's* Dictionary	1706
62	Vol. of Gazettes, 1693, 1694, 1695	
63	*Sandy's* Travels	1670
64	*Fabian's* Chronicle	1533
65	Laws and Statutes of the Stannary of *Devon*	1600
66	Case of the Dutchy of *Cornwal*	1613
67	King *Charles's* Works, large paper	1687
68	*Hooker's* Polity	1666
69	Quo Warranto	1690
70	*Brady's* Introduction	1684
71	*De la Valle's* Travels	1665
72	*Hollingshead's* Chronicle, 3d vol.	1587
73	*Knolles's* Hist. of the *Turks*	1603
74	*Hammond* on the New Testament	1671
75	*More's* Philosophical Writings	1662
76	*Meige's* French Dictionary	1688
77	*Favine's* Theatre of Honour	1623
78	Irish Tenure	1639
79	Votes	1690
80	Almahide	1677
81	*Townshend's* Collections	1680
82	*Shakespear's* Works	1632
83	*Eachard's* Ecclesiastical History	1702
84	*Dew's* Journal	1682
85	Book of Martyrs, 3 vol.	1684
86	*Brooks's* Catalogue of the Nobility	1619
87	*Bacon's* Resuscitatio	1657
88	*Grew's* Rarities	1681
89	*Daniel's* Hist. of *England*	1621
90	*Burnet's* Theory	1697
91	*Martin's* Chronicle	1615
92	*Beaumont* and *Fletcher*	1679
93	*Boccalin's* Parnassus	1656
94	Council of *Trent*	1676
95	*Phillips* of Monarchy and Parliaments	1687
96	*Hackluyt's* Voyages, 3d vol.	
97	Acts of Parliament, 1st, 5th, 6th, *William* and *Mary*, 2 vol.	
98	Tryals in the Popish Plot, 4 vol.	

 99 *Eachard*'s Hist. of *England*, 3 vol.   1718
100 *Spencer*'s Works   1679
101 Prince *Arthur*   1695
102 *Rushworth*'s Collections   1659
103 *Plott*'s Staffordshire   1686
104 *Rycault*'s Lives of the Popes   1688
105 Bp *Grindal's* Life   1710
106 *Douglas*'s Virgil   *ibid.*
107 *Johnson*'s Works   *ibid.*
108 Acts of Queen *ANN*, 9th Year
109 *Leigh*'s Lancashire   1700
110 *Bayle*'s Dictionary, 4 vol.   1710
111 Collection of Poems on the Victories of *Blanheim*, &c.   1708
112 *Stevens*'s Spanish Dictionary   1706
113 Hist. of *Philip de Commines*   1674
114 *Bentivoglio*'s Wars of *Flanders*   1678
115 *Burnet*'s Memoirs of D. *Hamilton*   1677
116 *Blackmore* on *Job*   1700
117 *Blount*'s Philostratus   1680
118 *Chaucer*'s Works   1602
119 *Whitlock*'s Memorials   1709
120 Tryal of the Seven Bishops—*Atkins* of Penal Statutes
121 Gazettes, 4 vol. 1674, 75, 76, 80, 81, 82, 83, 85, 86, 87
122 British Chronicle   1493
123 MSS. 23 vol. (all Law)
124 _____ ditto, 5 vol. (4°)
125 _____ ditto, 3 vol. (8°)
126 *Purcell*'s Orpheus Britan.   1706

° °

Libri Gr. Lat. &c. *in* QUARTO.

 1 *CAussin* de Eloquentia   1651
 2 *Platina* de Vitis Pontificum   1626
 3 *Herbert* de Veritate   1645
 4 *Ruvius* in Aristotelis Logica   1641
 5 Reformatio Legum Ecclesiasticarum   *ibid.*
 6 *Stierii* Logica   1659
 7 Processionale in usum Sarum
 8 *Vinnius* in Justinian   1655
 9 *Taciti* Opera Lipsius   1606
10 *Lucani* Pharsalia   1551
11 *Balæus* de Scriptoribus Britannicis   1549
12 *Curtii* Radices Hebrææ   1649
13 *Godwin* Antiquitates   1685
14 *Bythner*'s Lyra Prophetica
15 *Waræus* de Scriptoribus Hiberniæ   1639
16 *Gassendi* Vita Piereski   1655
17 D'Avila *Histoire de France*, 2 vol.   1657
18 *Littleton*'s Dictionary   1703
19 *Oeuvres de St.* Evremont, 3 *vol.*   1705

70   Four Vol. of Plays, by *Shirley, Heywood, Shakespear, Massinger*

●●

Libri Gr. Lat. &c. *in* Octavo.

1	JUvenal Delph.		1699
2	*Buxtorf* Lexicon	*Bas.*	1676
3	Apologia pro ejectis Ministris Angliæ		1664
4	Zouch de Politica Eccles. Anglicanæ		1683
5	Gradus ad Parnassum		1691
6	*Selden*'s Jani Anglorum		1610
7	*Polydore Virgil.* Hist. Angliæ		1651
8	Virgil Delphini		1695
9	Epicteti Enchiridion		1659
10	*Apollidorus* in Usum Schol. *Westm.*		1686
11	Buchanan de Rebus Scoticis		1594
12	*Vossius* de Studiis		1658
13	*Sleidan* de quattuor Summis Imperiis		1611
14	*Zouch* Quæstiones Juris-Civilis		1682
15	*Grotii* Epistolæ ad Gallos		1650
16	*Gulston* in Aristotelem		1696
17	*Thucydides* Historia		1589
18	*Curanza* summa Consiliorum		1668
19	*Minellius* in Horace		1676
20	*Vinnius* Justinian		1663
21	*Plauti* Comœdiæ 24°	*Amst.*	1652
22	*Lower* de Corde		1669
23	*Grævius* Suetonius		1697
24	Epigrammatum Dilectus		1680
25	*Augustini* Confessiones		1619
26	*Bythner* Clavis Linguæ Sanctæ		1618
27	*Martialis* Epigrammata		1689
28	*Livy* Historia, 2 vol.	*Cantabr.*	1679
29	Lucan (Variorum)		1669
30	*Colbert* Philosophia, 2 vol.		1685
31	*Zouch* Elementa Jurisprudentiæ		
32	Enchiridion Titulorum Juris		1565
33	*Juelli* Apologia		1591
34	*Grotii* Epistolæ ad Israelem		1670
35	Catullus, Tibullus (24°)		1686
36	Velleius Peterculus	*Elz.*	1639
37	*Farnaby*'s Virgil		1634
38	Nugæ Venales		1663
39	*Johannis* secundi Opera		1631
40	*Ovidii* Epistolæ (Delph.)		1702
41	Salustius (*Minellii*)		1685
42	*Saunders* de Schismate Anglicani		1585
43	*Mori* Utopiæ		1655
44	Liturgia Græca & Testamentum		
45	*Cowelli* Institutio Juris-Civilis		1676
46	Vita Cardinalis *Poli*		1690
47	*Tulii* de Natura Deorum		1596

48	*Usserii* Opuscula duo		1687
49	*Rog. Baconi* de Senectute		1591
50	*Sharrock* Provinciale		1664
51	*Homeri* Iliados, gr. & lat.		
52	*Heinsius* de Constitutione Tragœdiæ		1611
53	*Barclaii* Argenis		1674
54	*Robertson*'s Hebrew Psalms, 2 vol. interleaf'd		1685
55	*Bartholini* Historia Anatom. 2 vol.		1654
56	*Clerici* Vita		1711
57	*Selden* de Diis Syris		1662
58	*Buchanani* Psalmorum	*Elz.*	1628
59	Ignoramus		1630
60	Hist. Romanæ Epitome (24°)		*ibid.*
61	*Gurtleri* Historia Templariorum		1701
62	*Duck* de Authoritate Juris Civilis		1679
63	Biblia sacra Latina		1534
64	*Plinii* Epistolæ & Panegyr.	*Elz.*	1623
65	Salust		1591
66	*Campanella* de Monarchia Hispanica		
67	*Blebelius*'s Hebrew Grammar		1587
68	*Farnaby*'s Epigrams		1650
69	*Bellarmini* Symboli Apostolici		1624
70	*Machiavel* Princeps		1560
71	Heinsius Horace		1676
72	Q. Curtius	*Amst.*	1660
73	Athenagoras	*Oxon.*	1682
74	Greek Testament	*Elz.*	1656
75	*Robertson*'s Hebrew Psalms		*ibid.*
76	Corn. Tacitus		1621
77	*Quintiliani* Opera		1641
78	*Malpighius* de Hepate		1669
79	*Tullii* Orationes		1686
80	Philosophia Physica	*Paris,*	1646
81	*Grotius* de Veritate Relig. Christianæ		1674
82	_____ de Jure Belli ac Pacis		1670
83	*Plinii* Hist. Naturalis, lst tom.	*Elz.*	1635
84	Sophoclis Tragœdiæ	*Cant.*	
85	*Johnson*'s Sophocles, 2 vol.		1705
86	*Cockman*'s Tullii de Oratore		1706
87	*Quillet*'s Callipœdia		1708
88	Lucan	*Lugd.*	1564
89	*Strada* Prolusiones		1658
90	*Burgersdicius* Logica		1660
91	Musæ Britannicæ		1711
92	*Trapp*'s Prælectiones		*ibid.*
93	Macrobius (Variorum)		1694
94	Poetæ minores		1635
95	*Cowlei* Poemata		1678
96	*Plinii* Epistolæ	apud *Seb. Gryph.*	1552
97	*Justini* Historia		1687
98	*Bartholini* Anatomia		1669
99	*Barclaii* Euphormion		1655
100	Dionysius Longinus		1663

101	*Ovidii* Opera, 3 vol.		1715
102	*Hippocratis* Aphorismus		1582
103	*Bentley's* Horace, 2d vol.		1712
104	*Heinsius* de Constitutione Tragœdiæ		1643
105	Cæsaris Comment.		1686
106	Rutgersius Horace		1699
107	*Erasmi* Colloquia (24°)	*Amst.*	1650
108	Claudian		1688
109	Ovidii Metamorph. (24°)		1664
110	Val. Maximus		1626
111	*Homeri* Odyssea (24°)		
112	*Oeuvres de Rabelais, 4 vol.*		1711
113	*Lucien d'Ablancourt, 3 vol.*		1707
114	*Lettres de Patin, 2 vol.*		1692
115	*Hist. Divorce Hen. VIII. 3 vol.*		1688
116	_____ *de Florence, 2 vol.*		1694
117	*Oeuvres de Rapin, 2 vol.*		1686
118	*Contes de la Fontaine*		1699
119	*Theatre Italien, 6 vol.*		1701
120	*Histoire Imaginations Oufle*		1710
121	*Soupirs d'Europe*		1712
122	*Relation d'Inquisition Goa*		1688
123	*Retraite dix Milles de Xenephon*		1695
124	*Tragedies de Sophocles*		1693
125	*Histoire des Oracles*		1701
126	*Characteres de Theophraste, 3 vol.*		1705
127	*Histoire de France, par Mezeray, 6 vol.*		1682
128	*Voyage de Brazile, 2 vol.*		1717
129	*Horace Tarteron, 2 vol.*		1710
130	*Vie de Pythagoras, 2 vol.*		1706
131	*Lettres de Richelieu, 2 vol.*		1695
132	*Histoire de Louis XIV. 2 vol.*		1693
133	*Voyage de Siam*		1687
134	*Dacier's Horace, 10 vol.*		1699
135	*Oeuvres de Corneille, 8 vol.*		1665
136	*Hist. Heliodore*		1636
137	*Rosalinda*		1651
138	*Lettres du Count de Bussy*		1700
139	*Geographie de Croix, 1st, 2d, & 4th vol.*		1693
140	*Bertram*		1673
141	*Memoires d'Estrades, 2d tom.*		1709
142	*Histoire de Charles IV. Duc de Lorraine*		1693
143	*Poesies Anacreon & Sappho*		1681
144	*Vie de Oliver Cromwell, 2 vol.*		1694
145	*Voyage du Nort*		
146	*Histoire de Foundation des Ordres Religieux*		1688
147	*Description des Ordres Religieux*		
148	*Heureux Esclave*		1674
149	*Intrigues du Cour de Rome*		1677
150	*Memoires de Beaujeu*		1700
151	*Allix de France Historique*		1686
152	*Vie du Dutchess Valiere*		1695
153	*Histoire de la Republique de Venise*		1680

204	Account of *Denmark*	1694
205	*Dennis* on modern Poetry	1701
206	*Welwood*'s Banquet of *Xenophon*	1710
207	*Carr*'s Hist. of the Popish Plot	1681
208	*Anderson*'s Scotland's Independency	1705
209	*Nelson*'s Office of a Justice	1710
210	*Montfaucon*'s Travels	1712
211	*Temple*'s Letters, lst vol.	
212	_____ Memoirs, 3d vol.	
213	*Misson*'s Voyage to *Italy,* 2d vol.	1695
214	*La Hontan*'s Voyage, 2d vol.	1703
215	*Ludlow*'s Memoirs, 3d vol.	1699
216	Hist. of Monastical Orders	1693
217	Abridgment of the Statutes, 2d vol.	
218	*Perrault*'s Characters, 1st vol.	1704
219	Life of Cardinal *Richelieu,* 1st vol.	1703
220	Ductor Historicus	1698
221	*Coke*'s Detection, 1st vol.	1696
222	Phædra and Ajax, 2 vol.	1714
223	*Dacier*'s Homer, 5 vol.	1712
224	*Bethel*'s Interest of Princes	1680
225	Account of the *Pyrmont* Waters	1717
226	*Evremont*'s Works, 1st vol.	1700
227	*Waller*'s Poems	1705
228	*Congreve*'s Works, 3 vol.	1710
229	*Wilkins*'s Natural Religion	1678
230	Debates of the House of Commons in 1680	
231	*Rozel*'s Life	1709
232	*Nelson*'s Feasts and Fasts	1705
233	Two *Phillips*'s Poems, one large paper, one small	1710
234	*De Foe*'s Works	1703
235	*Davenant*'s Essays	1704
236	*Swift*'s Miscellanies	1711
237	*Ovid*'s Art of Love	1709
238	_____ Epistles	1701
236[sic]	*Betterton*'s Life	1710
240	*Creech*'s Theocritus	1684
241	*Otway*'s Plays, 2 vol.	1712
242	*Gildon*'s Art of Poetry, 2 vol.	1718
243	Gilblas, 2 vol.	1716
244	State of Persia	1695
245	*Anton*'s Spanish Grammar	1711
246	*Cent Leivre*'s Cruel Gift	1717
247	*Baxter*'s Church-Divisions	1670
248	*Brady*'s Answer to *Pettit*	1681
249	Funnel's Voyages	1707
250	*Galtrucius*'s Heathen Gods	1674
251	*Hoadley* on Government	1710
252	Reports in Chancery, 2d part	1694
253	*Hale*'s Contemplations	1685
254	*Smith*'s Memoirs of Secret Service	1699
255	Case stated, Jurisdiction of the House of Lords	1660
256	_____ of Bankers and Creditors	1675

362	Lingua Tersancta; or, Allegorick Dictionary	1703
363	*Hobbes*'s Homer	1686
364	The Moralists	1706
365	*Burnet*'s Rights of Princes	1682
366	*Long* against *Julian*	1683
367	*Howe*'s Living Temple	1675
368	*Lambards* Archian	1635
369	*Brerewoods* Enquiries	1674
370	*Dennis*'s Battle of Ramillies	1706
371	Present State of *America*	1687
372	*Zenophons* Cyrus	1685
373	*Youngs* Spelling-book	
374	*Alsops* Melius Inquirendum	1681
375	Account of the Storm	1704
376	*Dampiers* Voyages	1698
377	*Temples* Miscellanies	1680
378	*Sympsons* Hydrologia Chymica	1669
379	*Denhams* Poems	1684
380	*Hollis*'s Memoirs	1699
381	Memoirs of the English Court	1708
382	*Maundrels* Journey from *Aleppo*	1703
383	*Dionis*'s Surgery	1710
384	*Beaumont* of Spirits	1705
385	*Dunstars* Horace (large paper)	1712
386	Cyder (large paper)	1708
387	*Gays* Trivia (large paper)	
388	*Fentau*'s Poems (large paper)	1707
389	*Popes* Rape of the Lock (large paper)	1714
390	The Wanderer	1718
391	*Edgars* Book of Rates	1714
392	Classical Dictionary	1715
393	*Burchets* Memoirs at Sea	1703
394	*Plutarch*'s Lives, 5 vol.	1712
395	*Kennets* Roman Antiquities	1713
396	*Potters* Antiquities of Greece, 2 vol.	1706
397	*Etheridge*'s Works	1704
398	*Du Pin*'s Universal Library, 2 vol.	1709
399	*Littleburys* Herodotus, 2 vol.	*ibid.*
400	*Lake* on the Sacrament	1703
401	*Miltons* Paradise lost	1711
402	*May*'s Lucan	1635
403	*Ovids* Metamorphosis, Eng.	1717
404	Volume of Almanacks	*ibid.*
405	Characteristicks, 3 vol.	1711
406	*Drydens* Miscellanies, 6 tom. 5 vol.	1702
407	*Clarendons* Hist. of the Rebellion, 6 vol.	1705
408	*Bacons* Essays	1701
409	*Godfrey* of *Bulloigne*	1687
410	*Drydens* Fables	1713
411	*Whistons* Astronomical Lectures	1717
412	*Shakespears* Works, 7th vol.	1710
413	*Montaigne*'s Essays, 1st and 2d vol.	1693

FINIS.

Bibliographies

A

A Tentative Twentieth-Century Bibliography on Rowe's Tragedies

EDITIONS

Collections

The Dramatick Works of Nicholas Rowe, Esq. 2 vols. 1720; rpt. Farnborough, Hants., Eng.: Gregg International Publishers, Ltd., 1971.

The Fair Penitent and Jane Shore, ed. Sophie Chantal Hart. Belles-Lettres Series. Boston: Heath, 1907.

Nicholas Rowe (Tragedies): The Fair Penitent (*1703*), The Tragedy of Jane Shore (*1714*), The Tragedy of Lady Jane Grey (*1715*). Rpt. from Bell's and Inchbald's editions. Vol. IX of *British Theatre: Eighteenth-Century English Drama*, ed. Natascha Würzbach. Frankfurt: Minerva, 1969.

Three Plays: Tamerlane, The Fair Penitent, Jane Shore, ed. James R. Sutherland. London: Scholartis, 1929.

Individual Plays

The Fair Penitent, ed. Malcolm Goldstein. Regents Restoration Drama Series. Lincoln: University of Nebraska Press, 1969.

————, in *Eighteenth-Century English Drama*, ed. Joseph Wood Krutch. New York: Bantam, 1967.

————, in *Five Restoration Tragedies*, ed. Bonamy Dobrée. World's Classics. London: Oxford University Press, 1928.

————, in *Plays of the Restoration and Eighteenth Century*, ed. Dougald MacMillan and Howard Mumford Jones. New York: Holt, 1931.

————, in *Six Eighteenth-Century Plays*, ed. John Harold Wilson. Boston: Houghton, 1963.

Tamerlane, a Tragedy, ed. Landon Crawford Burns, Jr. The Matthew Carey Library of English and American Literature. Philadelphia: University of Pennsylvania Press, 1966.

————, in *Nicholas Rowe*, by Ottakar Intze. Heidelberg: K. G. Nachfolger, 1910.

The Tragedy of Jane Shore, ed. Harry William Pedicord. Regents Restoration Drama Series. Lincoln: University of Nebraska Press, 1974.

————, in *British Dramatists from Dryden to Sheridan*, ed. George H. Nettleton, Arthur E. Case, and George Winchester Stone, Jr. 2d ed. rev. Boston: Houghton, 1969.

————, in *British Plays from the Restoration to 1820*, ed. Montrose Jonas Moses. 2 vols. Boston: Little, 1929.

————, in *Eighteenth-Century Plays*, ed. John Hampden. Everyman's Library. London: Dent, 1928.

————, in *Eighteenth-Century Plays*, ed. Ricardo Quintana. Modern Library. New York: Random, 1952.

————, in *Representative English Dramas from Dryden to Sheridan*, ed. Frederick and James W. Tupper. Rev. ed. New York: Oxford University Press, 1934.

————, in *Types of English Drama, 1660–1780*, ed. David Harrison Stevens. Boston: Ginn, 1923.

————, intro. James L. Harner. 1714; rpt. London: Scolar Press, 1973.

The Tragedy of Lady Jane Gray, in *On the Boards of Old Drury,* ed. Lynette Feasey. London: George G. Harrap, 1951.

CRITICISM°

Behrend, Alfred. *Nicholas Rowe als Dramatiker.* Diss. Königsberg 1907. Leipzig: August Hoffman, 1907.
Borgwardt, Paul. *The Royal Convert von Nicholas Rowe 1707.* Diss. Rostock 1909. Rostock: W. H. Winterberg, 1909.
Budig, Willy. *Untersuchungen über* Jane Shore. Diss. Rostock 1908. Schwerin: Bärensprungschen Hofbuchdruckerei, 1908.
Bünning, Eduard. *Nicholas Rowe* Tamerlane, *1702.* Diss. Rostock 1908. Schwerin: Bärensprungschen Hofbuchdruckerei, 1908.
Burns, Landon Crawford, Jr. "The Tragedies of Nicholas Rowe." Diss. Yale 1958.
Canfield, John Douglas. "Nicholas Rowe's Christian Tragedies." Diss. Florida 1969.
Clark, Donald Bettice. "An Eighteenth-Century Adaptation of Massinger." *MLQ,* 13 (1952), 239 ff.
————. "Nicholas Rowe: A Study in the Development of the Pathetic Tragedy." Diss. George Washington 1947.
————. "The Source and Characterization of Nicholas Rowe's *Tamerlane.*" *MLN,* 65 (1950), 145 ff.
Conley, Irene Grace. "The Influence of Shakespeare on the Dramas of Nicholas Rowe." M.A. Thesis Minnesota 1929.
Dammers, Richard Herman. "Female Characters and Feminine Morality in the Tragedies of Nicholas Rowe." Diss. Notre Dame 1971.
————. "Recent Scholarship on Nicholas Rowe." *British Studies Monitor,* 5 (1975), 24–27.
————. "Rowe's Tragedies and Women: A Modern Approach." Paper delivered at the fourth annual meeting of the East Central Regional Conference of the American Society for Eighteenth-Century Studies, Indiana University of Pennsylvania, October 1973.
Dussinger, J. A. "Richardson and Johnson: Critical Agreement on Rowe's *The Fair Penitent.*" *ES,* 49 (1968), 45 ff.
Gilde, Alfred. *Die dramatische Behandlung der Rückkehr des Odysseus bei Nicholas Rowe, Robert Bridges und Stephen Phillips.* Diss. Königsberg 1903. Königsberg: R. Leupold, 1903.
Gilliard, Frederick William. "Nicholas Rowe's Men: A Playwright's Dramatic and Thematic Approaches to Characterization." Diss. Utah 1971.
Goldstein, Malcolm. "Pathos and Personality in the Tragedies of Nicholas Rowe," in *English Writers of the Eighteenth Century,* ed. John H. Middendorf. New York: Columbia University Press, 1971.
Jackson, Alfred. "The Life and Work of Nicholas Rowe." M.A. Thesis London 1929.
————. "Rowe's Historical Tragedies." *Anglia,* 54 (1930), 307 ff.
Jenkins, Annibel. "Passion and Penitence: Love and Innocence in Dante, Rowe, and Goethe." Paper delivered at the thirty-eighth annual meeting of the South Atlantic MLA in Jacksonville, Fla., November 1968. Précis publ. in *The South Atlantic Bulletin,* 34 (1969), 9.

°Exclusive of summary treatment in general works. See also Carl J. Stratman et al., eds., *Restoration and Eighteenth Century Theatre Research: A Bibliographical Guide, 1900–1968,* s.v. Rowe. Father Stratman's bibliography has been invaluable.

Kearful, Frank J. "The Nature of Tragedy in Rowe's *The Fair Penitent*." *PLL*, 2 (1966), 351 ff.

Kleitz, Philip Rex. "Nicholas Rowe: Developer of the Drama of Sympathy." Diss. Minnesota 1967.

"Nicholas Rowe." *TLS*, October 10, 1929, p. 773 f.

Rowan, D. F. "Shore's Wife." *SEL*, 6 (1966), 447 ff.

Schuster, Sister Celine. "Nicholas Rowe and the Whig Movement." M.A. Thesis Oregon 1941.

Schwarz, Alfred. "An Example of Eighteenth-Century Pathetic Tragedy: Rowe's *Jane Shore*." *MLQ*, 22 (1961), 236 ff.

————. "The Literary Career of Nicholas Rowe." Diss. Harvard 1951.

Schwarz, Ferdinand H. *Nicholas Rowe's* Fair Penitent: *A Contribution to Literary Analysis*. Diss. Berne 1906. Berne: Buchler & Co., 1907.

Stahl, Ludwig. *Nicholas Rowes Drama* The Ambitious Stepmother, *1700*. Diss. Rostock 1909. Rostock: Carl Hinstorff, 1909.

Sutherland, James R. "Nicholas Rowe." B. Litt. Thesis Oxford 1926.

Swern, Nancy Peter. "Nicholas Rowe: A Study." M.A. Thesis Columbia 1953.

Swindell, Alice Blanche. "Nicholas Rowe as an Exponent of Eighteenth-Century Drama." M.A. Thesis Columbia 1926.

Thorp, Willard. "A Key to Rowe's *Tamerlane*." *JEGP*, 39 (1940), 124 ff.

Whiting, George W. "Rowe's Debt to *Paradise Lost*." *MP*, 32 (1935), 271 ff.

Wikander, Matthew Hays. "History in Drama from Shakespeare to Rowe." Diss. Michigan 1975.

Williamson, Julia. "Nicholas Rowe's Theory of Tragedy." M.A. Thesis Illinois 1941.

Wyman, Lindley A. "The Tradition of the Formal Meditation in Rowe's *The Fair Penitent*." *PQ*, 42 (1963), 412 ff.

B

A List of Works Cited

Adams, Henry Hitch. *English Domestic or, Homiletic Tragedy 1575 to 1642: Being an Account of the Development of the Tragedy of the Common Man Showing its Great Dependence on Religious Morality, Illustrated with Striking Examples of the Interposition of Providence for the Amendment of Men's Manners.* 1943; rpt. New York: Blom, 1965.

Aldridge, A. Owen. "The Pleasures of Pity." *ELH,* 16 (1949), 76 ff.

Allen, Don Cameron. *Doubt's Boundless Sea: Skepticism and Faith in the Renaissance.* Baltimore: Johns Hopkins Press, 1964.

———. *The Harmonious Vision: Studies in Milton's Poetry.* Baltimore: Johns Hopkins Press, 1954.

Annotations upon All the Books of the Old and New Testament. London, 1645.

Arkell, Ruby Lillian. *Caroline of Ansbach, George the Second's Queen.* London: Oxford University Press, 1939.

Attwater, Donald, et al., eds. *A Catholic Dictionary.* New York: Macmillan, 1943.

Aubignac, François Hédelin, abbé d'. *The Whole Art of the Stage,* trans. anon. London, 1684.

Ault, Norman. *New Light on Pope.* London: Methuen, 1949.

Avery, Emmett L. "The Popularity of *The Mourning Bride* in the London Theatres in the Eighteenth Century." *Research Studies of the State Coll. of Washington,* 9 (1941), 115 f.

Baker, Herschel. *The Wars of Truth: Studies in the Decay of Christian Humanism in the Earlier Seventeenth Century.* Cambridge: Harvard University Press, 1952.

Banks, John. *The Innocent Usurper: or, The Death of the Lady Jane Gray.* London, 1694.

Barbeau, Anne T. *The Intellectual Design of John Dryden's Heroic Plays.* New Haven: Yale University Press, 1970.

Barrow, Isaac. *The Theological Works of Isaac Barrow,* ed. Alexander Napier. Cambridge: Cambridge University Press, 1859.

Battenhouse, Roy W. *Marlowe's* Tamburlaine: *A Study in Renaissance Moral Philosophy.* Nashville: Vanderbilt University Press, 1941.

Behrend, Alfred. *Nicholas Rowe als Dramatiker.* Diss. Königsberg 1907. Leipzig: August Hoffman, 1907.

Blackmore, Sir Richard. *A Paraphrase on the Book of Job.* London, 1700.

———. *Prince Arthur: An Heroick Poem in Ten Books.* London, 1695.

Borgwardt, Paul. *The Royal Convert von Nicholas Rowe 1707.* Diss. Rostock 1909. Rostock: W. H. Winterberg, 1909.

Bray, René. *La Formation de la doctrine classique en France.* Lausanne: Payot, 1931.

Brittain, Kilbee C. "The Sin of Despair in English Renaissance Literature." Diss. UCLA 1963.

Budig, Willy. *Untersuchungen über* Jane Shore. Diss. Rostock 1908. Schwerin: Bärensprungschen Hofbuchdruckerei, 1908.

Burnet, Gilbert. *The History of the Reformation of the Church of England.* London, 1679–1715.

Burns, Landon Crawford, Jr. "The Tragedies of Nicholas Rowe." Diss. Yale 1958.

———, ed. *Tamerlane, a Tragedy,* by Nicholas Rowe. Matthew Carey Library of English and American Literature. Philadelphia: University of Pennsylvania Press, 1966.

Burton, Robert. *The Anatomy of Melancholy,* ed. Holbrook Jackson. Everyman's Library. London: Dent, 1932.

Campbell, Lily Bess. *Shakespeare's Tragic Heroes: Slaves of Passion.* Cambridge: Cambridge University Press, 1930.

Canfield, John Douglas. "Nicholas Rowe's Christian Tragedies." Diss. Florida 1969.

A Catalogue of the Library of Nicholas Rowe, Esq. London, 1719.

Certain Sermons or Homilies, Appointed to be Read in Churches in the Time of Queen Elizabeth of famous Memory: and Now thought to be Reprinted by Authority from the Kings most Excellent Majesty. Oxford, 1683.

Chambers, E. K. *The Elizabethan Stage.* Rev. ed. Oxford: Clarendon, 1951.

Cioranescu, Alexandre. *Bibliographie de la littérature française du dix-septième siècle.* Vol. II. Paris: Centre National de la Recherche Scientifique, 1966.

Clark, Donald Bettice. "An Eighteenth-Century Adaptation of Massinger." *MLQ*, 13 (1952), 239 ff.

————. "Nicholas Rowe: A Study in the Development of the Pathetic Tragedy." Diss. George Washington 1947.

————. "The Source and Characterization of Nicholas Rowe's *Tamerlane*." *MLN*, 65 (1950), 145 ff.

Clarke, Samuel. *Seventeen Sermons.* 2d ed. London, 1724.

Collier, Jeremy. *Second Defence of the* Short View of the Profaneness and Immorality of the English Stage. London, 1700.

A Comparison between the Two Stages: A Late Restoration Book of the Theatre, ed. Staring B. Wells. Princeton: Princeton University Press, 1942.

Compton, Gail H. "The Metaphor of Conquest in Dryden's *The Conquest of Granada*." Diss. Florida 1968.

Congreve, William. *The Complete Plays of William Congreve,* ed. Herbert Davis. Curtain Playwrights. Chicago: University of Chicago Press, 1967.

————. The Mourning Bride, *Poems, and Miscellanies,* ed. Bonamy Dobrée. World's Classics. London: Oxford University Press, 1928.

Corneille, Pierre. *Œuvres complètes,* ed. André Stegmann. Paris: Editions du Seuil, 1963.

Courtney, William Leonard. *The Idea of Tragedy in Ancient and Modern Drama.* 1900; rpt. New York: Russell and Russell, 1967.

Crane, Ronald S. "Suggestions Toward a Genealogy of the 'Man of Feeling.' " *ELH*, 1 (1934), 205 ff.

Dammers, Richard Herman. "Female Characters and Feminine Morality in the Tragedies of Nicholas Rowe." Diss. Notre Dame 1971.

————. "Recent Scholarship on Nicholas Rowe." *British Studies Monitor*, 5 (1975), 24 ff.

Dennis, John. *The Critical Works of John Dennis,* ed. Edward Niles Hooker. Baltimore: Johns Hopkins Press, 1939–43.

Dimock, George. "Crime and Punishment in the *Odyssey*." *Yale Review*, 60 (1971), 199 ff.

Dobrée, Bonamy. *English Literature in the Early Eighteenth Century, 1700–1740.* Oxford History of English Literature, vol. VIII. Oxford: Clarendon, 1959.

————. *Restoration Tragedy 1660–1720.* Oxford: Clarendon, 1929.

Donne, John. *The Sermons of John Donne,* ed. Evelyn M. Simpson and George R. Potter. Berkeley: University of California Press, 1953-62.

Drake, James. *The Antient and Modern Stages Survey'd.* London, 1699.

Dryden, John. *John Dryden: Four Tragedies,* ed. L. A. Beaurline and Fredson Bowers. Curtain Playwrights. Chicago: University of Chicago Press, 1967.

————. Of Dramatic Poesy *and Other Critical Essays,* ed. George Watson. Everyman's Library. London: Dent, 1962.

————. *The Poems of John Dryden,* ed. James Kinsley. Oxford: Clarendon, 1958.

Ebbs, John Dale. "Milton's Treatment of Poetic Justice in *Samson Agonistes*." *MLQ*, 22 (1961), 377 ff.

————. *The Principle of Poetic Justice Illustrated in Restoration Tragedy.* Salzburg Studies in English Literature: Poetic Drama, 4. Salzburg: Institut für englische Sprache und Literatur, 1973.

Elledge, Scott, and Donald Schier, eds. *The Continental Model: Selected French Critical*

Essays of the Seventeenth Century, in English Translation. Minneapolis: University of Minnesota Press, 1960.

Farquhar, George. *The Complete Works of George Farquhar,* ed. Charles Stonehill. 1930; rpt. New York: Gordian Press, 1967.

Fénelon, François de la Mothe-. *Les Aventures de Télémaque, fils d'Ulysse.* Brussels, 1699.

Ferry, Anne Davidson. *Milton and the Miltonic Dryden.* Cambridge: Harvard University Press, 1968.

Filmer, Edward. *A Defence of Plays: or, The Stage Vindicated.* London, 1707.

Fisher, Dorothea Frances (Canfield). *Corneille and Racine in England: A Study of the English Translations of the two Corneilles and Racine, with Especial Reference to their Presentation on the English Stage.* New York: Columbia University Press, 1904.

Fleischmann, Wolfgang Bernard. *Lucretius and English Literature, 1680–1740.* Paris: Nizet, 1964.

Foxe, John. *Acts and Monuments of Matters Most Special and Memorable Happening in the Church: with an Universal History of the Same.* 9th ed. London, 1684.

Garth, Helen Meredith. *Saint Mary Magdalene in Medieval Literature.* Johns Hopkins University Studies in Historical and Political Science, 67, No. 3. Baltimore: Johns Hopkins Press, 1950.

Gasté, Arnaud, ed. *La Querelle du* Cid: *pièces et pamphlets publiés d'après les originaux.* Paris: H. Welter, 1899.

Gendrot, F., and F.-M. Eustache, eds. *Auteurs français: dix-septième siècle.* Paris: Hachette, 1951.

Gilbert, Allan H., ed. *Literary Criticism: Plato to Dryden.* 1940; rpt. Detroit: Wayne State University Press, 1962.

Gildon, Charles. "Charles Gildon's *A New Rehearsal, or Bays the Younger,*" ed. George L. Anderson. Diss. Pennsylvania 1953.

Goldstein, Malcolm. "Pathos and Personality in the Tragedies of Nicholas Rowe," in *English Writers of the Eighteenth Century,* ed. John H. Middendorf. New York: Columbia University Press, 1971.

————, ed. *The Fair Penitent,* by Nicholas Rowe. Regents Restoration Drama Series. Lincoln: University of Nebraska Press, 1969.

Greene, Donald. "Augustinianism and Empiricism: A Note on Eighteenth-Century English Intellectual History." *ECS,* 1 (Fall 1967), 33 ff.

Hadzits, George Depue. *Lucretius and His Influence.* New York: Longmans, 1935.

Harrison, Charles T. "The Ancient Atomists and English Literature of the Seventeenth Century." *Harvard Studies in Classical Philology,* 45 (1934), 1 ff.

Hart, Thomas Alonzo. "The Development and Decline of the Doctrine of Poetic Justice from Plato to Johnson." Diss. Michigan 1941.

Hathaway, Baxter. "John Dryden and the Function of Tragedy." *PMLA,* 58 (1943), 665 ff.

————. "The Lucretian 'Return upon Ourselves' in Eighteenth-Century Theories of Tragedy." *PMLA,* 62 (1947), 672 ff.

Heywood, Thomas. *The First and Second Parts of King Edward IV,* ed. Barron Field. Shakespeare Society. London, 1842. Also included in *The Dramatic Works of Thomas Heywood,* gen. ed. J. Payne Collier. Shakespeare Society. London, 1853.

Hnatko, Eugene. "The Failure of Eighteenth-Century Tragedy." *SEL,* 11 (1971), 459 ff.

Homer. *The Odyssey,* trans. A. T. Murray. Loeb Classical Library. London: Heinemann, 1924.

Horace. *Satires, Epistles, and Ars Poetica,* trans. H. Rushton Fairclough. Loeb Classical Library. Rev. ed. Cambridge: Harvard University Press, 1929.

Horne, Mark Daniel. "The Villain in Restoration Tragedy." Diss. Louisiana State University 1939.

Hunter, J. Paul. *The Reluctant Pilgrim: Defoe's Emblematic Method and Quest for Form in Robinson Crusoe.* Baltimore: Johns Hopkins Press, 1966.

Jackson, Alfred. "Rowe's Historical Tragedies." *Anglia,* 54 (1930), 307 ff.

Jenkins, Annibel. "Passion and Penitence: Love and Innocence in Dante, Rowe, and Goethe." Paper delivered at the thirty-eighth annual meeting of the South Atlantic MLA in Jacksonville, Fla., November 1968. Précis publ. in *The South Atlantic Bulletin,* 34 (1969), 9.

Jonson, Ben. *Ben Jonson: Volpone,* ed. Alvin B. Kernan. The Yale Ben Jonson. New Haven: Yale University Press, 1962.

Kearful, Frank J. "The Nature of Tragedy in Rowe's *The Fair Penitent.*" *PLL,* 2 (1966), 351 ff.

_____. "The Rhetoric of Augustan Tragedy." Diss. Wisconsin 1966.

Kern, Edith G. *The Influence of Heinsius and Vossius upon French Dramatic Theory.* Johns Hopkins Studies in Romance Literature and Languages, extra vol. 26. Baltimore: Johns Hopkins Press, 1949.

Kingston, Richard. *A Discourse on Divine Providence.* London, 1702.

Knolles, Richard. *The General Historie of the Turkes.* London, 1603.

La Mesnardière, Jules de. *La Poëtiqve.* Paris, 1640.

Loftis, John Clyde. *The Politics of Drama in Augustan England.* Oxford: Clarendon, 1963.

Lord, George DeForest. *Homeric Renaissance: The Odyssey of George Chapman.* Yale Studies in English, vol. 131. New Haven: Yale University Press, 1956.

Loughead, Flora H. *Dictionary of Given Names with Origins and Meanings.* Rev. ed. Glendale, Calif.: Arthur H. Clark, 1966.

Mackie, J. D. *The Earlier Tudors, 1485–1558.* The Oxford History of England, vol. VII. Oxford: Clarendon, 1952.

MacMillan, Dougald, and Howard Mumford Jones, eds. *Plays of the Restoration and Eighteenth Century.* New York: Holt, 1931.

Magill, Lewis M. "Poetic Justice: The Dilemma of the Early Creators of Sentimental Tragedy." *Research Studies of the State Coll. of Washington,* 25 (1957), 24 ff.

Mairet, Jean de. *La Silvanire.* Paris, 1631.

Marshall, Geoffrey. *Restoration Serious Drama.* Norman: University of Oklahoma Press, 1975.

Masani, Rustom. *Zoroastrianism: The Religion of the Good Life.* 1938; rpt. New York: Crowell-Collier, 1962.

Massinger, Philip, and Nathan Field. *The Fatal Dowry,* ed. T. A. Dunn. Fountainwell Drama Texts. Edinburgh: Oliver and Boyd, 1969.

Mayo, Thomas Franklin. *Epicurus in England (1650–1725).* Dallas: Southwest Texas Press, 1934.

McDermott, John J. "Mary Magdalene in English Literature from 1500–1650." Diss. UCLA 1964.

McNeill, John T., and Helena M. Gamer. *Medieval Handbooks of Penance: A Translation of the Principal* Libri Poenitentiales *and Selections from Related Documents.* New York: Columbia University Press, 1938.

Milton, John. *Complete Poems and Major Prose,* ed. Merritt Y. Hughes. New York: Odyssey, 1957.

Mintz, Samuel I. *The Hunting of Leviathan: Seventeenth-Century Reactions to the Materialism and Moral Philosophy of Thomas Hobbes.* Cambridge: Cambridge University Press, 1962.

Moulton, Richard G. *Shakespeare as a Dramatic Artist.* 2d ed. Oxford: Clarendon, 1888.

Nicoll, Allardyce. *A History of English Drama 1660–1900.* Vol II: *Early Eighteenth Century Drama.* 3d ed. Cambridge: Cambridge University Press, 1955.

Oldmixon, John. *Reflections on the Stage, and Mr. Collyer's Defence of the* Short View *in Four Dialogues.* London, 1699.

Otway, Thomas. *The Works of Thomas Otway: Plays, Poems, and Love-Letters,* ed. J. C. Ghosh. Oxford: Clarendon, 1932.

Patrick, Symon. *The Works of Symon Patrick,* ed. Alexander Taylor. Oxford: University Press, 1858.

Patrides, C. A. *The Phoenix and the Ladder: The Rise and Decline of the Christian View of History.* University of California Publications, English Studies, 29. Berkeley: University of California Press, 1964.

Peake, Charles Howard. "Domestic Tragedy in Relation to Theology in the First Half of the Eighteenth Century." Diss. Michigan 1941.

Petrie, Charles. *The Jacobite Movement: The First Phase, 1688–1716.* London: Eyre and Spottiswoode, 1948.

Pope, Alexander. *The Twickenham Edition of the Poems of Alexander Pope,* gen. ed. John Butt. London: Methuen, 1939–69.

Quinlan, Michael A. *Poetic Justice in the Drama: The History of an Ethical Principle in Literary Criticism.* Notre Dame, Ind.: University of Notre Dame Press, 1912.

Racine, Jean. *Œuvres de J. Racine,* ed. M. Paul Mesnard. Paris: Hachette, 1865.

A Review of the Tragedy of Jane Shore. London, 1714.

Ribner, Irving. *The English History Play in the Age of Shakespeare.* Rev. ed. London: Methuen, 1965.

Rothstein, Eric. *Restoration Tragedy: Form and the Process of Change.* Madison: University of Wisconsin Press, 1967.

Rowan, D. F. "Shore's Wife." *SEL,* 6 (1966), 447 ff.

Rowe, Nicholas. *The Dramatick Works of Nicholas Rowe, Esq.* 2 vols. 1720; rpt. Farnsborough, Hants., Eng.: Gregg International Publishers, Ltd., 1971.

————. *The Works of Nicholas Rowe, Esq.* London, 1792.

————, ed. *The Works of Mr. William Shakespear.* London, 1709.

————, trans. *Lucan's* Pharsalia. London, 1718.

Rudé, J. Leland. "Poetic Justice: A Study of the Problem of Human Conduct in Tragedy from Aeschylus to Shakespeare." Diss. Harvard 1934.

Scaliger, Julius Caesar. *Poetices Libri Septem.* Lyons, 1561.

Schwarz, Alfred. "An Example of Eighteenth-Century Pathetic Tragedy: Rowe's *Jane Shore.*" *MLQ,* 22 (1961), 236 ff.

————. "The Literary Career of Nicholas Rowe." Diss. Harvard 1951.

Schwarz, Ferdinand H. *Nicholas Rowe's* Fair Penitent: *A Contribution to Literary Analysis.* Diss. Berne 1906. Berne: Buchler & Co., 1907.

Shakespeare, William. *The Complete Plays and Poems of William Shakespeare,* ed. W. A. Neilson and C. J. Hill. Cambridge, Mass.: Houghton, 1942.

————. *Five Restoration Adaptations of William Shakespeare,* ed. Christopher Spencer. Urbana: University of Illinois Press, 1965.

Sherlock, William. *A Discourse Concerning the Divine Providence.* London, 1694.

Singh, Amrik. "The Argument on Poetic Justice (Addison *versus* Dennis)." *The Indian Journal of English Studies,* 3 (1962), 61 ff.

Singh, Sarup. *The Theory of Drama in the Restoration Period.* Bombay: Orient Longmans, 1963.

Smith, G. Gregory, ed. *Elizabethan Critical Essays.* 1904; rpt. London: Oxford University Press, 1937.

South, Robert. *Forty-Eight Sermons.* London, 1715.

The Spectator, ed. G. Gregory Smith. Everyman's Library. London: Dent, 1907.

The Stage Acquitted. London, 1699.

Stanford, William Bedell. *The Ulysses Theme: A Study in the Adaptability of a Traditional Hero.* Rev. ed. Oxford: Basil Blackwell, 1963.

Stanley, Arthur Penrhyn. *Historical Memorials of Westminster Abbey.* Philadelphia: George W. Jacobs & Co., 1899.

Steele, Sir Richard. *The Christian Hero,* ed. Rae Blanchard. London: Oxford University Press, 1932.

Stevenson, Burton, ed. *The Home Book of Proverbs, Maxims, and Familiar Phrases.* New York: Macmillan, 1948.

Stratman, Carl J., et al., eds. *Restoration and Eighteenth Century Theatre Research: A Bibliographical Guide, 1900–1968.* Carbondale: Southern Illinois University Press, 1971.

Stroup, Thomas Bradley. *Microcosmos: The Shape of the Elizabethan Play.* Lexington: University of Kentucky Press, 1965.

Sutherland, James R., ed. *Three Plays*: Tamerlane, The Fair Penitent, Jane Shore, by Nicholas Rowe. London: Scholartis, 1929.

Swedenberg, Hugh Thomas, Jr., ed. *Essential Articles for the Study of John Dryden.* Hamden, Ct.: Archon, 1966.

Swift, Jonathan. *The Poems of Jonathan Swift,* ed. Harold Williams. 2d ed. Oxford: Clarendon, 1958.

Temple, Sir William. *Five Miscellaneous Essays,* ed. Samuel Holt Monk. Ann Arbor: University of Michigan Press, 1963.

Thorp, Willard. "A Key to Rowe's *Tamerlane.*" *JEGP*, 39 (1940), 124 ff.

Tillotson, John. *The Works of John Tillotson.* 2d ed. London, 1717.

Tuveson, Ernest Lee. "The Importance of Shaftesbury." *ELH*, 20 (1953), 267 ff.

Tyre, Richard H. "Versions of Poetic Justice in the Early Eighteenth Century." *SP*, 54 (1957), 29 ff.

Ussher, James. *A Body of Divinitie.* 4th ed. rev. London, 1653.

Varchi, Benedetto. *Lezzioni.* Florence, 1590.

A Vindication of the Stage, with the Usefulness and Advantages of Dramatick Representations. London, 1698.

Virgil. *Virgil,* trans. H. Rushton Fairclough. Loeb Classical Library. Rev. ed. London: Heinemann, 1965.

Waith, Eugene. *Ideas of Greatness: Heroic Drama in England.* New York: Barnes & Noble, 1971.

————. "Tears of Magnanimity in Otway and Racine," in *French and English Drama of the Seventeenth Century: Papers Read at a Clark Library Seminar, March 13, 1971,* intro. Henry Goodman. Los Angeles: Clark Memorial Library, 1972.

Walker, John David. "Moral Vision in the Drama of Thomas Otway." Diss. Florida 1967.

Wallace, John M. "Dryden and History: A Problem in Allegorical Reading." *ELH*, 36 (1969), 265 ff.

Wasserman, Earl R. "The Pleasures of Tragedy." *ELH*, 14 (1947), 283 ff.

White, Helen C. *Tudor Books of Saints and Martyrs.* Madison: University of Wisconsin Press, 1963.

Whiting, George W. "Rowe's Debt to *Paradise Lost.*" *MP*, 32 (1935), 271 ff.

Williams, Aubrey. "The 'Just Decrees of Heav'n' and Congreve's *Mourning Bride,*" in *Congreve Consider'd: Papers Read at a Clark Library Seminar, December 5, 1970,* intro. H. T. Swedenberg. Los Angeles: Clark Memorial Library, 1971.

————. "Poetical Justice, the Contrivances of Providence, and the Works of William Congreve." *ELH*, 35 (1968), 540 ff.

Wyman, Lindley A. "The Tradition of the Formal Meditation in Rowe's *The Fair Penitent.*" *PQ*, 42 (1963), 412 ff.

Index